Truth and Hope

Essays for a Perilous Age

WALTER BRUEGGEMANN

*Compiled, Edited, and with
a Foreword by Louis Stulman*

WESTMINSTER
JOHN KNOX PRESS
LOUISVILLE · KENTUCKY

Contents

Foreword

During the past fifty years, Walter Brueggemann has emerged as one of the most influential figures in biblical studies and U.S. Protestant Christianity. This impact is not limited to his distinguished writing career, which includes a repertoire of well over one hundred books; it is also the upshot of his passionate work in the seminary classroom (at Eden Theological Seminary and Columbia Theological Seminary) as well as hundreds of lectures and sermons given at churches, universities, and conferences across the United States and abroad. A recent conversation at Baltimore-Washington Airport reminded me of Walter's enormous impact. While waiting for my flight to Detroit, I lent a hand to a person carrying three massive bags. He had spent two months in the Northwest Pacific Wilderness and was now traveling to Baltimore to visit a grandchild teaching at Johns Hopkins. When he learned I was a religious studies teacher, he told me his partner had taken a doctoral class in Atlanta on the book of Jeremiah. "I'm not sure if you're familiar with the instructor, Walter Brueggemann, but this extraordinary individual almost singlehandedly revolutionized the way the U.S. church interprets the Bible." This serendipitous meeting only reinforced my conviction that Walter Brueggemann—preacher, teacher, scholar, social critic, organic intellectual—has indeed played a formative role in the church and the academy.

This book may conclude Walter Brueggemann's publishing career. If so, take special note. As we have come to expect from Walter, *Truth and Hope* is rich in insight, subversion, and imagination. It inspires, disturbs, and pulsates with astonishing clarity. It relishes interpretive complexity, acknowledges a multiplicity of textual voices, and never tires of dialogue over monologue. And like a good number of his books, it is markedly wide-ranging, as if to address as many pressing issues as possible under one cover: public faith, consumerism, intolerance, drifts toward fascism, immigration, loss of wonder, hegemony—all, of course, through the interpretive lens of Christian Scripture. The present book parses Hebrew texts on prayer and justice, inclusion, hope, truth-telling, stewardship, generosity, and fidelity, as well as greed and fear. Like every other work of Walter's, it moves briskly and organically into contemporaneity, refusing to relegate biblical texts to antiquity and never shrinking from the most pressing issues of our time. Accordingly, it is not only a robust reading of the Bible and a biting social critique; it is also rich theological engagement, which, I think, is its distinguishing mark. Put directly, this book is unabashedly theological. Whether tackling religion and higher education, homiletics, modern reductionism, or neighborly materiality, Walter, as is his custom, enters the fray and broaches questions of transcendence. He dares to speak of God, even though it is increasingly difficult to do so with intellectual integrity. Kathleen O'Connor reminded me recently that people don't talk much about God these days. And I thought to myself, "That's right, and for good reason."

God hasn't been getting high marks in the polls of late. Church attendance is on the decline. The number of religious "nones" and "religiously unaffiliated" is on the rise. According to the Barna Group, "Substantial majorities of millennials who don't go to church say they see Christians as judgmental (87%), hypocritical (85%), anti-homosexual (91%), and insensitive to others (70%)."[1] The devout are center stage for acting out unseemly behavior. In God's name, believers are disparaging immigrants, supporting white privilege, and championing various forms of extremism. Clearly not the best track record!

This bad behavior was on display in the 2016 U.S. election cycle. Prominent Christian leaders leveraged positions of power and privilege over civility and the common good. Some deployed sacred texts and theological language to sanction male aggression and disparaging rhetoric against the poor and vulnerable. This demeaning language was even leveled against victims of one of the worst humanitarian crises of our time, the Syrian civil war. In this conflict over 400,000 people have died. Seven million people have been internally displaced. Over five million Syrians are now refugees,[2] more than half of whom are children.[3] The face of Omran Daqneesh, the traumatized child from Aleppo, embodied the catastrophe.

You would think such a tragedy would have generated an outpouring of sympathy, but instead it incited a frenzy of fear. The presidential campaign of Donald Trump provided a platform for this intense xenophobia. The presumptive Republican nominee had no qualms in telling Syrian refugee children, "You can't come here." "We don't know where their parents come from. They have no documentation whatsoever. . . . There's absolutely no way of saying where *these people* [my emphasis] come from. They may be from Syria, they may be ISIS, they may be ISIS-related."[4]

This harsh language alongside "promises" to purge the U.S. of "illegals," ban Muslims, and build a "great wall to our south" appealed to our worst selves, not to the people we truly desire to be. Pope Francis understood this immediately and responded, "A person who thinks only about building walls, wherever they may be, and not building bridges, is not Christian. This is not the Gospel."[5]

Ideologies of exclusion and rhetoric against "others" may calm the fears of some, but they do little to address the biblical mandate to improve the lives of many in need. They do little to unite us in authentic ways with the rest of humanity.

Unfortunately and disconcertingly, millions of Christians supported this vitriolic campaign, support that hasn't waned since the election, as the sign of one enthusiast indicates, "Thank you Lord Jesus for President Trump," or as Jerry Falwell Jr. exclaimed, "I think Evangelicals have found their dream president" (April 29, 2017). [6]Apparently, 75 to 80 percent of white evangelical voters ignored accusations of aggravated sexual harassment and contempt for those with disabilities, people of color, Mexicans, and other minorities. Those who cherish a sacred text that champions the dignity of all people and identifies with the broken and vulnerable, "the least of these" (Matt. 25:31–46), more than tolerated ideologies rooted in xenophobia and bigotry. The reasons for such support are no doubt complex and well beyond the scope of this foreword,[7] but I can't help wonder if the incongruence did not lie in part with the lure of power and influence.[8] Regardless, the alignment of large cross-sections of the church with such ideologies was and continues to be a tragedy of massive proportion.

Not unrelated, and complicating theological discourse even more, we are currently witnessing seismic shifts in cultural, political, and religious landscapes. The litany of damage is nothing less than staggering:

- Deepening fissures in American culture, unprecedented in our lifetime
- The rejection of democratic norms
- The rise of authoritarianism and ethnic tribalism
- Disturbing signs of despotic leadership in the United States and Europe
- The resurgence of white nationalism
- The dismantling of civic discourse and civil society
- A greater tolerance of racial bigotry
- Horrifying gun violence in schools
- Dehumanization of immigrants, even the seizure of children from parents at the border
- Increasing economic disparities
- Assaults against woman's rights, environmental protections, the judiciary, and the free press
- Contempt for truth
- Disturbing alliances of Christian communions with autocratic political systems
- The long and dangerous reach of ideologies of power and transactional ethics in the guise of Christian faith
- Deep disruptions in theological education, including the closing, merging, and relocations of seminaries
- Disillusionment with long-standing forms of religious life, especially among millennials
- Resultant widespread despair and palpable cynicism

Put succinctly by a group of our elders, including Walter, "We are living through perilous and polarizing times as a nation, with a dangerous crisis of moral and political leadership at the highest levels of our government and in our churches. We believe the soul of the nation and the integrity of faith are now at stake."[9]

Not all is bleak, though. Already emerging from the wreckage are signs of resistance, creativity, and empowerment. We are witnessing grassroots movements with renewed commitments to the teachings of Jesus, communities confronting animus toward Muslims, sexual violence, and the dehumanization of refugees and minorities. In this fight for "the soul of the nation and the integrity of faith," a number of community leaders are confronting "the resurgence of white nationalism, racism, and xenophobia; misogyny; attacks on immigrants, refugees, and the poor; the regular purveying of falsehoods and consistent lying by the nation's highest leaders; and moves toward autocratic political leadership and authoritarian rule."[10] In all, we can discern a fresh openness to the Spirit, a commitment to reflection and action, and the audacity to reembrace biblical faith, hope, and love, expressed in manifestos that say yes to life, yes to others, yes to compassion, and no to injustice and intolerance.

Walter Brueggemann is a lead voice in this chorus. The present collection is a case in point. Even though it developed over a period of years, it still, uncannily, speaks to our particular crisis in history. It is faithful to the witness of the Jewish and Christian Scriptures, attentive to contemporary exigencies, alert to the value of inclusion and empathy, and audacious enough to believe that God still speaks through and to the fractures of the current mélange. The present volume attends to the central concerns and theological constructions that emerge from pain-filled and dislocated spaces, including land seizure, exile, injustice, shame, and confinement. It explores theological strategies for survival and resistance as well as gestures of hospitality to the outsider whose defender is the divine stranger: "Don't mistreat or oppress an immigrant, because you were once immigrants in the land of Egypt. Don't treat any widow or orphan badly. If you treat them badly and they cry out to me, you can be sure that I'll hear their cry" (Exod. 22:21–22 CEB). Along the way, it pays close attention to fractures in culture and faith, while listening to voices of despair and hope, domination and hegemony, and to an alien God who enters the fray to address the concrete needs of wounded people—then and now.

No wonder so many are reluctant to talk about God today. In settings such as ours, theological dialogue is scandalous, not because it dares to enter a secular terrain but because it is so easily misconstrued as power brokerage and opportunism. Yet to relinquish this engagement comes at great cost, for theological discourse not only shapes personal piety but also collective imagination. What is at stake, or more precisely *who* is at stake, is the divine and human Other, the Stranger, the Guest, the Poor,[11] who are often the victims of market-driven religions of certitude, or what Jean Vanier, the founder of L'Arche, has called elsewhere the 'religion of winning . . . which "leave[s] behind those who are weaker."[12]

We are grateful, indeed indebted, Walter, for your audacity to take, bless, break, and give the word of life, rich in meaning and mercy, resistant to closure and certitude, laden with dialogical possibility, ever new and transformative, yet wounded and vulnerable, and always aligned with the disempowered and marginalized. Thanks for the chutzpah to speak of God in such challenging times.

Louis Stulman

Preface

I have taken my title for this collection from one of these essays that was a presentation to the Wisconsin Council of Churches. In that presentation, I began with an appeal to three contemporary Christian confessions: Barmen, Kairos, and Martin Luther King's "Letter from the Birmingham Jail." On the first page, I suggested that our general social situation is not unlike that of German National Socialism. That judgment turned out to be an anticipation of the more recent Christian confession, "Reclaiming Jesus," a statement that is intentionally patterned after the Barmen Declaration. Or as Jim Wallis, the principle author of "Reclaiming Jesus," avers, "This is our Bonhoeffer moment." In that presentation a bit ago, I suggested that these confessions, after the manner of the long prophetic trajectory of the Bible, focus characteristically on the two acts of truth-telling and hope-telling.

There is no doubt that the prophetic tradition regularly engages in truth-telling, in order to expose social reality as a systemic act of "falseness" that contradicts the purposes of God. The prophetic tradition of Jeremiah, for instance, is preoccupied with truth-telling that exposes "falseness."

> For from the least to the greatest of them,
>   everyone is greedy for unjust gain,
> and from prophet to priest,
>   everyone deals falsely.
>   6:13; see also 8:10

> This is your lot,
>   the portion I have measured out to you, says the LORD,
> because you have forgotten me and trusted in lies.
>   13:25

They are prophesying to you a lying vision, worthless divination, and the deceit of their own minds. (14:14)

The prophet exposes the deceit of dominant culture. That same prophetic tradition (like many others) turns eventually to the work of hope-telling:

For surely I know the plans I have for you, says the LORD, plans for your welfare and not for harm, to give you a future with hope. (29:11)

For I will restore health to you,
    and your wounds I will heal, says the LORD.
                                30:17

For thus says the LORD of hosts, the God of Israel: Houses and fields and vineyards shall again be bought in this land. (32:15)

Such hope does not doubt that the faithful God can create futures, a way out of no way. The sequence from truth to hope in the book of Jeremiah is characteristic of the prophetic books of the Old Testament. These several prophetic voices (that gave canonical shape to the prophetic books) knew that this sequence is definingly important. There can be no hope until truth is told. Our temptation, of course, is to do the work of hope without the prior work of truth.

This sequenced work of truth and hope is theologically rooted. Truth-telling is grounded in the God who will not be mocked by our illusions. Hope is God-grounded in the conviction that even our wayward resistance does not negate God's good resolve for fidelity in the creation of futures. Without that God-groundedness, truth-telling can readily become nothing more than harping, and hope-telling only wishful thinking.

In Christian tradition, that sequence of truth and hope is given dramatic articulation in the Friday and the Sunday of the life of Jesus. The Friday crucifixion of Jesus amounts to truth-telling against the Roman Empire—namely, that the lethal capacity of Rome can do its work, but it is not enough and will not bring well-being. And so Sunday is a dramatic embodiment of hope for the power of life over the scandal of death. And of course in church practice we would like to do the hope of Easter without the truth of Good Friday, as witnessed in the contrast in church attendance on those days.

As this dual God-grounded work is voiced in the prophets and performed in the life of Jesus, so now our work in the church is the same: to tell the truth about the way in which our dominant way of consumer militarism (under the guise of American exceptionalism) will fail, because it contradicts the purposes of God, and to tell the hope that God is at work for an alternative world of peace with justice. These two accents dominate the confessions I have named, not least the most recent, "Reclaiming Jesus." These themes variously permeate these essays and indeed all of my work. As early as *The Prophetic Imagination* (1978),

I had identified these two tasks. I hope the essays collected here usefully extend the exposition of these themes that are so urgent for our faithful practice.

These essays are varied; some are recent, some are not. Almost all of them are keyed to a specific occasion, most of them by invitation. In sum, they are an extended exposition of a variety of biblical texts, most often to connect to our contemporary realities of faith and life.

My finish is with gratitude in so many directions that I cannot begin to name them. Obviously, I am grateful to my dear friend, Louis Stulman, for helping me get this collection into a manuscript and providing a generous foreword. I am grateful, as always, to the folk at Westminster John Knox Press for their good and careful work, notably David Dobson and Julie Tonini. Most of all now, I am grateful to Tia, who knows my toils and snares of completing one of my final collection of essays.

Walter Brueggemann

Chapter 1

Holiness as Ground
for Knowing Mercy

I want to consider resources and guidance that may be found in the book of Daniel as we think about our response to the gospel for the sake of the world.

I.

The book of Daniel is most often disregarded among us because of its bizarre, enigmatic "apocalyptic" dimension. But the first half of the book, my focus, offers narratives that are not apocalyptic but are dramatically alive in agonistic ways. The antagonist for Daniel in this narrative is Nebuchadnezzar, a reference point that situates Daniel in the Babylonian Empire, where Jews were displaced and required to sing the songs of Zion in a strange land. In what is a litmus test for critical scholarship, the book of Daniel is commonly placed in the period of Antiochus, the Syrian heir to Alexander the Great, who brought with him an aggressive Hellenistic perspective that sought to override local traditions, including the traditions of Judaism. In that context, the book of Daniel offers a mode of faith that is aware of the violent effort of the Maccabees, who are dismissed in the book of Daniel as a "little help" (Dan. 11:34). Whether we take the proposed

1

Babylonian context for the narratives or the critical Hellenistic context, either way the Daniel narratives concern a crisis of Judaism when Jews were marginalized, and when the peculiar tradition and identity of Judaism were under assault from a large, hegemonic power. The wonder of the Daniel narrative is that this threatened Jew and his company did not withdraw from hegemonic society in order to nurture and maintain an alternative distinct identity. Rather, Daniel is perforce a quite public man in the narrative, boldly playing an assertive part in maintaining a particular presence in the affairs of that hegemonic society.

John Collins concludes that the purpose of such a diaspora hero as Daniel is to offer sustaining literature in order

> (1) to remind the Jews that their monotheistic religion is a glorious heritage infinitely superior to the paganism with its gross idol worship; (2) to encourage the Jews to remain loyal to that heritage like the outstanding protagonists of the book who were willing to risk their social, economic, and political status and even their lives by steadfastly refusing to compromise their faith, and (3) to show dramatically and imaginatively that the God of Israel comes to the rescue and delivers those who believe in him despite even the severest reverses, including death by martyrdom.[1]

Concerning faith lived in the diaspora, Daniel Smith concludes,

> If Daniel, Esther, and Joseph are examples of exilic hero stories, designed didactically to advise a "lifestyle for the diaspora," then the hero, as Abrahams, Meinhold, and Collins emphasized, is a focus for a group: one in whom hopes are placed and one who provides an example as well. It is significant that the result of virtually all the diaspora hero stories is a change of condition, either implied or explicitly stated, for the Jewish people as a whole. Thus, Jewish diaspora hero stories become deliverer stories as well.[2]

Smith, following the work of N. H. H. Graburn, proposes that displaced people, those who are powerless in their own land, are living in "the Fourth World," in order to maintain identity when the dominant culture is bent on marginalizing—if not crushing—that identity:

> The alternative worldview presented in this study could be called a "Fourth World" perspective. In modern sociological literature, exiled peoples have come to be included among those otherwise collectively known as "the Fourth World." Graburn's definition of the Fourth World provides a helpful beginning:
>
> > All aboriginal or native peoples whose lands fall within the national boundaries and techno-bureaucratic administrations of the countries of the first, second, and third worlds. As such, they are peoples without countries of their own, peoples who are usually in the minority, and without the power to direct the course of their collective lives.[3]

In what follows, I propose, mutatis mutandis, that the Daniel narrative may be a resource for the church in the midst of the national security state in the

United States. I am aware that that is a huge mutatis mutandis, but I believe it is an accurate description of our situation of faith and ministry. For all the religious talk among us, it is the case that the dominant ideology of our culture, which I term "military consumerism"—an ideology that totalizes much of the imagination of both conservatives and liberals—is profoundly inimical to the primal claims of the gospel. Thus, our context is not unlike that of the early church in the book of Acts wherein proclamation of resurrection was a sufficient reason to be summoned before the authorities. I will work with that analogue, even though one must not press it too far. I believe that a faithful response to the gospel for the sake of the world may begin in a recognition of our true place in that world. And I judge that our evangelical claims are in deep contradiction to the claims of the global empire that is our societal habitat.

Thus, I propose this analogue: Daniel's work is to practice his Jewish identity in generative ways in an alien hegemony, to protect that identity, and to impinge upon that hegemony in transformative ways. The church's work is to practice our baptismal identity in generative ways in an alien hegemony, to protect our baptismal identity, and to impinge upon that hegemony in transformative ways.

II.

I will consider three narratives of confrontation in the book of Daniel, with particular attention to the third one. I will be partly interested in the conduct and utterance of Daniel, because he is the key "Fourth World" figure amid the dominant world wherein he finds himself.

1. In the long narrative of Daniel 2, Nebuchadnezzar, a cipher for the ancient and for the contemporary national security state, has a disturbing dream that is propelled by the impingement of the holy truth upon an otherwise hermetically sealed system. The "magicians" of the empire, the intelligence community, are required by Nebuchadnezzar not only to interpret the dream but to tell the dream. But they cannot! In his frustration with his own intelligence apparatus, Nebuchadnezzar decrees that all of them should be executed.

In the midst of a hegemonic violent rage comes Daniel, carrier of a distinct faith identity, a man with "prudence and discretion." In preparation for his work, Daniel

- urges his companions to pray for mercy for himself and for the imperial wise men (v. 17);
- offers a doxology to the God of heaven, praise to God for sovereign power and wisdom (vv. 20–23); and
- urges that the lives of the imperial magicians be spared (v. 24).

These three actions taken altogether amount to a vigorous intervention in the world of Nebuchadnezzar and reflect deep rootage in Jewish tradition concerning mercy, wisdom, and divine power.

In verses 25–45, Daniel reiterates the dream and gives its interpretation. It is about the rise and fall of great empires, including that of Nebuchadnezzar. This is a formidable philosophy of history that reflects the world of the late Persian and early Hellenistic periods, all of which pertains to YHWH's rule. Daniel allows himself two claims for his distinct faith. First, he asserts that it is the God of heaven who knows the mysteries that he is about to disclose:

> There is a God in heaven who reveals mysteries, and he has disclosed to King Nebuchadnezzar what will happen at the end of days. Your dream and the visions of your head as you lay in bed were these. . . . But as for me, this mystery has not been revealed to me because of any wisdom that I have more than any other living being, but in order that the interpretation may be known to the king and that you may understand the thoughts of your mind. (Dan. 2:28, 30)

The coming course of events is beyond the ken of the empire that imagined its own unchallengeable sovereignty. There is a plan beyond worldly power that is carried by Daniel. Second, there is coming a rule that will supersede all human pretensions:

> And in the days of those kings the God of heaven will set up a kingdom that shall never be destroyed, nor shall this kingdom be left to another people. It shall crush all these kingdoms and bring them to an end, and it shall stand forever. (2:44)

The upshot of this narrative is a remarkable one. Given such assurance, Nebuchadnezzar turns out to be benign. Daniel has tamed the violent rage of the empire with his larger perspective on the coming governance of the God of heaven. Nebuchadnezzar for an instant issues a doxology to the God of Daniel:

> The king said to Daniel, "Truly, your God is God of gods and Lord of kings and a revealer of mysteries, for you have been able to reveal this mystery!" (2:47)

And Daniel himself, as response to his exhibit of bold courage, is presented to the king and given many gifts. Without interpretive comment, the narrative has shown how it is that Daniel the Jew emerges, by his bold wisdom, with transformative impact on the empire. And his God is praised by the empire!

2. In the second narrative, chapter 3, the relationship of Daniel to Nebuchadnezzar—that is, Jew to empire, local identity in the face of hegemonic power—is much more aggressive and violent. In this narrative, Nebuchadnezzar now has the self-aggrandizing statue before which all shall bow down. The action to follow is situated in appropriate state liturgy:

> Therefore, as soon as all the peoples heard the sound of the horn, pipe, lyre, trigon, harp, drum, and entire musical ensemble, all the peoples, nations,

and languages fell down and worshiped the golden statue that King Nebu-chadnezzar had set up. (3:7)

All of that worked smoothly, and it was in any case just liturgy. But such a hegemonic power has an immense and effective surveillance system. It did not take long before Nebuchadnezzar got a report: "Certain Chaldeans came forward and denounced the Jews" (v. 8):

> There are certain Jews whom you have appointed over the affairs of the province of Babylon: Shadrach, Meshach, and Abednego. These pay no heed to you, O King. They do not serve your gods and they do not worship the golden statue that you have set up. (3:12)

It mattered in that ancient world, as now, in what liturgy one participates. After all, even back in Egypt, all that was asked was "Let my people go that they may worship me." The management of a liturgical system is a life-and-death matter for the maintenance of public power. For that reason, Jewish passive resistance to imperial liturgy immediately evoked imperial aggressiveness:

> Then Nebuchadnezzar in furious rage commanded that Shadrach, Meshach, and Abednego be brought in; so they brought those men before the king. . . . "Now if you are ready when you hear the sound of the horn, pipe, lyre, trigon, harp, drum, and entire musical ensemble to fall down and worship the statue that I have made, well and good. But if you do not worship, you shall immediately be thrown into a furnace of blazing fire, and who is the god that will deliver you out of my hands?" (3:13, 15)

It seemed innocuous enough. Join the liturgy, and then go home and be an absent Jew. But these Jews could not hide their particular identity. They could not withdraw to safe practice. And so the Jews respond to hegemonic power with a simple but comprehensive refusal:

> Shadrach, Meshach, and Abednego answered the king, "O Nebuchadnez-zar, we have no need to present a defense to you in this matter. If our God whom we serve is able to deliver us from the furnace of blazing fire and out of your hand, O king, let him deliver us. But if not, be it known to you, O king, that we will not serve your gods and we will not worship the golden statue that you have set up." (3:16–18)

The answer is a double "if" concerning both eventualities:

> If we are delivered . . .
>
> If we are not delivered . . .

Either way, we will not worship. We will not serve. We will not concede our identity. A great deal is staked on the delivering power of "our God." But not

everything is staked on divine intervention. The rest is staked on Jewish stubbornness, on Jewish identity even when miracles are lacking. The remarkable
statement is a profound act of defiance. And the threat of the furnace surely
draws an allusion back to the exodus deliverance in Deuteronomy 4:20:

> But the LORD has taken you and brought you out of the iron-smelter, out
> of Egypt, to become a people of his very own possession, as you are now.
> (Deut. 4:20)

This has all happened before, and we are ready and resolved as it happens this
time.

The rest of the narrative is history, or legend, or imagination, or whatever.
Nebuchadnezzar is yet again in a rage (Dan. 3:19). The maintenance of absolute power that lacks any persuasive legitimacy keeps people edgy, nervous, and
prone to violence. The furnace is heated up seven times (3:19). In an oppressive
hegemony, every act must be performed in hyperbole. How else to implement
"shock and awe"? But as we expect, the courageous, defiant friends are endorsed
by the God of all asbestos:

> And the satraps, the prefects, the governors, and the king's counselors gath-
> ered together and saw that the fire had not had any power over the bodies
> of those men; the hair of their heads was not singed, their tunics were not
> harmed, and not even the smell of fire came from them. (Dan. 3:27)

And even Nebuchadnezzar, slow learner that he is, gets the point and breaks out
yet again in doxology:

> Blessed be the God of Shadrach, Meshach, and Abednego, who has sent his
> angel and delivered his servants who trusted in him. They disobeyed the
> king's command and yielded up their bodies rather than serve and worship
> any god except their own God. (3:28)

Nebuchadnezzar sees exactly what has happened. Not unlike Pharaoh, he is a
late learner. But he learns. By courageous defiance and testimony, so the narrator
attests, even hegemonic power can come to see the truth that subverts all phony
claims to authority. The outcome is a decree that the God of Jews must not be
disregarded:

> Therefore I make a decree: Any people, nation, or language that utters
> blasphemy against the God of Shadrach, Meshach, and Abednego shall be
> torn limb from limb, and their houses laid in ruins; for there is no other
> god who is able to deliver in this way. (3:29)

There is no other God who is able to deliver in this way. That is the judgment of
the empire! It is no wonder that the Jews are promoted in the imperial government (v. 38).

3. The third narrative, chapter 4, moves in the same pattern, again featuring Nebuchadnezzar versus Daniel in a way that subverts the absolute claims of the global reach of Babylon. As this narrative goes, Nebuchadnezzar is in a better mood. He sings to the Most High God (vv. 2–3). Not unlike the psalmist—"I shall not be moved" (Ps. 30:6)—he declares his prosperous ease: "I, Nebuchadnezzar, was living at ease in my home and prospering in my palace" (Dan. 4:4). But the prosperity only belongs to the daylight. At night, when one's guard is down, other stuff happens to Nebuchadnezzar beyond his favorite construal: "I saw a dream that frightened me; my fantasies in bed and the visions of my head terrified me" (Dan. 4:5).

Nebuchadnezzar now knows what to do, having learned from the events recounted in chapter 2. His own interpreters failed, but he knows about the Jews who can probe the mysteries:

> At last Daniel came in before me—he who was named Belteshazzar after the name of my god, and who is endowed with a spirit of the holy gods— and I told him the dream. (Dan. 4:8)

Nebuchadnezzar even recognizes Daniel's special gifts from God and asks these interpretive gifts to serve the empire:

> O Belteshazzar, chief of the magicians, I know that you are endowed with a spirit of the holy gods and that no mystery is too difficult for you. Hear the dream that I saw; tell me its interpretation. (4:9)

Nebuchadnezzar then tells the dream to Daniel; in contrast to chapter 2, Daniel does not need to recount the dream, only provide the interpretation. The dream is about a luxurious tree that fails. Mindful of the risk he takes in truth-telling, Daniel proceeds in a way not unlike that of Nathan before David: "It is you, O king" (v. 32). It is you who will be brought low, made to eat grass, humiliated, made powerless, "until you have learned that the Most High has sovereignty over the kingdom of mortals, and gives it to whom he will" (Dan. 4:25). It is the "until" that debunks Nebuchadnezzar's hegemony and that exhibits it as a fragile penultimate power arrangement that cannot prevail. Nebuchadnezzar's big learning yet to come is that "heaven is sovereign" (v. 26).

But then in verse 27, Daniel makes a move beyond interpretation. He dares to follow dream and interpretation with a policy proposal. This celebrated but uncredentialed Jew speaks Jewish truth to hegemonic power:

> Therefore, O king, may my counsel be acceptable to you; atone for your sins with righteousness, and your iniquities with mercy to the oppressed, so that your prosperity may be prolonged. (4:27)

Righteousness and mercy! Righteousness, which is to practice communitarian economics and ethics between haves and have-nots, and mercy, which is to yield to the neighbor in need. The outcome of these two practices is in order that your prosperity may be prolonged. The calculus is simple: the practice of mercy will lead to prosperity. The calculus is as old as the book of Deuteronomy. But what is old and steady in Jewish horizon must have been a stunner to hegemonic power. It is a stunner because hegemonic power does not major in righteousness and does not specialize in mercy. Indeed, Daniel may have read Second Isaiah, in which Babylon is condemned for its treatment of Israel:

> I was angry with my people,
>   I profaned my heritage;
> I gave them into your hand,
>   you showed them no mercy;
> on the aged you made your yoke
>   exceedingly heavy.
>
>   Isa. 47:6

The proposal of Daniel to his overlord is that the crown may open its settled imperial truth to the counter-truth that has been kept and nourished in this local tradition of Torah.

When Daniel finished speaking, the narrative tersely reports, "all this came upon Nebuchadnezzar" (Dan. 4:28). All this dream came upon him. All this dream of deconstruction and humiliation. All this dream came because Nebuchadnezzar had not grasped the Jewish "until," had not understood that his power was penultimate and held to account. All this came upon him, but none of it would have surprised any serious Jew. Nebuchadnezzar is presented as still being buoyantly full of himself:

> The king said, "Is this not magnificent Babylon, which I have built as a royal capital by my mighty power and for my glorious majesty?" (Dan. 4:30)

But, says the narrator,

> while the words were still in the king's mouth, a voice came from heaven: "O King Nebuchadnezzar, to you it is declared: The kingdom has departed from you!" (4:31)

The drama of self-sufficiency is interrupted by another voice, this one the transcendent voice of heaven beyond the reach of the superpower. This interrupting voice is the same one that will sound again in the parable of the Rich Fool in Luke 12:

> God said to him, "You fool! This very night your life is being demanded of you. And the things you have prepared, whose will they be?" (Luke 12:20)

It is the big hovering question that is always asked of absolute power. That voice to Nebuchadnezzar lays out the dismantling and then reiterates "until you have learned that the Most High has sovereignty over the kingdom of mortals and gives it to whom he will" (Dan. 4:32).

The turn in the narrative occurs in verse 34, when Nebuchadnezzar himself attests, "My reason returns to me." He had been, he now acknowledges, unreasonable. Indeed, he had been insane. Absolute power, in its mix of anxiety and self-sufficiency, does indeed become insane. It becomes insane in acquisitiveness, in aggressive violence, in the seizure of goods that belong to others, in its craving disregard of local traditions. And when reason returns to the dominant culture, it issues in doxology (vv. 34–35). This is not an idle "praise hymn," but a genuine acknowledgment and ceding over of authority. Nebuchadnezzar has finally, under the tutelage of Daniel, arrived at the inescapable "until" of penultimacy, where he never could have arrived himself without this Jewish witness. The narrative ends with restoration, on the other side of yielding:

> At that time my reason returned to me; and my majesty and splendor were restored to me for the glory of my kingdom. My counselors and my lords sought me out, I was re-established over my kingdom, and still more greatness was added to me. (Dan. 4:36)

But the reiteration is grounded in an acknowledgment:

> Now I, Nebuchadnezzar, praise and extol and honor the king of heaven,
>
>> for all his works are truth,
>>   and his ways are justice;
>> and he is able to bring low
>>   those who walk in pride.
>
> (4:37)

Truth and justice, not deception and exploitation. Not falseness and injustice. Nebuchadnezzar is sobered by his situation before the God of heaven.

That is as far as I will go now in the narrative of the hegemonic power of Nebuchadnezzar in the book of Daniel. Here are three narratives of confrontation in which an exemplar Jew responds out of his saving tradition for the sake of the empire. I suggest these are three narrative pictures that pertain to our theme of response to the gospel for the sake of the world.

1. In chapter 2, Daniel, unlike the magicians of the empire, knows "the mysteries." He knows them for the sake of Nebuchadnezzar:

> But as for me, this mystery has not been revealed to me because of any wisdom that I have more than any other living being, but in order that the interpretation may be known to the king and that you may understand the thoughts of your mind. (Dan. 2:30)

It is important that this king should come to know, but he can only know by submitting to the truth entrusted to Daniel. There is a long tradition in biblical narrative of turning to this unlikely source:

- In Exodus 12:32, Pharaoh at long last comes to Moses and says, "And bring a blessing on me too."
- In Jeremiah 21:2, Zedekiah pleads with Jeremiah for the sake of Jerusalem: "Please inquire of the LORD on our behalf, for King Nebuchadrezzar of Babylon is making war against us; perhaps the LORD will perform a wonderful deed for us, as he has often done, and will make him withdraw from us" (Jer. 21:2)
- In John 18:38, the governor asks Jesus, "What is truth?"

In the biblical horizon, the world of power and control does not know the mystery that makes life possible. It is this mystery that has been entrusted to the unassimilated people of God. In Christian confession, that mystery is this:

Christ has died.
Christ is risen.
Christ will come again.

In Jewish tradition, that mystery is that you cannot circumvent the requirement of righteousness and mercy. It is the same mystery. It is the truth that raw power and brutal control cannot generate the safety, well-being, or joy for which creaturely life is destined. The church, as an heir to Daniel, has frittered most of its authority away on lesser matters. But here it is. It is the great "until" that Moses and Jeremiah and Jesus all know so well.

2. In chapter 3, Daniel and the three young Jews are so clear and so sure of their identity and destiny as the people of God that they refuse to bow down to the icons of hegemony. They refuse to credit, even for an instant, that the exhibition of power and glory by Nebuchadnezzar holds any gift for the future. Refusing to bow down is an act of bold defiance; Daniel and these courageous Jews refuse to entertain the thought that Nebuchadnezzar has in his power to make any claim on their life. This either/or defiance is, as we know, not the whole of Scripture. There are models of accommodation, not least in the Joseph narrative that in some ways is a counterpoint to the Daniel narrative. Thus, the Daniel narrative may not be our last, best word on the matter. But it is a word that we may ponder for a season in order to ask how to recover nerve for the hope that has been entrusted to us, for without such recovered nerve we likely cannot act "for the sake of the world."

3. In chapter 4, it is clear that Daniel and the three young Jews' defiance in chapter 3 is not just stubbornness. It is, rather, stubbornness as a way of making distinctions and maintaining distance from which to articulate an alternative. It is clear that Daniel's defiance is "for the sake of the world," that is, for the sake of the empire. Daniel very much wants Nebuchadnezzar to embrace the "until." That is why in verse 27 he offers the double imperative of the road back to security. It is, in a proper theological sense, crazy to practice high-handed, aggressive, acquisitive ultimacy at the expense of the rule of the God of heaven. The news on the lips

of the Jew is that there is an alternative to the lethal system of Nebuchadnezzar. There is a road back to well-being and even back to authority. It is a conversion from exploitation to righteousness. It is a transformation from arrogance to mercy.

The news is that there is an alternative to the mad pursuit of commodity; it is the maintenance of the neighbor. There is an alternative to aggressive consumerism; it is the sharing of resources. There is an alternative to imperial militarism; it is to yield ultimacy in the interest of a peaceable order. The issue is articulated in the narrative as addressed to high worldly power. But the same news is offered to every person who is bewitched by the ideology of autonomy that lies just beneath the surface of conservative starchiness and liberal accommodation.

So imagine this Daniel,

- entrusted with the life to which Nebuchadnezzar has no claim;
- empowered in boldness to defiance for the sake of an alternative destiny;
- Knowledgeable about the conversion whereby the world may come to well-being;
- Knowledgeable as a practical theologian.

He is indeed a person of faith for the sake of the world.

III.

Here is a man of faith *entrusted, empowered,* and *knowledgeable* who has an immense impact upon the world because of his faith. The narrative is surely intended as a model to Jews of faith about life in the world. Such models of courageous faith, moreover, are offered as a model for Christian courage:

> And what more should I say? For time would fail me to tell of Gideon, Barak, Samson, Jephthah, of David and Samuel and the prophets—who through faith conquered kingdoms, administered justice, obtained promises, shut the mouths of lions, quenched raging fire, escaped the edge of the sword, won strength out of weakness, became mighty in war, put foreign armies to flight. (Heb. 11:32–34)

To be sure, in that list the models come from an earlier period and Daniel is not named. But the phrases fit Daniel as well: "administered justice, obtained promises, shut the mouths of lions, quenched raging fire." My question now is this: How did Daniel become equipped for such a life of courageous witness? Or for that matter, any of those named in the recital of Hebrews 11 become so equipped? While most of us have no inclination for such heroism, we might learn from them how to be better equipped for such risk. The question is: How did Daniel come to this calling? I propose that the answer to the question is offered in Daniel 1, even though I am aware that the narratives have only incidental connection to each other. Perhaps there is a reason that chapter 1 comes in the book before chapters 2–4. In chapter 1, we learn of the reach of the empire into the Jewish community to equip suitable Jewish agents for civil service in the empire. To seek such Jews who are handsome, without physical defect, knowledgeable, insightful, and competent makes sense to me. It is rather like a government "out East" seeking good Midwesterners because they are reliable, or corporate executives preferring upper Midwestern Lutherans because people from Lake Wobegon are without guile and trustworthy. They knew that about Jews in the empire, and so they recruited young Jews for their imperial training program in service to the empire. The ones selected had to leave their Jewish families to enter the training program. To help them move from their Jewish rootage to the horizon of the empire, they received imperial names; Belteshazzar used to be Daniel, and Shadrach, Meshach, and Abednego are known in the narrative only by their imperial names, and not their old Jewish names of Hananiah, Mishael, or Azariah. Perhaps even our reading of them is already saturated in the reality of hegemony.

The pivot point of the training program and of the narrative is the training table at the imperial boot camp:

> The king assigned them a daily portion of the royal rations of food and wine. They were to be educated for three years, so that at the end of that time they could be stationed in the king's court. (Dan. 1:5)

But get this:

> But Daniel resolved that he would not defile himself with the royal rations of food and wine; so he asked the palace master to allow him not to defile himself. (1:8)

"Resolved"—set it upon his heart. Daniel refused the diet of the training table, an act that ordinarily would have gotten him dismissed from the program. It might be like training for IBM but insisting that your work will be done on an abacus. From his loyalty to Jewish perception, Daniel concluded that such alien imperial food would defile him and render him a disqualified Jew.

He asked the palace master, the director of recruits, to be given permission to eat other food. The palace master was not unsympathetic to Daniel but declared that if he gave permission and Daniel was seen to be unhealthy in any way, it would be his head. Interestingly, the narrative does not report what the palace master decided, but apparently he said to this stubborn Jew, "You work it out with your guard, but don't tell me about it." So Daniel's business is now with the guard who has charge over Daniel, Shadrach, Meshach, and Abednego. It is telling that midway through the narrative, the four are called by their Jewish names and not their new imperial names. The narrator trusts his implied audience to notice: still Jews! Because of the proposal to depart from the official rules of engagement at the training table, the guard agrees to extend the experiment. Ten days of Jewish vegetables and Jewish water contrasted with the rich royal rations. At the end of the ten-day experiment, the guard saw that the Jewish boys were "better and fatter" than all the others in the program. As a result, the guard, and perhaps the palace master as well, though he is not mentioned here, judged that there was no risk for them in the alternative, no risk for their jobs or for their lives. The Jewish proposal was free of such risk. Consequently, the guard permitted the four Jews an alternative for the three-year training program. No royal rations for them. And then, we are told,

> To these four young men God gave knowledge and skill in every aspect of lit-
> erature and wisdom; Daniel also had insight into all visions and dreams. (1:17)

It worked! They are still Jews!

At the end of the three-year program, at the graduation ceremony, Nebu-chadnezzar came for the awarding of prizes and diplomas and did not find other recruits to compare with the blessed four:

> In every matter of wisdom and understanding concerning which the king
> inquired of them, he found them ten times better than all the magicians
> and enchanters in his whole kingdom. (1:20)

Imagine that—ten times better! The narrative carries us stage by stage so that you can see the tension thicken:

> The recruitment . . .
>
> The offer and the refusal . . .
>
> The palace master . . .
>
> The guard and the ten-day experiment . . .
>
> The three-year training session . . .
>
> The verdict: ten times better.

Voila! Daniel is qualified and commended for service to the empire, but he has not compromised his Jewishness. It is his identity in faith that gives him a way to be in the world for the sake of the world.

Here is my thesis. It is Daniel's refusal to be "defiled" that gives him the power, the courage, and the authority in chapters 2, 3, and 4 to make a differ-ence in the empire. So I dwell on the term "defile." The term used twice here is, in the Old Testament, found only in the following literature:

- In Zephaniah 3:1, the term is juxtaposed to oppression and autonomy; the defiled city "accepted no correction."
- In Lamentations 4:14, the city is defiled with blood, that is, murder.
- In Isaiah 59:3, it is defiled by blood (murder), inequity, and lies.

- In Isaiah 63:3, it is "stained" by blood.
- In Malachi 1:7, 12, it is defiled by polluted offerings and profanation of the Lord's Table.
- In Ezra 2:62 it is defiled by impure genealogy for priests, so also Nehemiah 7:64 and 39:29.

That is the sum of all the uses of the term. The various occurrences of the term cluster around ritual and social activity that violate Torah and compromise Jewish identity. A strong tilt of the term is toward ritual contamination, though the references to murder are social rather than ritual. But if we take the term in context, according to this word usage, Daniel refused to engage in a diet that would violate his purity, thus offering a usage related to a ritual disqualification.

We can gain a fuller picture of the issue at stake if we push behind this later word *ga'al* to the more common word *timai'* attested frequently in what is likely earlier usage. All of these usages of the term in Leviticus cluster around the defining mandate in Leviticus 19:2: "Speak to all the congregation of the people of Israel and say to them: You shall be holy, for I the LORD your God am holy." The summons is to practice holiness, but the laws include a number of prohibitions, notably on homosexuality in Leviticus 18 and 20. While the tradition focuses on the negative, the mandate of Leviticus 19:2 is itself a positive invitation in that Leviticus 19 is preoccupied with concern for the poor and for the alien (Lev 19:9–10, 15–17, 32–34). The tradition liberally mixes ritual and social mandates. Now I am aware of how odd or perhaps repulsive the holiness traditions are to many of us, most especially to those of us whose theological tradition focuses upon grace without these punctilious requirements. I am aware, moreover, that Jesus joins issue with the matter of defilement with his dismissal of such regulations about defilement:

> Then he called the crowd again and said to them, "Listen to me, all of you, and understand: there is nothing outside a person that by going in can defile, but the things that come out are what defile." . . . He said to them, "Then do you also fail to understand? Do you not see that whatever goes into a person from outside cannot defile, since it enters, not the heart but the stomach, and goes out into the sewer?" (Thus he declared all foods clean.) And he said, "It is what comes out of a person that defiles. For it is from within, from the human heart, that evil intentions come: fornication, theft, murder, adultery, avarice, wickedness, deceit, licentiousness, envy, slander, pride, folly. All these evil things come from within, and they defile a person." (Mark 7:14–15, 18–23)

Specifically, the dismissal of food regulations by Jesus in verse 19, surely echoed in Peter's dream in Acts 10, extrapolates from David's sacrifice. (See 1 Sam. 21:1–6.) Perhaps my focus on this verse in Daniel 1 concerning defilement and my general consideration of the Daniel narrative is misguided.

But I return to the issue because I believe that the Daniel text and the holiness tradition may have a good word for us if we focus on the main point and are not distracted by the specificity of the requirements about which it is easy to take exception. If we consider defilement and pollution as a compromise of faithful identity, then holiness requires a distancing from the compromises offered by culture that erode identity, that subvert courage, and that ease resolve into accommodation. Clearly we do not know what lay behind the punctiliousness of Leviticus and, clearly, the countervision of Acts 10 means to reach beyond a holiness community that is too sure and exclusionary in its practices. That much is clear, and it is long clear in my theological tradition. But I take it in most mainline Protestant churches in the United States that the deep problem for response to the gospel is *not excessive punctiliousness*, though it may be in some quarters. Rather, the crisis is one of *easy cultural accommodation* so that the sharp edge of discipline is nearly lost—any form of discipleship being too readily slotted in legalism and moralism and narrowness. If the danger to the church's testimony is the loss of missional passion for response to the gospel, then I want to entertain the thought that we have something to learn from the Daniel traditions.

Another Daniel, Daniel Smith-Christopher, has suggested that the practice of purity is a mode of resistance to empire in that ancient Jewish tradition. Daniel's attention to dietary practice is not because he is a legalist, but because he is ready to engage in resistance against imperial hegemony for which Nebuchadnezzar is the cipher in the narrative. Daniel's dietary refusal is as much an act of defiance as the later refusal to bow down in chapter 3, even if the refusal to bow down is more dramatic and a compromise on food would have been no big deal. What Daniel does in this narrative is to refuse the junk food of the empire that would render him compromised and without standing ground in his identity. He refuses junk food and instead settles for Jewish health food (vegetables and water), which not only nourish his body in strength but nourish his faith identity in resolve. Thus, against the teaching of Mark 7 for an instant I entertained the thought that what goes in may defile, if defilement means the compromise of faith identity.

IV.

Thus I propose—with what you may think are too many doubtful interpretive nuances—that we may learn from the Daniel narrative that the capacity for faithful response to the gospel for the sake of the world begins in a disciplined practice of holiness that refuses junk food that compromises an evangelical identity. The empire always wants the faithful community to believe that its junk food is at least harmless and, at best, good for you.

At the first level such junk food is indeed "junk food," the offer of artificial foods that contain nothing of what is needed for health.[4] The politicization of the Centers for Disease Control in Atlanta is an indication of how much the food and drug industry wants to distort habits of usage in the interest of making money.

But at a second level, the real junk food that is offered by dominant ideology is the ideology of insecurity and anxiety that assumes that more commodities—more sex or beer or oil—can contribute to health and well-being and youth.

That commoditization of human possibility is fostered by the wonders of electronic liturgy: cell phones, email, Facebook, Twitter, Instagram, and all of the existing models of communication that lead to dumbing down and fake community. One does not need to be a Luddite—and I am not one—to see that the offers of a virtual society are a feeble substitute for serious human engagement that requires critical thought and genuine care. I do not want to defend all the rules and regulations of Leviticus and all of the attempts to regulate holiness into a sacerdotal system. And I do not want to applaud Daniel's resistance to the empire if it is to be understood as a thin moralism that simply wants to honor a code. But I believe that Daniel's resistance is not a regimented sacerdotal system or thin moralism. It is, rather, a knowing, intentional act of self-consciousness that a distinction must be made between the risky offers of Nebuchadnezzar and the realities of faith. That discipline did not cause Daniel to withdraw from Nebuchadnezzar's system of civil service. Indeed, verse 21 attests that Daniel continued in the service of Nebuchadnezzar until the first year of Cyrus the Persian.

Daniel was able to make a distinction that is grounded in the decree of Exodus 9 concerning the pestilence that will come upon Egypt:

> But the LORD will make a distinction between the livestock of Israel and the livestock of Egypt, so that nothing shall die of all that belongs to the Israelites.
> . . . And on the next day the LORD did so; all the livestock of the Egyptians died, but of the livestock of the Israelites not one died. (Exod. 9:4, 6)

That distinction is mostly lost among us. And the outcome, I suggest, is at best an anemic capacity to respond to the gospel for the sake of the world.

V.

So consider Daniel as a man *undefiled, unseduced* by empire, *uncompromised* in faith. He is just a model and not more. I understand that none of us and none of our parishioners are ready for that kind of heroic distinction, because it smacks too much of self-righteousness self-justification. But it would not hurt to raise the question about what kind of food the empire offers:

> Do not work for the food that perishes, but for the food that endures for eternal life, which the Son of Man will give you. For it is on him that God the Father has set his seal. (John 6:27)[5]

Or what kind of water gives life:

> Jesus said to her, "Everyone who drinks of this water will be thirsty again, but those who drink of the water that I will give them will never be thirsty.

The water that I will give will become in them a spring of water gushing up to eternal life." (4:13–14)

It is no wonder that the crowd said of his bread, "Sir, give us this bread always" (John 6:34). And on that occasion the woman said of the water, "Sir, give me this water, so that I may never be thirsty or have to keep coming here to draw water" (4:15). Thus, undefiled Daniel had no appetite for the junk food of Nebuchadnezzar:

- It is this Daniel who in chapter 2 knew the mystery that would let the empire receive true teaching about its future.
- It was Daniel's friend who in chapter 3 refused to bow down and in the end evoked a doxology for his God on the lips of the empire.
- It is this Daniel who in chapter 4 could instruct the king in the ways of righteousness and mercy, who permitted the empire to cover its sanctity by yielding its ultimacy to the God of heaven.

I am not sure that chapter 1 is the trigger in the book of Daniel for chapters 2, 3, and 4, but I suspect so. One last thought on this connection: After the vision in Acts 10 of eating what used to be unclean, the meeting in Acts 15 reached a conclusion that included the verdict of James:

Therefore I have reached the decision that we should not trouble those Gentiles who are turning to God, but we should write to them to abstain only from things polluted by idols and from fornication and from whatever has been strangled and from blood. (Acts 15:19–20)

Do not "trouble." The early church was invited to watch out for food polluted by idols:

For it has seemed good to the Holy Spirit and to us to impose on you no further burden than these essentials: that you abstain from what has been sacrificed to idols and from blood and from what is strangled and from fornication. If you keep yourselves from these, you will do well. Farewell. (15:28–29)

If this analysis is credible and the avoidance of defilement was urgent for the courage of faith amid the empire, then the pastoral teaching in the church must do the hard imaginative work of identifying *food that defiles*. The intent is not a community preoccupied with excessive disciplines. It is, rather, a community clear enough in its identity that it can bear witness precisely to the truth entrusted to it. What better than holy disciplines, whereby we, with Nebuchadnezzar, may recover the sanity of faith and sing songs of praise:

> For all his works are truth,
> and his ways are justice;
> and he is able to bring low
> those who walk in pride.
> Dan. 4:37

Chapter 2

Dialogic Thickness
in a Monologic Culture

The awareness that none of us can stay confined in our preferred disciplines is an invitation to us all. I take as my task a reflection on the ways in which my discipline, Christian Old Testament/Hebrew Scriptures, might be at an interface with the practice of pastoral counseling and pastoral care most broadly understood. I have made a first offer on that interface in extended pages in my *Theology of the Old Testament*.[1]

I.

More particularly, I have asked myself what a faithful practice of the Old Testament text and the discipline of pastoral care may have in common that biblical scholars and pastoral-care givers may celebrate together and about which we may learn from each. I have asked further what might be distinctive about these disciplines together that invite critical appreciation at the interface. The latter question I considered with reference especially to the theme of this conference, "Lightning, Risk, and Awe"[2]—in supervision or in any other serious human transition of accountability:

- I take *lightning* to mean a sudden intrusion that shakes our complacency, an intrusion that may shock and may for an instant illuminate.
- I take *risk* to be the work of placing in jeopardy things that seem to be settled, a danger that may be welcomed or perhaps resisted.
- I take *awe* to mean the stunned awareness that the real stuff is beyond our control and our explanatory categories.

Plus, considering the disciplines of biblical studies and pastoral care, and the reality of "sudden intrusion," "jeopardy for the way things are," and "beyond our critical control and explanation," I offer the notion that we share a sense of *thickness* about the human scene and the world we inhabit, a conviction of the complexity, ambiguity, and layered meaning that moves through our massive, irresolvable contradictions in order to mediate to us the sweet truth and truthful sweetness that is our destiny. That thickness, moreover, is practically (day to day) and ultimately (before the throne of mercy) a *practice of dialogue* wherein many voices—some invited, some unwelcome, some acknowledged and some not—sound in an unsorted cacophony whereby we are led where we had not intended to go, wherein things are called into existence that do not yet exist, wherein things we have treasured and relied upon are "brought to naught." I do not want you to miss the scriptural allusion in my latter statements, allusions that catch what are for me the most compelling claims of Paul:

- Concerning the crucifixion: "God chose what is low and despised in the world, things that are not, to *reduce to nothing things that are*" (1 Cor. 1:28, au. emph.).
- Concerning the resurrection: "(As it is written, 'I have made you the father of many nations')—in the presence of the God in whom he believed, who gives life to the dead and *calls into existence the things that do not exist.*" (Rom. 4:17, au. emph.).

The transactions that are definitional in these twinned disciplines concern nothing less than dying to what is treasured and being raised to newness we had not anticipated. The depth, complexity, richness, and threat of such thickness are urgent and difficult. Thus, I imagine that *thickness via dialogue*

- provides an arena wherein *lightning* strikes, we are shocked from complacency, and we are occasionally illuminated;
- exposes us to *risk*, for we are suddenly led where we had not thought or wanted to go; and
- generates *awe*, reminding us yet again that our explanatory categories are at best feeble, that our real life is lived not by sight but in faith—or in fear.

II.

I focus on the thick dialogic practices of life that the disciplines of biblical studies and pastoral care share, because our society—in every aspect—has a determined bent toward thinness and monologue that robs life of freedom and newness, miracle and forgiveness, possibility and reconciliation. Settled power arrangements, in every dimension of reality, always seek to move toward monologue as a way of maintaining the status quo, always seek to silence dialogue, always seek to prohibit the lightning, forego the risk, and deny the awe.

We now, in Western culture, live in a society and in a political economy that moves in every way it can imagine toward monologue. The most visible play in that monologic propensity is the global reach of U.S. imperialism, which is increasingly intolerant of local tradition or variation. That imperial reach, moreover, now is controlled by an oligarchy of the very wealthy and the very powerful that has the nerve and the capacity to operate largely in secret. That oligarchy, moreover, continues to foment fear and anxiety that in turn breed a hunger for certitude, simplistic formulation, and the dumbing down of human critical capacity.

There is no doubt that such a monological tendency reaches into personal lives that are dominated by technological conformity and by the pressures of compulsive consumerism. The same propensity reaches into local congregations through a culture of fear that cannot tolerate a thought or a gesture of openness. The predictable response is a desire, in Luther's categories, to eliminate the threat and risk of grace and reduce all to "law." I need only mention that the well-funded and brazen work of the Institute for Religion and Democracy reaches into our several church communities in the service of the same monologue that is frightened by any "other" and is determined to exclude any voice of the "other" that disputes the old treasures of certitude and entitlement. That same combination of political *ideology*, economic *conformity*, and theological *authoritarianism* reaches into our personal sense of self and invites denial and repression of the other "selves of the self" that are "unorthodox" or illegitimate. The large sweep of imperial monologue drives "the many selves of the self" into the closet, where they fester in grief and may from time to time emerge as controlled resentment or uncontrolled rage.[3] The connection between *large conformist ideology* rooted in fear and the damage to our *most intimate selves* is an important linkage between the disciplines of biblical studies and pastoral care.

But after we trace such *thinness* in public society, in church, and in our personal lives, we may also reflect on the way in which thinness has been powerfully definitional in our disciplines. In my discipline of Old Testament study—and in biblical studies more broadly—the thinness that refuses lightning, risk, and awe comes as the practice of historical criticism, a nineteenth-century Enlightenment project that thinned the text by submitting it to modern reason, thereby dissolving the thickness of contradiction, ambiguity, repetition, and all of the rhetorical maneuvers judged in that venue to be faulty. The obvious example that is familiar to us is the division of hard texts into various sources, thereby dissolving the contestation of many voices, a contestation that was indeed the point of the text and the glory of interpretation.

Recent decades have featured an effort in Old Testament studies to move beyond that rational thinness to recover, honor, and be led by the thickness that is the intention of the text. The primary means of recovery has been an effort to read the text closely, as much as possible on its own terms.[4] But that effort has been abetted by appeal to important theoretical points of reference that fall outside of Enlightenment rationality. Of these I will mention two. First, Mikhail Bakhtin, a Russian theorist who endlessly troubled the Soviet Union, understood and showed that great literature—especially his favorite genre, the novel—is inherently and intransigently dialogical.[5] The move from Bakhtin to Scripture study—highlighted in studies by Barbara Green and Carol Newsom—has been to show (or hear) that there are many voices in the text; these are not sources but voices arranged in an ongoing contestation that admits of no resolution and that has beneath it no absolute monologue.[6] Second, Emmanuel Levinas, a Jewish interpreter in Paris, opened new worlds with his 1969 book *Totality and Infinity*.[7] By these two terms, Levinas meant that "totality" on the one hand is an attempt to contain and control by totalizing explanation, whereas "infinity" is to appreciate and practice an openness of cascading meaning and interpretation that reach no finality. From Levinas we may indeed conclude that historical criticism was an attempt at totalism that tried to reduce the multivoiced text to a single line of reasoning that eventuated in a single hypothesis of unilateral evolution in the religion of Israel and in the development of Israel's literature. In such a maneuver of thinness, the text became manageable. Under the hermeneutical invitation of Bakhtin, Levinas, and others, recent interpretation has much more readily been led by the text itself in its offer of revelatory disclosure that refuses every closure, and that consequently opens to energy, courage, and freedom.

Having summarized the current crisis and possibility in Old Testament study, I dare as an outsider to suggest that the pastoral care movement has been engaged in a quite parallel venture. I will state this all tentatively, but so it seems to me. The pastoral care movement arose, with reference to pastors and churches and seminary faculties, because of an awareness that widespread one-dimensional absoluteness of a theological kind was unbearable, unhealthy, and unfaithful. As an access point, the early movement appealed to psychological categories even if framed in various theoretical frameworks. But that framework, perhaps most especially in the monologic model of Carl Rogers, was indeed very thin and left the "client" very much to her own resources. In more recent times, pastoral practice has moved toward a much thicker willingness to take notice of theological reality. While I am no expert at theory, my own impression, both from reading and from my own personal work, is that object relations theory in its various forms moved the agenda out of the solipsism of the individual person into dialogical transactions that require negotiation with the other and in the ongoing contestation between parties that are variously "good enough" or "not good enough."[8]

The recovery of dialogical thickness in the pastoral care movement, so it seems to me, has summoned the enterprise away from psychological thinness in the same way that Old Testament studies have been summoned away from the thinness of historical criticism. In the case of the movement, the recovery of dialogical thickness summons in two directions. First, psychological thinness must be necessarily resituated in the thickness of social, cultural interaction, because the self is inescapably formed, sustained, threatened, and renewed through social engagement. Thus the movement, in reclaiming social aspects of the self that have economic and political dimensions, recognizes a range of psychological possibilities that are generated by and impinged upon by cultural forces.

Second, after psychological thinness, the pastoral care movement is pressed to become more intentionally theological, not only by the vague reference to "larger meaning" but by the awareness of holy agency, whereby the creator-redeemer God is indeed defining for the emerging self. Thus the Holy God, when we take theological claims seriously, is not simply an enforcing superego, real or imagined, but is in fact the ultimate lover and generator of the self, the assertive destabilizer of the self, and the one who calls the self to vocation so that in any serious theology of creation, there are no "uncalled selves." Given the reality and defining character of the Holy One, it is not difficult to imagine that the core pathology among us is idolatry, a false rootage in an ersatz holiness that cannot save or bring joy.

The history of the contemporary pastoral care movement is much shorter than the history of modern biblical interpretation, and so the movement has passed through this history more rapidly. That being said, however, I suggest that both disciplines have faced the temptations of modern reductionism and are now working their way beyond that reductionism.

III.

My conviction is that the disciplines of biblical studies and pastoral care share a common rootage, a common urgency, and a common possibility.

1. The *common rootage* we have is profoundly Jewish, and the recovery of dialogical thickness requires the recovery of that Jewishness. What we are now required to learn in Old Testament studies is how to read from the long Jewish tradition of interpretation that honors the texts in its rich, multivoiced claim. Thus, from the work of Jon Levenson, Michael Fishbane, and James Kugel, among others, we are able to see the rabbis at their careful work lingering over the kind of inconvenient detail that discloses, without rushing to big shrill questions of "historicity" that are the specialty of Enlightenment Christians.[9] The outcome is a readiness to linger in close reading, to listen to nuance and hint

and trace, without reductionism, to stay with the text itself without immediate intrusion of either ideological claims or alienating interrogations.

In like manner, the pastoral care movement is singularly rooted in the daring venturesomeness of Freud, who was widely parsed as a scientist but was in fact a great humanist who appealed to metanarrative myths and who lingered over the detail of utterance in order to provide trace and hint and clue that are not on the surface for the utterer. There can be no doubt that Freud's mode of listening is one he learned from the way in which rabbis listen to texts, not searching for big conclusions but for moments of grace to disclosure.[10] *Rabbinic exegesis* and *Freudian listening* are rooted together in Jewish relational, covenantal, and dialogical ways of knowing that find the relational transaction itself revelatory, healing, transformational, and summoning. The matter is Jewish because Jews have lived, since the day they left Egypt, amid empires that traffic in big conclusions that will in turn foreclose the future and crush the human spirit. The move away from that Jewishness toward thin history or thin psychology has constituted a loss of the dialogical. And we hold as common ground rootage in dialogical thickness.

2. Our disciplines share *common urgency* because our contemporary world is bent on monologue that makes human life impossible. The monologue in Scripture study features either the loud, certain orthodoxy of right-wing fundamentalism that makes the Bible a package of nonnegotiable certitudes, or a reactive left-wing shrillness that also has no more feel for dialogical openness than does fundamentalism.

That same monologic pressure is before the pastoral care movement as it practices the mystery of human personhood in human community. For the dominant reductionist notions of human personhood want to reduce all to commodity, to make everyone into ideological conformists in support of the national security state, or into conformists who believe that shopping and hurrying and having and eating and controlling are the goals of human life.

The dominant passion of reductionism, evident in the political economy and evident in religious culture, seeks to eliminate all risk and with it all freedom, and ends by generating a kind of unbearable anxiety, not only anxiety before terrorism but anxiety about not getting into the right college or onto the right Little League team.

What we are witnessing is a drift, a propelled drift, toward fascism, the notion that there is only a single preferred option with every decision before us. In the process of reductionism, all human thickness is lost and all dialogical possibility is forfeited. The mood is one of meanness, fear, aggressiveness, certitude, privilege, and entitlement in which there is no more generative interaction.

3. Given common rootage in a Jewish openness and common urgency amid the widespread drift of fascism, our disciplines share a *common possibility* of entertaining the thought that Scripture study, with its irreducible dialogical text, and pastoral care, with its irreducible vision of fresh intentionality, stand together—with some other allies to be sure—as an offer of an alternative way in

the world, a way that refuses dominant idolatries, that fosters a presence in the world that is inherently and intentionally subversive and countercultural.

The subversion entrusted to us is a vision of the human future of the world—"sub" to be sure—that features a *Holy God* who will not be reduced to a static idol, a *holy neighborhood* in which the "other" is honored and accepted as a part of a common destiny, and a *holy self* that is not gelled in fearful ideology but that is open to the summons of newness. I imagine that this practice of dialogic, interactive covenantalism:

- counters *settled religion* by trusting interaction with God that invites God into *new modes and images* well beyond approved orthodoxy;
- counters *settled politics* by insisting that *the voice of the marginalized*, like an "importunate widow," is to be sounded in relentless and pestering ways, sounded in prophetic oracle, in daring narrative, and in insistent poetry, sounded until truth penetrates power on high and evokes a *novum*, even from political power that had thought itself immune to such inappropriate disturbance (Luke 18:1–8);
- counters *settled economics*, because for every authoritative decree that forecloses the claim of the needy for the sake of the wealthy, there is somewhere a *narrative of newness*, of loaves that abound, of jars of oil that run over, of bread and wine and oil and water given from the will of the Creator, gifts that are not administered by the World Bank or the International Monetary Fund; and
- counters *reduced selves* who have certitude and security as their goal, by bringing to speech the ongoing voices of the unfinished self, the sum of which offers a truthfulness never voiced in a single, resolved, settled self.

IV.

Having laid out the urgency of *dialogical thickness* and suggested that the common work of biblical studies and pastoral care is precisely that theological thickness, I now turn to matters more properly in my own discipline. I do so with an urging that practitioners of pastoral care might more fully and intentionally engage these texts as the clearest resources and models for dialogical thickness.

The Psalter, I propose, is inherently subversive because it speaks insistently and relentlessly against every closure. It speaks a *sub-version* of reality that inescapably will *subvert* settled versions of theology, politics, or economics. That subversion is the *voice of protest* that will not settle for any unjust worldly arrangement, but that subversion also is the *voice of wonder* that acknowledges and celebrates new gifts, new life, and new miracles beyond all that the rulers of this age can manage and administer. That subversion is an act of insistent imagination. For example:

- The Psalter imagines that the wound of the speaker is never forgotten, never finished in holy precincts, because our tears are "in your bottle" preserved to perpetuity (Ps. 56:8).
- The Psalter imagines that we are not self-sufficient but that we rely morning, noon, and night on the ready gift of breath that we cannot produce or hold, breath that we mistakenly render "spirit" but either way is a gift (104:29–30).
- The Psalter imagines that creation is amenable to the Creator, that even hills and mountains must tremble and yield before the terrible coming of the exodus God (114:1–6).
- The Psalter imagines that the pursuit of power and control by princes, and other military agents, is futile, because their plans perish when they try to take a deep breath (146:3–4).

This imagining is a sub-version of reality that we cannot, when we pay attention, resist. The congregation evoked by the Psalter is not anxious about the fearful restlessness of the world. Rather, it exults in such freedom and possibility. It gathers regularly in dialogue in order to defy the lethal closures of monologue.

When we recognize how deeply unsettling such dialogic interaction is, we can readily understand why the church has shunned the dialogic pattern of worship in the Psalter, why it has excluded the texts most frontally engaged in such exchange, and why the church has flattened the texts it uses into a settlement. Even when we recognize that, however, we may take a deep breath and imagine the people of God gathered, precisely in a monologic culture, in order to engage in such a dialogic transaction. We may imagine the congregation, pastor and people together, prepared yet again for the evangelical act that is intrinsically subversive and revolutionary, an act acutely urgent in a society wherein the dominant version of reality imagines that it may stifle and eliminate all such sub-versions. When it has been faithful, the church has always been irrevocably committed to the practice of such a transaction. On the other hand, when the church has lost the will, energy, and freedom for such bold interaction, it has settled for idolatry, a practice that offers immediate security and certitude, and a nodding approval from the powers that be that do not want to be disturbed. I speak of the church as gathered, but if care and counseling are "pastoral," then surely every such dialogical interaction is committed to the same engagement with the sub-version that is here so powerfully scripted.

When I press more specifically toward dialogical thickness, I propose that it is the psalms of lament that are the primal genre of speech in the Old Testament, a primal genre of speech that funds, invites, empowers, and authorizes the public processing of pain that permits pain in all of its dimensions—anger, fear, alienation, and despair—to be transformed into positive energy. I use the phrase "public processing of pain" because the subject in Old Testament laments is characteristically pain; the exercise is public in that the utterance is heard either in great liturgy or in intimate liturgy; the utterance affirmed and heard is itself processing whereby pain is validated, honored, transmitted, and released.

It is evident that with only one or two exceptions, Israel's laments characteristically end in some form of doxology, an outcome indicating that the hurt is heard and answered. The dominant hypothesis is that at the proper point in the recital there is a divine intervention of utterance, mediated by a responsible human agent.[11] That response characteristically is "Fear not, for I am with you," a statement of solidarity that has a transformative effect that permits a move toward doxology and an assurance of being heard. Because there is divine intervention and response, it is clear that the psalms of lament are authentically dialogical.[12] The lightning that strikes is the notion that a situation of abandonment is decisively and effectively transformed into an arena of solidarity. The risk of the speaker is that the lament may be rejected. The risk for the listening God is to be impinged upon in demanding ways. The awe of the process of utterance is a newness that emerges through dialogue, a newness neither party had anticipated in advance.

The genre of lament is a statement of candor before the God from whom no secret can be hid. The speaker tells the narrative of hurt in forceful detail. In such utterance the speaker asserts the primacy of the self even before God. We may mention two other characteristic features of the lament. First, there is almost never a statement of guilt.[13] The speaker characteristically does not believe troubles voiced are given as punishment. More likely, they are given by divine default, neglect, or absence. Second, such utterance is not a statement of helpless despair; it is rather a statement of insistent hope.[14] The speaker expects and claims as legitimate a transformative answer from God, not doubting that where God's attentiveness is secured God is fully able to transform the environment of pain.

The lament psalms stand in the Psalter alongside hymns of praise. It is worth noting that except for Psalm 22, the church has shunned the laments and focused on hymns. Taken by themselves, however, the hymns are monologic. Nothing happens in them. There is no divine answer. There is no process whereby things are any different at the end from the beginning. The church prefers hymns that are *monologic acts of deference* rather than laments that are *dialogic acts of hope, insistence, and transformation.* Even though the church avoids the laments and is unfamiliar with them, they are crucial for mature, effective faith. We may notice two uses that attest Israel's imaginative use of lament.

First, in the exodus narrative, the process begins with the lament of Exodus 2:23: "After a long time the king of Egypt died. The Israelites groaned under their slavery, and cried out. Out of the slavery their cry for help rose up to God" (Exod. 2:23). In the narrative, moreover, Israel's groan received divine response that set in motion the drama of emancipation:[15] "God heard their groaning, and God remembered his covenant with Abraham, Isaac, and Jacob. God looked upon the Israelites, and God took notice of them" (2:24–25).

Second, in the exile, the book of Lamentations is Israel's great voice of grief, with a steady word of bereftment:[16]

> She weeps bitterly in the night,
>   with tears on her cheeks;
> among all her lovers
>   she has *no one to comfort her*;
> all her friends have dealt treacherously with her,
>   they have become her enemies.
>   Lam. 1:2 (au. emph.)

> Her uncleanness was in her skirts;
>   she took no thought of her future;
> her downfall was appalling,
>   with *none to comfort her*.
> "O LORD, look at my affliction,
>   for the enemy has triumphed!"
>   1:9 (au. emph.)

> Zion stretches out her hands,
>   but there is *no one to comfort her*;
> the LORD has commanded against Jacob
>   that his neighbors should become his foes;
> Jerusalem has become
>   a filthy thing among them.
>   1:17 (au. emph.)

> They heard how I was groaning,
>   with *no one to comfort me*.
> All my enemies heard of my trouble;
>   they are glad that you have done it.
> Bring on the day you have announced,
>   and let them be as I am.
>   1:21 (au. emph.)

It is the uncomforted voice through which Israel goes public with pain.

It is most plausible, as many scholars have noted, that the great lyric of emancipation and homecoming in Second Isaiah is a divine response to the lament.[17] The great poem begins with "comfort," a precise antidote to despair:

> Comfort, O comfort my people,
>   says your God.
> Speak tenderly to Jerusalem, and cry to her
>   that she has served her term,
>   that her penalty is paid,
> that she has received from the LORD's hand
>   double for all her sins.
>   Isa. 40:1–2

Thus, the two great moments of need and deliverance, of death and resurrection, in the Old Testament are scripted according to lament and divine response. In its dialogical mode, Israel is bold to insist in ways that evoke divine engagement. It is clear that when such a practice of speech prevails, the world is kept open. Neither partner can settle; both are available and at risk, vulnerable to lightning. I submit that such texts serve as a model whereby pastoral care may line out the dialogic act in a way that makes clear that the transaction concerns the needy speaker and the trusted human mediator, but it also concerns the Holy God who inhabits Israel's texts.

V.

Thus I conclude,

- that the disciplines of biblical studies and pastoral care share the responsibility for *thick dialogue*;
- that they share (1) *common roots* in Jewishness, (2) *common urgency* in a monologic society, and (3) *common possibility* that dialogue makes all things new; and
- that lament psalms *script the several voices* that belong to dialogue.

I want now to consider Psalm 35 as a stunning example of Israel's capacity for dialogic interaction as a mode of faith, worship, and life. This psalm offers the conventional components of the genre of individual lament. First, it features a series of *petitions* that reflect urgency, that address YHWH in an imperative. The opening verses articulate that urgency in military figures, though the initial verb might suggest judicial confrontation:

> Contend, O LORD, with those who contend with me;
>   fight against those who fight against me!
> Take hold of shield and buckler,
>   and rise up to help me!
> Draw the spear and the javelin against my pursuers.
> Ps. 35:1–3a

The second set of imperative petitions is even more insistent:

> You have seen, O LORD; do not be silent!
>   O Lord, do not be far from me!
> Wake up! Bestir yourself for my defense,
>   for my cause, my God and my Lord!
> Vindicate me, O LORD, my God,
>   according to your righteousness,
>   and do not let them rejoice over me.
> 35:22–24

Second, the imperative petitions are matched by *imprecations*. The hope of the psalmist is that YHWH will not only do good for the speaker but will retaliate against the enemy:

> Let them be put to shame and dishonor
>   who seek after my life.
> Let them be turned back and confounded
>   who devise evil against me.
> Let them be like chaff before the wind,
>   with the angel of the LORD driving them on.
> Let their way be dark and slippery,
>   with the angel of the LORD pursuing them.
> . . . .
> Let ruin come on them unawares.
> And let the net that they hid ensnare them;
>   let them fall in it—to their ruin.
> . . . .
> Let all those who rejoice at my calamity
>   be put to shame and confusion;
> let those who exalt themselves against me
>   be clothed with shame and dishonor.
>   35:4–6, 8, 26

Third, the *complaint* properly characterizes for YHWH the acute jeopardy of the psalmist and the urgency of divine intervention:

> For without cause they hid their net for me;
>   without cause they dug a pit for my life.
> . . . .
> Malicious witnesses rise up;
>   they ask me about things I do not know.
> They repay me evil for good;
>   my soul is forlorn.
> . . . .
> Do not let my treacherous enemies rejoice over me,
>   or those who hate me without cause wink the eye.
> For they do not speak peace,
>   but they conceive deceitful words
>   against those who are quiet in the land.
>   35:7, 11–12, 19–20

Fourth, the petition, imprecation, and complaint are supported by *motivations* that declare the innocence and merit of the speaker, reason enough that YHWH should act:

> But as for me, when they were sick,
>   I wore sackcloth;
>   I afflicted myself with fasting.
> I prayed with head bowed on my bosom,
>   as though I grieved for a friend or a brother;

I went about as one who laments for a mother,
    bowed down and in mourning.
But at my stumbling they gathered in glee,
    they gathered together against me;
ruffians whom I did not know tore at me without ceasing;
they impiously mocked more and more,
    gnashing at me with their teeth.

                                        35:13–16

The contrast between good speaker and evil adversaries is complete. The ground for divine help is the entitlement of the speaker, who has been faithful and has contributed to the well-being of the community.

It is clear that the entire sequence of *petition, imprecation, complaint,* and *motivation* constitute together a speech addressed to the God of the covenant who has made promises to this Israelite and who has offered sanctions that guarantee succor to those who remain faithfully in the covenant.

The speaker of the psalm is able to articulate—construct, imagine—*the ongoing conversation of faith.* In this rendition, the psalmist boldly speaks all of the parts to the conversation that is constitutive of faith. This is a daring project because the speaker ventures to anticipate what each party in the conversation may say. In the first instant, we may judge that this is an *internal* dialogue; that internal exchange, however, has profound implications for the *external* conversation that is subsequently to be enacted. We may identify five parties to the conversation that make the exchange of faith fruitfully complex. What is remarkable in this psalm is that each voice among the contesting parties is given explicit rendition.

First, the psalm itself is *the voice of the suppliant.* That voice is of course the pervasive one, because the entire psalm is on his lips. But for all the stylized convention of this voice, we should not minimize its importance for the larger picture of faith. All such suppliants follow in the wake of Moses, who himself dared implore YHWH in order to evoke a change in YHWH's intention (Exod. 32:11–13; Num. 14:13–19). This is faith "from below," in which, for an instant, the petitioner has the upper hand and addresses YHWH in an imperative. In such utterance there is provisional role reversal; the petitioner assumes the role of senior partner in the exchange, and YHWH is summoned to respond.

The second voice to this exchange is *the voice of YHWH,* who is given one line in the psalm. Well, it is not YHWH who speaks. Rather, the psalmist proposes what YHWH should say, thus assigning lines for the exchange to God. After the series of imperatives in verses 1–3a, the psalmist follows with yet one more imperative to YHWH, the verb "say": "Say to my soul, I am your salvation" (v. 3).

The words assigned to YHWH are of course a standard salvation oracle, only not introduced by the customary "Fear not." The proposed utterance is an assurance of YHWH's attentiveness and YHWH's presence, YHWH's readiness and capacity to intervene transformatively in the vexed life of the speaker. It is the voice of faith that evokes the divine voice of rescue.[18] The divine response is of course not automatic, as is made evident in the poem of Job. It is, however, regularized enough that the psalmist dared count on it and assume YHWH's readiness to answer the petition. It is also possible to think that the psalm intends to head off and preclude other, less affirmative divine responses, such as those eventually offered by YHWH to Jeremiah and to Job. The psalmist knows the utterance from YHWH that is needed and desired, and takes an initiative to ensure that YHWH speaks what is needed and not some other word YHWH could in freedom have uttered. The psalmist prays in uncommon confidence and with daring freedom, with a sense of entitlement that belongs to a covenantal, dialogic life.

Third, in verses 9–10 the speaker *quotes himself in anticipation* of what he will say after deliverance by YHWH:

> All my bones shall say,
>   "O LORD, who is like you?
> You deliver the weak from those too strong for them,
>   the weak and needy from those who despoil them."
>   35:10

It is instructive that the anticipated declaration of praise is not only to be given in words, not only by mouth, but by "all my bones," his whole being, every part of his delivered life that is now to be postured in doxology. It is of course obvious that his anticipated doxology is in total contrast to his present circumstance and present utterance of complaint. The speaker exhibits sufficient self-control and critical distance to imagine an utterance other than his current one in a transformed insistence.

That anticipated utterance of doxology is a "formula of incomparability," an affirmation that YHWH is unlike any other God.[19] That familiar conventional formula insists, characteristically, on two claims for YHWH—namely, that YHWH is stronger than any other and that YHWH is fully allied with the weak and the needy, for whom the psalmist is a representative speaker. That this utterance on the lips of the speaker is anticipated, based upon the anticipated intervention of YHWH, means that the praise of Israel is propelled and sustained by the most recent transformative intervention of YHWH. Where there is no such recent intervention by YHWH, Israel's praise is not forthcoming. Thus, the pledge to praise YHWH is at the same time an implied conditionality of praise, a conditionality that bespeaks a transaction in which both parties are freely and vigorously in play.

Fourth, Claus Westermann has shown that in the psalms of complaint, the issue is always a triangle that includes, along with YHWH and Israel, the enemy.[20] Of course, it is possible that the psalmist is simply paranoid. But such paranoia is grounded in the awareness that social life is deeply and always contested, that the petitionary speaker is at risk and without resources and that therefore everything depends upon the intervention of YHWH, which is anticipated but not this next time certain.

Because of that vigorous and threatening contestation in which the petitioner always finds himself, the adversary must be given full play in the psalm that is itself the arena of that contestation. In order to dramatize and underscore the contestation, the adversary is given full voice in the exchange of the psalm.[21] As the speaker can imagine what YHWH ought to say and will say in the future and can anticipate what he himself will say upon deliverance, so the speaker in jeopardy is also able to imagine what the adversary might say in one possible outcome of the dispute. One possible resolution to the stated crises of the complaint is that the enemy will triumph, a possibility that is only thinkable if YHWH is not mobilized.

The psalmist anticipates that in such triumph (with the implied failure of YHWH) the adversary will gloat:

> They open wide their mouths against me;
>> they say, "Aha, Aha, our eyes have seen it."
>>> 35:21

If YHWH does not act to vindicate the psalmist, moreover, the adversaries are sure to gloat even more:

> Do not let them say to themselves,
>> "Aha, we have *our heart's desire.*"
> Do not let them say, "We have swallowed you up."
>> 35:25 (au. emph.)

"Our heart's desire" is a translation of "our *nephesh.*" That is, as the *nephesh* of the psalmist may be addressed by the saving God in verse 3, and as the *nephesh* of the psalmist may praise YHWH in verse 9, so the victory of the adversary will give the adversary greater *nephesh*, surely at the expense of the *nephesh* of the psalmist. In the dispute, the matter of more or less *nephesh* is presented as a zero-sum game, more *nephesh* for the adversary, less *nephesh* for the psalmist. There is no doubt that the anticipated, gloating self-congratulations of the adversary are designed to motivate YHWH, for the defeat of the psalmist is inescapably a defeat for YHWH as well, a divine defeat that will be noted by other adversaries of YHWH, both human and divine.

Fifth, that imagined defeat of speaker and of YHWH, however, is not the anticipated outcome of the dispute that the psalmist commends. Rather, it is anticipated that YWHH will indeed say, "I am your salvation," and will act to make it so. Thus the psalm ends, as do many of the psalms of complaint, with an immense celebration of YHWH's deliverance of the psalmist and the defeat of the adversary. That celebration is enacted by the psalmist himself in his "formula of incomparability" (v. 10). Such deliverance, however, requires more than one voice of praise. The psalmist mobilizes the entire community of those who stand in solidarity with him and who hope for his acquittal. All in that company are to exult in the vindication of their friend and so are summoned to praise:

> Let those who desire my vindication
>> shout for joy and be glad,
>> and say evermore,
> "Great is the LORD,
>> who delights in the welfare of his servant."
>>> 35:27

They recognize, in their doxology, that YHWH is great, greater than the adversary, greater than any threat or any other deliverer. What constitutes that divine greatness, as already anticipated in the speaker's doxology in verse 10, is that YHWH delights in the *shalom* of the speaker who is reckoned to be among the weak and needy. YHWH not only delights in such *shalom* but also effects *shalom* in a circumstance where no such well-being could have been imagined. The end result of the psalm is that the psalmist is restored to the *shalom* that only YHWH can give.

VI.

There is no doubt that the psalmist is permitted, since it is his psalm, to manage the dialogue and place the accents where he will. The controlling capacity of the psalmist, who for the course of the psalm holds leverage over the entire process and over YHWH, is evident in three anticipations of praise and thanks to YHWH for saving intervention.

First, in verse 9 the anticipated formula of incomparability on the lips of the psalmist is stated:

> *Then* my soul shall rejoice in the LORD,
>> exulting in his deliverance.
>>> 35:9

The "then" of the NRSV is only a *waw*-consecutive in Hebrew, but it is enough to indicate that praise is withheld from YHWH until rescue and that it depends upon that rescue.

Second, in verse 18 a parallel statement again withholds thanks until rescue:

> *Then* I will thank you in the great congregation;
>> in the mighty throng I will praise you.
>>> 35:18 (au. emph.)

Here there is no indication in Hebrew at all of the "then" of the NRSV, but the point is self-evident. Here the speaker is the one who will give thanks, but the thanks is in the midst of the "great congregation." This anticipated thanks is the connecting point between the praise of the psalmist in verse 10 and the praise of the congregation in verse 27, for here it is the psalmist but in the midst of the congregation. Thus, verse 18 concerns both thanks and praise—thanks for concrete deliverance, and praise for generic celebration and affirmation based on the concrete deliverance.

Third, in verse 28 the "then" is again a *waw*-consecutive in Hebrew:

> *Then* my tongue shall tell you of your righteousness
> and of your praise all day long.
>
> 35:28

Praise concerns YHWH's capacity to make things right for the speaker.

All three uses of "then" as rendered in the NRSV (and, I believe, rightly informed by the Hebrew) withhold praise and thanks until deliverance is granted. In this way, assuming that YHWH desires praise and thanks, YHWH is at the behest of the speaker, who is no easy touch but who bargains hard and holds the upper hand in the process. The psalm offers a dialogic exchange in four voices—*YHWH, the psalmist, the enemy,* and *the congregation*—or five if we distinguish between the *present complaining voice* of the psalmist and the *anticipated doxological voice* of the psalmist in time to come. The strategic articulation of the psalm situates the speaker and the faith of the speaker in the midst of a vigorous dialogic contestation, the place where faith is characteristically at risk and at work.

VII.

If it is true that we share the task of dialogic thickness, and if it is true that dialogic thickness is an urgent countercultural activity in a monologic society, and if the drama of the lament psalm is the primal script for dialogic thickness, then I propose that Psalm 35 is a model script, a classic verbatim of dialogic practice that gives airtime to all of the voices in the contestation of faith and life. I take the trouble with this particular psalm because the current practices of *textual exposition* and of *dialogic interaction in supervisory relationships* are ongoing works of lightning, risk, and awe that break the monologue of control, reductionism, certitude, and absoluteness. In our disciplines, we work in the wake of Israel's textual practice that models, authorizes, and summons to an alternative way that refuses closure but is an act of hope in two directions: (1) that we may yet say more in truthful ways and (2) that we may be yet again addressed by the Holy One in ways that heal and call to new vocation.

On the basis of this authorization of dialogical thickness I draw four conclusions. First, this psalm most directly and others less directly witness to *the many-voiced reality of the human self.* In the history of spirituality there is regular reference to "the many selves of the self." Roy Shafer has detailed the same reality in his psychoanalytic practice.[22] But the many-voiced reality of human life is not simply the self in conversation *with the self*. Rather, the human conversation is the self involved *with many other persons and many other voices*, so that an engaged human person is a party to a dialogue if that dialogue has not been repressed or silenced. Ministry takes place in the midst of people who are conducting a conversation of contestation that includes present self, anticipated self, remembered self, caring community of companions, the adversary, and the Holy God who may be brought to active intervention. There may be other voices, but at least there are these that are to be heard, honored, and taken seriously. It may be that such a conversation, if it becomes a cacophony, is a form of destructive, compulsive rumination.

Or taken more positively, it may be a pastoral mode of constructing a life with prospects of new possibility wrought by enough self-regard to utter a withholding "then" that awaits good outcomes from God. Either way, if the conversation is honored, it is plausible that the processing, hearing, and speaking of life turns to energy, even energy for mission. Conversely, when that conversation is stifled, censored, or dismissed, the shutdown of such internal conversation produces resentment and negativity toward self or toward others, and eventually a readiness for violence. It is a treasure of Jewish tradition that such speech in contestation is a mode of newness. YHWH is a vigorous player in such contestation, but by no means always the one with the best, last word.

Second, the psalm is an act of prayer. Lament psalms were likely scripts that were designed and used for local and intimate worship, perhaps even personal prayer. But even such personal practice of the Psalms is a mapping of social power and an anticipation of social engagement and contestation. That is, the Psalms cannot be kept "private." Thus, I imagine that such prayer, even if it is intimate and personal, functions willy-nilly as "practice" for social engagement.

The very process of hearing one's own voice in such exchange, the capacity to hear and refute the voice of the adversary, the capacity to hear and appreciate the voice of celebrating companions, the capacity to assign lines to YHWH to be subsequently uttered and enacted, all constitute a construction of social identity and a readiness to participate in an external arena of social contestation. Such utterance is an act of social imagination, but it is never conducted in a vacuum. Rather, such a practice of speech is an act that imagines social transactions in time to come will be ordered in this way and not in some other. The speaker of such psalms can at least entertain the possibility of such future utterance that is not in secret. Thus:

- It is imagined that YHWH is a present and powerful force of transformation.
- It is imagined that the adversary is real and formidable but finally impotent before holy power.
- It is imagined that the speaker is not alone but is surrounded by those "who desire my vindication," who will be present at the vindication.

- It is imagined that I am not fated to this needy petition but that I have a future and in time to come will be in a posture of praise for transformations that will have been enacted on my behalf.

The very process of this script of imagined utterance, when grounded in memories of ancient fidelity, is itself empowering. I would imagine that people who participate in such dialogic transformative liturgy, preaching, education, and pastoral care are persons with revived identity, energy, courage, and freedom that monologue never allows.

Third, beyond personal prayer and social imagination, it is also possible that such prayers are more directly acts of social power. Gerald Sheppard (following the social mapping of Norman Gottwald) has proposed that the prayers that refer to the enemy are designed, intended, and enacted as speeches of revolutionary social criticism to be overheard by actual social adversaries:

> Prayers are not considered in general elsewhere in the Old Testament to be secretive, silent, or private exercises. The capacity of a prayer to be overheard is a characteristic rather than an incidental feature of it. . . . I am proposing . . . that prayers are assumed to be overheard or, later, heard by friends and enemies alike; and, furthermore, "enemies" mentioned in these prayers, as often as not, belong to the very same social setting in which one prays. The presence of overhearing "enemies" is integral to the prayer situation and influences the perceived function of prayer socially, rhetorically, religiously, and politically.[23]

In reference to the complaints of Job and Jeremiah, Sheppard judges that

> these prayers are not portrayed as silent agonies, but complaints and indictments shared with an audience to which the enemies belong.
> Applying this insight to the psalms, I find three principal ways in which the enemy is indirectly addressed in these prayers: (1) as someone whom the psalmist, through overheard prayer, implicitly exposes in public and from whom protection is now sought; (2) through indictments or threats against the enemy; and (3) by harsh commands, advice, or instruction given to the enemy, often in hope for the conversion of the enemy. . . .
> Prayer provides protection for the supplicant in various ways. For one, exposure of an enemy, even though not explicitly named, brings an end to abuse denied or endured in silence. Especially in a tight-knit peasant society, these prayers about enemies undoubtedly invited those "in the know" to interpret the prayer in ways that could make obvious who the enemies were and what was the nature of their wrongdoing. The prayers could easily be "reused" to some effect by other parties. From the content of the psalms, we can see that the situation itself is presumed to be common knowledge already. . . .
> Moreover, the words of prayer are distinguished from words used in gossip and can, consequently, be unusually blunt and graphic. In this regard, prayer becomes a significant alternative to gossip because, unlike gossip, it makes God the primary listener, maintains the intimacy of that discourse by not naming the enemy, and directly asks God, rather than neighbors, to

respond in word and deed in behalf of the petitioner. As prophets are protected, despite their denunciations, by claiming that their words are God's
rather than their own, the psalmist can argue that only God is directly
addressed rather than the public. . . . The biblical psalms of lamentation
and praise are filled with asides to those who overhear to join in prayer, to
take up shouts, or even to repeat specific pious formulas. In this way, prayer
offers the prospect of protection both by God and by other persons who
overhear and who join both in prayer and care for the one who suffers.[24]

Sheppard suggests that by going public in utterance, the speaker gathers protection in real-life contexts of threat. In addition to such protection, Sheppard
opines that such an exercise leads to freedom, authority, and energy that may
redress the circumstance of vulnerability for the weak and needy.

If Sheppard is right about overhearing by the enemy, then I suggest we may
also imagine two other overhearings. On the one hand, the companions in support may overhear and rally in support. On the other hand, YHWH may overhear and rally to the rescue. In the end, the speaker may have sufficient critical
distance to hear and derive from the utterance a completely reorganized mapping of social power. Again, notice that it is the dangerous potential of social
construction through the practice of the Psalms that has caused these psalms to
disappear from the repertoire of the settled church.

Fourth, if we bring these insights (a) concerning the empowerment of the
many selves of the self, (b) concerning reimagining the ways of the social map
of social power, and (c) concerning overhearing that reconstitutes social power,
we may finally bring our discussion to the specific agenda of supervision in
which the novice is mentored to responsible maturity. I submit that responsible
maturity is the capacity for dialogical thickness that subverts every monologic
temptation:

- the monologic temptation to *despair*;
- the monologic temptation to *anger*;
- the monologic temptation to *denial*; and
- every monologic temptation that keeps one from being engaged with
  the present truth of life in the presence of all of our companions.

It has occurred to me that "supervision" is a misnomer, which I take to mean
to "see over" or to "oversee." Better to call that mentoring process "superaudi-
tion," the capacity to hear better, or "superutterance," the capacity to speak more
truthfully, more hearingly.

There is no doubt that the mentoring process aims to evoke agents who can
engage in a profoundly countercultural process of thickness wherein God's holiness seeks us out and may from time to time bivouac among us for an instant.
This countercultural process is something expositors and pastors are always
relearning. Expositors are tempted to the *thinness of criticism*. Pastors are tempted
to the *thinness of assurance*. The primal script of the biblical text reminds us that

our community has been doing verbatims forever in which we have the very words

- of the present self;
- of the anticipated self;
- of the Holy God;
- of the adversary; and
- of the good companion.

This script resists every silencing reductionism. The disciplines of biblical studies and pastoral care may together move back and forth more intentionally than we have done between *present verbatim* and *ancient verbatim*. Between the lines in those scripts is thickness that cannot be hurried. Imagine this alternative community rooted in Sinai with contested fidelity, waiting between the lines while our monologic culture rushes to conclusions.

Chapter 3

On Knowing, Not Knowing, and Being Known

I.

The relationship between the church and higher education is immensely important and deeply problematic just now.[1] It opens us to recurring tensions that require rethinking. It poses the large question of *faith and reason*, the notion from the Enlightenment that reason must be autonomous and that faith of any particular kind is a compromise of reason. It poses the issue that we must *believe in order to understand*, a view that takes faith as a premise of sound reason, and the notion that our reason is as corrupt as all else and stands in need of the repentance of faith. It also poses the equally large issue of *Christ and culture*, and of course the classical discussion of H. Richard Niebuhr, flawed as it is now seen to be, has led most of us to hold a view that "Christ," by which we have generally meant the mission of the church, is to transform "culture." What we now witness in our society, however, is that culture powerfully transforms the church and produces a deeply distorted, compromised community of faith that itself lacks transformative capacity.

The recent narrative of the church and higher education, now frequently recited, is a simple one:

- In the United States, it was largely church communities that *founded and funded* the initial institutions of higher learning in the schools that long preceded land grant institutions.
- Through the twentieth century, these church-based schools tended to resonate so fully with American cultural reality that inside the schools themselves faith came to be seen as an authoritarian check on free inquiry. As a consequence, the model of free inquiry by scholars who were schooled in *skeptical criticism* found it necessary to eschew the categories of faith.
- At the outset of the twenty-first century, we are now *rethinking and seeking to recover* the connection of church to higher education, but that reconnection is exceedingly difficult as it moves between the *temptation to authoritarianism* and a *deep commitment to skepticism* that occupies many institutions.

In what follows I will reference what I have to say to Elmhurst College and then turn the discussion to the Old Testament, my own field of competence.

II.

Since our theme is higher education, I will begin by commenting a bit on my experience at Elmhurst College, my own beginning point in higher education.

The themes I wish to explore arose for me in a course in philosophy by William J. Halfter. He was a keen thinker but, I thought at the time, a bit complicated in his articulation. That course in philosophy began with the Ionian philosophers concerning air, earth, fire, and water. And when we reached the Middle Ages in our survey, Professor Halfter led us through the mystery of "nominalism and realism," an issue I think none of us grasped; certainly we did not grasp the cruciality of the question for the modern period.

The part of Halfter's presentation to which I want now to refer was his delineation of *information, knowledge,* and *wisdom.* We did not spend much time on information, as that point was obvious, though I now suppose we would say "data." But the distinction between knowledge and wisdom was difficult and complex for us. Knowledge—*gnosis*—was an attempt to decode the mystery into manageable technique. Such knowledge made it possible to give access to the secret ways of the gods and therefore to harness the mysterious powers of the universe. By contrast, wisdom—*sophia*—is a perspective of discernment that honors and respects mystery and that seeks to respond to that mystery without reducing it to manageable proportion.

Though I did not think so then and Halfter did not say so, I suggest now that the distinction between knowledge as *mystery decoded for management* and wisdom as *respect for and response to mystery* gives us an access point to the theme of the church and higher education. The theme connects because higher education trades in knowledge, especially now that the agenda of institutions has become so pragmatic; and without taking such knowledge lightly, moreover, the church has a deep stake in wisdom, with which our pragmatic culture is profoundly impatient.

Reinhold Niebuhr, our most distinguished alum, whose piercing eyes grace the center of the campus, was not a deep philosophic Christian thinker, though he knew the philosophic tradition well. One can see the dialectical edge of his thinking and many of his most famous and repeatable aphorisms to be an acute awareness of the distinction between knowledge and wisdom. In Niebuhr's categories, knowledge might be taken as pragmatic realism about power in the world, but Niebuhr's sense of wisdom, "mystery beyond control," caused a sustained awareness on his part that human knowledge is always penultimate and is contained within holiness that will not be administered. Niebuhr is known for his critical pragmatism; he understood power and its root reality, ideology, and its self-deception, and the illusions generated by knowledge. In the end, however, Niebuhr's greatest gift was irony, the recognition that nothing is as it seems or purports to be. It is this embrace of irony that cautioned Niebuhr away from pretensions of every kind that took the form of self-interested idolatry. Thus Niebuhr, surely characteristic of Elmhurst College at its best and of higher education at its most alert, worked the deep riddle of faith and reason. He was Lutheran enough to mistrust reason. In his own way, he understood finally that while his articulation of faith was often abbreviated in his pragmatism, his faith was only barely beneath the surface of what he said, wrote, and thought.

H. Richard Niebuhr—interestingly, "Helmut" until he went to Yale—was president of Elmhurst College and surely the generator that transformed Elmhurst into an American institution. His thought was more subtle than that of his older brother Reinhold, and his was of a somewhat different tack. He was less pragmatic than Reinhold, more attuned to the community of faith as a defining force in public reality. I cite two particular instances. First, in the most famous exchange between the two brothers concerning World War II and American engagement, Reinhold was something of a hawk and ready to act. H. Richard's response was entitled, "The Grace of Doing Nothing." In this phrase, he moved against easy knowledge and equally easy power, and understood about a cunning at the core of history that is not easily decoded into policy. His formulation allowed much more for God's decisive inscrutability in the public process. The implication of H. Richard's formulation is that the pragmatic management of knowledge and power toward which Reinhold was inclined must be recognized as finally penultimate.

Second, H. Richard was commencement speaker at my Elmhurst College graduation in 1955. Even though Elmhurst College was thoroughly secularized—its church relatedness by 1955 largely truncated—preacher that he was, H. Richard took a biblical text as his theme. His text struck me then and still strikes me as quite remarkable for the occasion:

For thus said the Lord GOD, the Holy One of Israel:
In returning and rest you shall be saved;
    in quietness and in trust shall be your strength.
But you refused and said,
"No! We will flee upon horses"— therefore you shall flee!
and, "We will ride upon swift steeds"—
    therefore your pursuers shall be swift!

                            Isa. 30:15–16

Imagine saying that at a graduation exercise in can-do America!

In the book of Isaiah, the voice of the text is a prophetic reprimand for royal policy in Jerusalem that relied on its own military capacity and would, so Isaiah is sure, lead to disaster—which it finally did. In 1955, H. Richard was issuing a warning against an easy, simple assumption that can-do energy—perhaps not unlike that of his brother Reinhold—could have its day but finally could not succeed. Heard now from Isaiah via H. Richard, the voice sounds a warning against military unilateralism that is every time a harbinger to disaster. Thus, H. Richard is himself a model of Christ speaking to culture, a word of faith in a context of reasoned autonomy.

I cite Halfter, Reinhold Niebuhr, and H. Richard Niebuhr first as representative practitioners of church and higher education, but then second to indicate that these issues have been cooking at Elmhurst College for a long, long time. H. Richard insisted that Elmhurst College must engage U.S. culture, but he never compromised his conviction of restraint that U.S. culture—and its schools of higher learning—may never be regarded as autonomous in their knowledge. That restraint of faith is hidden, slow, indirect, and inscrutable. But it is a given for which current articulation in every new circumstance remains a significant challenge.

III.

In order for me to say anything of my own on the subject of the church and higher education, I must transpose that topic into my own field of Old Testament studies. The theme of church and higher education is, I suggest, adumbrated in the Old Testament in the wisdom traditions—in the first instance in the book of Proverbs and ultimately in the book of Job. It is agreed by scholars that these sapiential traditions participated in the common culture of learning in the Ancient Near East and that they eschewed the more "sectarian" categories of narrative and prophets.

There is a consensus among scholars, moreover, that the methods of wisdom teachers are profoundly empirical; what they offered is a reflection upon the accumulated deposit of lived experience in the community. The wisdom material in the mouth of teachers and the principal mode of utterance is surely instruction, albeit in quite artistic form. That wisdom is done by empirical method in the mouth of teachers for the purpose of instruction thus gives us "education." What makes this material "higher education" is that the data upon which reflection is based is treated in a critical fashion in a highly urbane theoretical and even speculative way. This is education that is "higher" in the sense that it is not content simply to reiterate old conventions or settle for things gotten at first glance. This is rather a more or less systemic method whereby lived experience is "troped," that is, cast in highly imaginative form whereby the teaching makes an observation, but it also, at the same, hides and transforms, invites and teases. It seems evident that even if wisdom sayings to some extent originated in folk society, they are now taken up in a more learned way, perhaps in schools and certainly in court systems of the most urbane intelligentsia. And of course the prime example of "higher" in this education is the book of Job, a remarkably learned poem that until now defies any simple decoding. It defies simple decoding because its artistic authors recognize that behind the dilemma upon which they reflect stands mystery. The literature is shaped to invite the reader into the mystery, here posed through the image of whirlwind. Thus, the wisdom material is *education* and it is *higher*.

But it is also, in an odd sort of way, *church* higher education, because the literature is filled with faith. Proverbs both asserts and assumes that YHWH is the governor who upholds and sustains the created order to give reliable coherence to life. In the poem of Job, however, the name of YHWH, the God of Israel, is for a long time withheld so that the poem uses only generic names for God, as a student of religion might prefer. It is only in Job 38, after the long cycle of exchanges between Job and his friends, in the speech from the whirlwind, that faith finally utters the name of YHWH and so places at risk all of the previously held generic reflections on religion. This is an extraordinary achievement wherein faith sits at the interface with urbane education and invites that education beyond its assumed categories into mystery. This wisdom in the Old Testament then is *higher education* vis-à-vis the *church*, a design and an artistic articulation that invite the very best critical thought but that in the end are compelling in their faith commitment.

This is not to say that these wisdom teachers are naive fideists, for the book of Job lets faith be subjected to the accusation of injustice, but that assault in the end is contained by faith that is itself stretched by the argument. Thus, the tension works both ways in the book of Job, so that faith pushes learning beyond itself, but learning pushes faith to new venturesome extremity. One can see here, I believe, an extraordinary case of faith and reason, of "Christ and culture" that gives the church its hard work in higher education. In what follows, I will explore three aspects of our topic: on knowing, on not knowing, and on being known.

IV. ON KNOWING

I begin with a proverb that states the two sides of our issue:

It is the glory of God to conceal things,
  but the glory of kings is to search things out.
                                    Prov. 25:2

I want to highlight here the second half of the Proverb—that it is the glory of kings to search things out.

It is the business of higher education to know, to accumulate, to fashion, to preserve, and to transmit knowledge. In the ancient world, the king at the center of the cult, the economy, and high culture was the great engine of knowledge, the one who could mobilize limitless resources not only to satisfy the practical needs of the state but to engage in the luxury of artistic and aesthetic ventures. In the Old Testament, Solomon is the quintessential model of the king whose glory it is to seek things out. Indeed, for reasons political, economic, and symbolic, the royal administration could maintain a virtual monopoly on knowledge. In the modern world, that capacity for knowledge is somewhat democratized but not completely so. Knowledge continues to be a primal mark of government, though government has many satellites in business and industry and higher education, all of which engage in research and development. It is obvious that most scientific breakthroughs are of a quite pragmatic kind and most often in the service of the military. The state works at a monopoly of power and must do so in order to stay at the front edge of knowledge.

If, however, we ponder things more specifically and do not think simply of grand research engines but of schools like Elmhurst College, it is still a knowledge industry. In hundreds of schools like this one, there are faculty members who every day do their small bit to advance learning. They complain about overwork and too many committee meetings, but sometime during the day or the week, they finish another paragraph or another lab report or another formula or another poem that has never been done in precisely that way before. And alongside them, there are students in every such school who learn. Some learn because they must. Some learn to advance a career. Some learn for the sheer ecstasy of it. The reason such learning is so demanding is that learning is always toward *the not known* that upon the day of embrace becomes *the known*. Such students pore over old poems and cut pig's eyes. They write papers and do research. Sometimes they imagine a new idea, only to be deflated to find it already known. What they are doing in the humanities and the sciences and the arts and the social sciences is mostly to learn so that they can be situated in the already known. They learn the codes and the formulations, the lore and the methods to participate in symbolic culture, an adventure of great work. But in Elmhurst College and in every such school, from this pool of students situated in the already known, some few will join the process of formulating new knowledge, and so Elmhurst College produces its small but impressive number of knowledge producers who in time to come will shape the world.

But of course there is more to *the known* than simply knowledge. The modern world is premised on the aphorism of Frances Bacon that "knowledge is power."[2] One can take that aphorism generically to recognize that knowledge is a primary access point to the halls of influence; quite concretely, knowledge does lead to power in every discipline. Thus higher education, with its accent upon the known, concerns empowerment—empowerment over "nature," empowerment with words and symbols to manage and shape and manipulate, empowerment of the self and the conduct of self in community.

The formula "knowledge is power" has as well a more ominous overtone, for autonomous knowledge leads to unbridled power. It is important to remember that kings—or governments or corporations—pursue knowledge precisely for the use of power. It is possible that power may be used to enhance the community; it is more probable, however, that an autonomous king or an autonomous government or an autonomous corporation—allied with knowledge-producing higher education—will use power in self-serving, self-enhancing ways without reference to the common good.

It is clear in the ancient world of Solomon that knowledge turned to military and commercial power that eventuated in state slavery. It is unmistakable that the knowledge that emerged after Bacon in the modern world moved, very quickly, to the Thirty Years' War and the emergence of the absolute nation-state. And in our time, moreover, it is beyond doubt that it was knowledge as power that produced the hysteria and anxiety of the Cold War and the concentration of huge wealth in the hands of a few. It is beyond doubt that it was knowledge as power that evidently produced the Vietnam War and a dozen other acts of state violence. It is a sad but true commentary on knowledge as power that fixed Lyndon Johnson in our imagination as a futile, bewildered president with his Vietnam face hopelessly in his hands, surrounded by the wise men of his generation who had not a clue.[3] That shamelessness culminated perhaps in the verdict of McGeorge Bundy, the primary architect of the Vietnam War, who said of himself, his brother William, and their cohorts, "We were good, but we were not as good as we thought we were."[4] And now we have the chance to watch former Secretary of Defense Robert McNamara stammer his way, yet again, through *The Fog of War*, the pathos-filled retrospective on the Vietnam War, in sadness and a reach of courage. Finally, it is beyond doubt that knowledge as power is what propelled Cheney and Rumsfeld and Wolfowitz in their ignorant pursuit of hegemony in initiating the unprovoked war in Iraq, unembarrassed without blushing at violence in the name of democracy.

You may think that these are only extreme cases that I cite in an excessively partisan way. I insist, however, that as we think about higher education, these cases are representative of the end result of *limitless knowledge* that is shameless and autonomous and that makes available *limitless power* that imagines that the whole of life may be made accessible to a very particular agenda. It is indeed the glory of kings to seek out knowledge!

V. ON *NOT KNOWING*

The other part of the proverb I have cited is this: "It is the glory of God to conceal things." This line in the proverb serves to qualify and limit the line about seeking out knowledge. The reference to God is a sapiential way of speaking about the ultimate hiddenness of the sources and purposes of life that are beyond and unavailable to our self-serving ideologies and our shameless idolatries. What a mouthful! The line shows that these wisdom teachers, these early advocates of higher education, were not mere pragmatists. They were not interested in simple analytic treatment of the data of life. They were, rather, faith-grounded people who did not need to parade or call attention to their faith in God, but who were unable to come at the empirical data of life except by reference to that hidden mystery of life that is actively kept beyond human discovery. My thesis is that the church's vocation vis-à-vis higher education is to be one important witness to the awareness that *knowledge is given in limit* and *power is curbed* by a restraint that is intrinsic to the creative processes of life.

In the first instance, that is why the church historically has been deeply allied with the humanities—with literature, history, and philosophy. In the second instance, it is this great triad that provides a tradition of pondering the mystery that constitutes lived reality and that situates the human pursuit of knowledge and power in a holy coming that defies our mastery.

Philosophy stands at the heart of higher education. And while philosophy has in recent times been twisted and distorted for trivial usage, it is always concerned with *metaquestions*—first, an acknowledgment that there are indeed *metaquestions*; second, the probe of the oddness of change and constancy, of one and many, of particular and universal, of transient and permanent, all questions that keep us from committing blindly to the fashionable currents of the day.

History stands at the heart of higher education as a memory not just of wars and rumors of wars and officeholders, but an inventory of the odd mistakes, strange miscalculations, and inscrutable convergences that have left the world scarred and warped and occasionally new. We may, through such a reentry into memory, be empowered by human choice to be agents in our own history—not objects of fate but choosers in more freedom than our ideologies can entertain.

The study of *literature* stands at the heart of higher education as, on the one hand, the capacity to parse grammar correctly, because reality must be well said if it is to be well lived. On the other hand, literature provides any society with a written chronicle of self-critical reflection, from Shakespeare and Milton through Melville and Hawthorne and on to John Updike and Alice Walker and Mary Oliver in our English-speaking world.

The import of the humanities that self-serving knowledge and unbridled power cannot drive out is that the learner is located in a cloud of witnesses, each of whom continues to give testimony that matters even now.

But the church is not simply an advocate of old-fashioned disciplines that lack market value. The church has a stake in *the natural sciences* to insist that the object of study is not just "nature" as an autonomous system but is a *creation*, a coherent life-giving whole willed and loved and empowered by the Creator, who has provisionally entrusted the processes of life to creation but has not given the mystery of that process over to us.[5] The church's stake in the natural sciences is that we learn to order, love, respect, enhance, and serve the creation as a milieu of life and not simply an object of exploitation.

The church has a stake in *the social sciences* in order to insist that the human community is an ongoing construction of human imagination. That work of human imagination requires ongoing sustenance and human effort. It continues to form and construct and correct and enhance what is possible in human community. The social sciences, alongside the humanities, are interested not only in analysis of crowds but in *the maintenance of a public* that is served and empowered by a citizenry under obligation.

The church has a stake in *the arts*. The church has a provisional alliance with the artistic articulation of the absurd, but it also has a mandate to be honest beyond the truth of absurdity to affirm that absurdity is not a final statement. Pondering the absurd is itself a sign of meaningfulness that resists absurdity and nihilism. What the church knows is that *truth about pain* is peculiarly *allied with hope*. And so the arts in their several articulations keep at the task of vision, now among us a modest, scarred vision, but nonetheless a vision that insists that endless brutality—whether by terrorists or by state policy—is not the story of the world.

And beyond all of these classical disciplines, now *international studies* and *global studies*, while relatively new among us, are a more disciplined embrace of the world than the old imperial mission practices of the church. Autonomy in knowledge and power results in the view that *we*—wherever *we* are—are the norm for all of life. But now there are burgeoning studies to remind us of the *other*, the other unlike us but alongside us, not only trading partners and political threats, but an *other* with whom to exchange gifts of culture and trust and hope, to give of our Western largesse but also to receive at the point of our glaring deficits.

The church's preoccupation with the hiddenness of God makes testimony that our knowledge is at best penultimate, partial, distorted, and never "successful." The proverb I have quoted says more than that hiddenness is in the nature of things. More than that, it is God's glory to hide knowledge, a cat and mouse game conducted by a Divine Trickster who moves against everyone who imagines that we know enough to be masters.

I suggest that the church's testimony to the hiddenness of God must, in the first instance, resist the current U.S. religious temptation to reduce God to a friendly, good-buddy eminence and, conversely, to bear witness to the God who is beyond all of our categories: "Am I a God near by, says the LORD, and not a God far off?" (Jer. 23:23).

1. The church witnesses amid higher education that at the core of reality is *holiness, an inapproachability* that invites respect, modesty, and humility. The narrative in 2 Samuel 6:6–12 witnesses to the risk of touching the holy ark and being killed. This God is not mocked, but the church must say so in ways that do not smack of authoritarianism, for the church's own claims are properly made with modesty, humility, and respect. That may be a model for all claims of truth.

2. The holiness that stands at the center of reality is not an amorphous blob but is *infused with moral purpose* that transcends our pet projects. The Creator

has shaped and formed creation so that there are undeniable mandates imposed upon every creature, upon every human creature. Thus, Proverbs characteristically is an attempt to articulate in artistic form the mandates that are not imposed in revelation but are visible and inescapable in the processes of creation itself. Of course, it is hazardous to offer a simple formulation of these holy mandates, even though Moses likely gave the best offer, for every such formulation runs the risk of ideology. Nonetheless, it is clear that this Holy Urge who governs the world is bent toward justice, mercy, truth, and compassion, in the end directed toward neighbor love, which includes the love of neighbors in need, neighbors across all lines of race, territory, tongue, class, and so forth, but also vulnerable neighbors like radishes and rabbits and catfish and elm trees. That mandate touches what is taught in higher education, but it also invites critical reflection upon the allocation of resources and access.

3. That holiness with moral purpose is *Other*, unlike us, or with Karl Barth "wholly other" (*ganz Anders*). This vision of holy otherness keeps us aware that even in our most thoughtful imagination, our best efforts at knowledge can never approximate divine purpose. Thus, higher education has a mandate in this context to teach self-criticism and self-transcendence, that this Holy Other stands over against our best partisan commitments. It is surely a measure of the failure of higher education that just now the voting public in the United States is so susceptible to ideology that traffics in an alliance of religious commitment and military adventurism.

4. The holy reality with moral purpose that is other is a *Thou* who addresses us as a *Thou*. This has been known among us since God's first utterance to the anxious couple in the garden of Eden. God engages in two-way conversation even while God holds the initiative in that conversation. Human agents, peculiarly among God's creatures, are *addressed, called by name*, termed "*Thou*" and *summoned* to answer. This means that reality is fundamentally relational and that the human enterprise is ultimately dialogical. We may equip ourselves to uphold our end of the dialogue for direct, fearful engagement with the Holy One. The idea that human life is dialogical is not a new thought in the humanities, but it is a *novum* in much religious thought that wants to freeze God as an absolute who is beyond impingement by a dialogical partner. Such a dialogic notion of God deabsolutizes every easy claim for God; it also deabsolutizes human claims—political, economic, cultural, or religious—that are made in an absolutist way as though to echo the absoluteness of God. Thus, commitment to the holy dialogic God means that the church has an immense stake in higher education that is itself dialogic, that knows that every settlement of truth is provisional and contextual and must be revisited beyond settlement. That it is God's glory to conceal from us God's own purposes (Prov. 25:2).

5. It is nonetheless the claim of the church that we have seen glimpses of that Holy Other fleshed among us in Jesus of Nazareth, who is the truth as well as the way and the life. Now I understand that any direct confession of Jesus Christ pushes higher education excessively in a direction that smacks of

authoritarianism and that presumes ready closure. At best, the church's confession is at the interface with higher education but not imposed upon it.

We may consider this interface by holding together the most elemental claim for Jesus and the most sweeping theological claim made for him. The elemental claim is this: "For I handed on to you as of first importance what I in turn had received: that Christ died for our sins in accordance with the scriptures, and that he was buried, and that he was raised on the third day in accordance with the scriptures" (1 Cor. 15:3–4). The church, in its scandal of particularity, confesses that the Messiah was crucified, that the carrier of God's truth died, and that in his death, "the things that are are reduced to nothing" (1 Cor. 1:28). This acknowledgment of the death sentence over all things creaturely is of course matched by the Easter claim that on Sunday we see at work the God who "calls into existence the things that do not exist" (Rom. 4:17). These two claims, of the failure of the creaturely and the resilient power of God to make things new, become a frame for rethinking and reliving the world in the presence of the holy God. It is of course unfortunate that this twofold claim has not been understood, articulated, or appropriated as a critical principle that destabilizes all knowledge and power, and that invites work toward new truth yet to be given.

This most elemental and oft-repeated claim for Jesus may be linked to the most sweeping theological claim I know: "He himself is before all things; and in him all things hold together" (Col. 1:17). This statement, so characteristically sapiential in tone, dares to claim that Jesus of Nazareth is the force of coherence for all of creation. Or as Gene Wehrli has said, "Jesus is the glue of the universe." What a claim that has become jaded among us, that knowledge and power finally are given, measured, and curbed by the story of creature deathliness and divine newness, a wonder of loss and a greater wonder of gift. It is no wonder then that God delights in concealing. And authentic higher education leads to the awareness that after truth is searched out, still more is withheld. To be educated is *to know* and *not to know*.

VI. ON BEING KNOWN

If we now move in wisdom teaching, an ancient form of higher education, from Proverbs to Job, we may move beyond *knowing* and *not knowing*. Job—a righteous man, an eloquent poet, a considerable theologian—knows. He knows about the moral expectation of God, and he knows the calculus of obedience and blessing. He knows how to gather evidence and draw conclusions. He knows how to make arguments and go to court to make the case.

As the argument moves in the book of Job, however, halfway through it dawns on Job that he does not know. It begins to occur to him that his knowledge is futile and beside the point. It is not adequate to be a knower. At midpoint, in Job 28, there is a remarkable soliloquy about the hiddenness of wisdom that lives elusively beyond knowledge. Job does an inventory of knowledge of a scientific sort about the energy resources in the earth that are beyond human access. And then, in a moment of awareness, he asserts:

> But where shall wisdom be found?
>   And where is the place of understanding?
> Mortals do not know the way to it,
>   and it is not found in the land of the living.
> The deep says, "It is not in me,"
>   and the sea says, "It is not with me."
> It cannot be gotten for gold,
>   and silver cannot be weighed out as its price.
>   Job 28:12–15

And then, a second time, comes the same awareness:

> Where then does wisdom come from?
>   And where is the place of understanding?
> It is hidden from the eyes of all living,
>   and concealed from the birds of the air.
>   28:20–21

And then the conclusion that only God fully knows:

> God understands the way to it,
>   and he knows its place.
> For he looks to the ends of the earth,
>   and sees everything under the heavens.
> When he gave to the wind its weight,
>   and apportioned out the waters by measure;
> when he made a decree for the rain,
>   and a way for the thunderbolt;
> then he saw it and declared it;
>   he established it, and searched it out.
>   28:23–27

Now Job must occupy a place in the world where we all live, knowing but in fact not knowing. He continues in this dilemma of knowing and not knowing through chapter 31, and in that chapter he is still vigorous in his self-assertion.

But then, dramatically, the poem turns in chapter 38; for the first time, God speaks. Now for the first time in the poetry the proper name for God, "YHWH," is used. Heretofore we have had only generic names for God, but now we enter Israel's particularity, thus signaling the scandalous particularity of the Israelite God:

> Then the LORD answered Job out of the whirlwind:
> "Who is this that darkens counsel by words without knowledge?
> Gird up your loins like a man,
>   I will question you, and you shall declare to me.
> Where were you when I laid the foundation of the earth?
>   Tell me, if you have understanding.

Who determined its measurements—surely you know!
    Or who stretched the line upon it?
On what were its bases sunk,
    or who laid its cornerstone
when the morning stars sang together
    and all the heavenly beings shouted for joy?
Or who shut in the sea with doors
    when it burst out from the womb?—
when I made the clouds its garment,
    and thick darkness its swaddling band,
and prescribed bounds for it;
    and set bars and doors,
and said, 'Thus far shall you come, and no farther,
    and here shall your proud waves be stopped'"?
                        38:1–11

The one who has been making speeches is now addressed by God. The one who has known so much is now submitted to questioning:

Gird up your loins like a man,
    I will question you, and you shall declare to me.
                        38:3

The questions, of course, are rhetorical. But even rhetorical questions invite the hosting of an imagined answer. We may imagine Job imagining answers to this divine probe:

Where were you?—"Nowhere."

Who determined its measure?—"Not me."

Have you commanded the morning since your days began?—"Never."

Have you entered the springs of the sea?—"No."

Have you comprehended the expanse of the earth?—"No, I never tried."

Where is the way to the dwelling of light?—"I don't know."

The questions go on and on. The answers are cumulative: "Nowhere; Not me; Never; No; No, I never tried; I don't know." The first impact of these questions and their implied answers is to end the bombast of Job, to reduce Job to silence, and to invite a new humility. Job is shown to be a nonplayer in the world of real knowledge and real power. The Holy One concludes, "Anyone who argues with God must respond" (40:2). Job does give an answer, but it is the tamed response of a dethroned speaker:

See, I am of small account; what shall I answer you?
    I lay my hand on my mouth.
I have spoken once, and I will not answer;
    twice, but will proceed no further.
                    40:4–5

But the second realization from this barrage of questions is, I suggest, different. Job now moves out of his role as objective advocate who in *dubito* can therefore *sum*. Now he is engaged and is the lesser party, the one called to account. It must dawn on Job as an easy, objective learner who finds himself now under question: *God knows about me and has placed me into question.* Job thought he knew, and the friends thought they knew; they, however, are living in a world of objective reason and now are drawn into a dialogue where one is called into account and into question.

What faith knows and must say to reason is that *we are known* in a way that completely repositions us. The movement of Job from being *the knower* to being *known* causes me to imagine something like a transfer from a busy, anonymous city to a closely knit village. In the former, one can engage in deception and self-deception and posturing. But in the village, there is always someone observing who knows, and being known changes everything. It robs one of autonomy. It denies one sheer freedom. It invites to accountability. It brings one under expectation. And so Job must end his posturing. He is a learner, but now he has been learned about. His response at the end may be one of submission or one of defiance; either way, it is from a very different angle than that of an objective knower (42:6).

We may take Psalm 139 as a primal commentary on the movement of Job from *knowing* to *not knowing* (Job 28) to *being known* (Job 38–41). The speaker of Psalm 139 knows what it is like to be under surveillance by the Holy One:

> O LORD, you have searched me and known me.
> You know when I sit down and when I rise up;
>   you discern my thoughts from far away.
> You search out my path and my lying down,
>   and are acquainted with all my ways.
> Even before a word is on my tongue,
>   O LORD, you know it completely.
> You hem me in, behind and before,
>   and lay your hand upon me.
> Such knowledge is too wonderful for me;
>   it is so high that I cannot attain it.
>   Ps. 139:1–6

The psalmist discovers that he has no choice now to flee back to autonomy. He is presently in the crosshairs of the Almighty and has no choice to be alone again. As he reflects on being known, he is astonished:

> For it was you who formed my inward parts;
>   you knit me together in my mother's womb.
>   139:13

He moves to glad doxology for the wonder of his own life that he had not known before or had valued:

I praise you, for I am fearfully and wonderfully made.
  Wonderful are your works;
that I know very well.
  My frame was not hidden from you,
when I was being made in secret,
  intricately woven in the depths of the earth.
Your eyes beheld my unformed substance.
In your book were written all the days that were formed for me,
  when none of them as yet existed.
How weighty to me are your thoughts, O God!

139:14–17

The reality of God becomes defining and all comprehensive for him, but the final outcome is companionship, not the deciphering of the holy:

I try to count them—they are more than the sand;
  I come to the end—I am still with you.

139:18

The loneliness of knowing is overcome by being known. In the end, this Joban psalmist wants to be better known by God and wants life to conform to the moral righteousness of the Holy One:

Search me, O God, and know my heart;
  test me and know my thoughts.
See if there is any wicked way in me,
  and lead me in the way everlasting.

139:23–24

VII.

There is a remarkable movement about *education* when the depth of *faith* pervades it. One is driven more closely to the core of communion that is one's true habitat. *To know* is a vocation. *Not to know* is to enter beyond autonomy into dialogue. *To be known* is to see oneself truly with, alongside, and before holiness that is the truth of our life.

I suggest that this is a journey made in the process of maturity. In the move from *information* to *knowledge* and then to *wisdom* comes the capacity to accept one's penultimate place in God's creation. Education, of course, does not end there. For the next day, the faithful must go back to school, must engage in higher education, and must take up the task of knowledge. There is more yet to be discovered, so much granted us around the edges of holiness. As we relate to the truth, however, there is a soberness and a modesty, an easing of anxiety, for everything does not depend on our knowing. Postdialogical knowing is a new kind of freedom, the freedom born of companionship that need no longer take knowledge as dispute and achievement.

The move from *knowing* to *being known* by way of *not knowing* is an endless negotiation among us:

- Roy Shaffer has characterized sexual reciprocity as the capacity variously to be milieu for the partner and agent with the partner.[6] He says that maturity is the capacity to embrace both these roles.
- Elie Wiesel has characterized rabbis who expostulate against God but then on cue turn and bow in humility.[7]

The flexibility suggested in various venues by Shaffer and Wiesel is the flexibility that belongs to good education, education that is centered in the buoyancy of faith. The church need not fear knowledge but takes the pursuit of knowledge as a proper vocation. But the church must hold up its end of the conversation to keep knowledge in context, to invite learners by way of knowledge to wisdom. One can imagine such wisdom is possible only in and through knowledge. That is of course the hope of the best higher education. Such education is thick; it lives in modesty. But while modest, those who engage it find themselves fully empowered to be their true selves, alive for God's world.

Chapter 4

Three Waves of Certitude

Almost every pastor with whom I speak says that the deepest problem faced in the day-to-day practice of ministry is a small-minded certitude among people who have faith tied up in a box that keeps faith safe and beyond penetration. That small-mindedness

- tends to be simplistic, so that there is a great dumbing down;
- tends to be uncritical, so that there can be no real engagement with it;
- tends to be disconnected from the daily reality of life around us and of the life in the larger world;
- tends to be marked by acute ideological passion, largely on the right, but not limited to the right;
- tends to turn all energy inward in a defensive closure, so that there is nothing left for missional energy; and
- tends to be reflective of deep, unarticulated, and unacknowledged anxiety, with a tight lid that precludes discussion, exploration, openness, or change.

Such a practice of certitude presents a minefield for the pastor. A certitude that knows all the answers before the questions are posed is stultifying and saps the community of energy. Given the fact that the pastoral task is to assist and equip the saints to process their lives toward the newness of God's rule, this environment for ministry is an almost unbearable milieu.

In this chapter, I want to consider the practice of certitude in the Old Testament and hope to show that every effort at certitude is, sooner or later, subverted and deconstructed by the ongoing dynamism of life. I take up this question in the hope that we might think about the challenge of ministry in a social context of fear, and the ways in which scriptural resources may be of value as we do the pastoral work that is faithful and important to the church.

I.

Consider Solomon, the temple builder, as the great purveyor of certitude in the Old Testament.[1] He is the son of David, the king who received a blank check of assurance from the God of the exodus (2 Sam. 7:1–16). Nathan the prophet spoke words of assurance to David that carried with them an offer of certitude concerning his son:

> I will be a father to him, and he shall be a son to me. When he commits iniquity, I will punish him with a rod such as mortals use, with blows inflicted by human beings. But I will not take my steadfast love from him, as I took it from Saul, whom I put away from before you. Your house and your kingdom shall be made sure forever before me; your throne shall be established forever. In accordance with all these words and with all this vision, Nathan spoke to David. (2 Sam. 7:14–17)

The oracle of Nathan is echoed in the Psalms:

> But I will not remove from him my steadfast love,
>   or be false to my faithfulness.
> I will not violate my covenant,
>   or alter the word that went forth from my lips.
> Once and for all I have sworn by my holiness;
>   I will not lie to David.
> His line shall continue forever,
>   and his throne endure before me like the sun.
> It shall be established forever like the moon,
>   an enduring witness in the skies.
>   Ps. 89:33–37

The son lived amid the certitudes of the father. When Solomon had seized power in a contest with his brother Adonijah, he was duly installed as heir to David's power and authority, heir as well to divine assurance and royal certitude:

> There let the priest Zadok and the prophet Nathan anoint him king over Israel; then blow the trumpet, and say, "Long live King Solomon!" You

shall go up following him. Let him enter and sit on my throne; he shall be king in my place; for I have appointed him to be ruler over Israel and over Judah. Benaiah son of Jehoiada answered the king, "Amen! May the LORD, the God of my lord the king, so ordain. As the LORD has been with my lord the king, so may he be with Solomon, and make his throne greater than the throne of my lord King David." (1 Kgs. 1:34–37)

That pageant of assurance was confirmed, so the narrative claims, in a night visitation as the Lord appeared to Solomon in a dream. Solomon was invited by the dream lord, "Ask what I should give you" (1 Kgs. 3:5), and Solomon, in a mood of pious deference, asks only for the gifts in order to be a good king:

> Give your servant therefore an understanding mind to govern your people, able to discern between good and evil; for who can govern this your great people? (3:9)

Solomon answered rightly and so was rewarded by the dream lord with much more than he asked:

> God said to him, "Because you have asked this, and have not asked for yourself long life or riches, or for the life of your enemies, but have asked for yourself understanding to discern what is right, I now do according to your word. Indeed I give you a wise and discerning mind; no one like you has been before you and no one like you shall arise after you. I give you also what you have not asked, both riches and honor all your life; no other king shall compare with you." (3:11–13)

Solomon is assured of every blessing that will make him without parallel on the earth.

The Solomon narrative is dominated by "the king's great thing," the building of the temple.[2] In the construction of the temple—which involves careful planning, good craftsmen, and limited budget resources—the king builds a self-congratulatory monument that acknowledges his divine guarantee. There, in downtown Jerusalem for all to see, Solomon is visibly the most pious, most successful, most-to-be-admired king. The temple is there for taxpaying peasants to see him in their regular pilgrimages. The temple is there for other kings to see in their trade missions to Jerusalem.

Finally, at long last the temple is completed; it must have been the talk of the Near East:

> Thus all the work that King Solomon did on the house of the LORD was finished. Solomon brought in the things that his father David had dedicated, the silver, the gold, and the vessels, and stored them in the treasuries of the house of the LORD. (7:51)

All that remained was the elaborate, extravagant service of dedication that would be, in Israel, the great ecumenical consolidation of religious loyalty, economic resources, and political authority. The dedication was accomplished in a great pageant, so that the populous would not doubt that something great had happened that had decisively turned history toward its culmination in Jerusalem.

- The pageant included all the leadership of every sector of Israelite society:

> Then Solomon assembled the elders of Israel and all the heads of the tribes, the leaders of the ancestral houses of the Israelites, before King Solomon in Jerusalem. (8:1a)

- All of them, either willingly or grudgingly, were recruited for the occasion.

- The pageant featured the ark, the symbol of the old tribal tradition, so that the old tribal loyalties were confiscated for the new enterprise in the royal city and transported to the temple:

> . . . to bring up the ark of the covenant of the LORD out of the city of David, which is Zion. All the people of Israel assembled to King Solomon at the festival in the month Ethanim, which is the seventh month. And all the elders of Israel came, and the priests carried the ark. So they brought up the ark of the LORD, the tent of meeting, and all the holy vessels that were in the tent; the priests and the Levites brought them up. (8:1b–4)

- The pageant exhibited the king's extravagant piety by the expenditure of huge wealth in religious devotion, the offering of valuable animals that made clear that the king could afford everything and would spare no expense:

> King Solomon and all the congregation of Israel, who had assembled before him, were with him before the ark, sacrificing so many sheep and oxen that they could not be counted or numbered. (8:5)

At last everything was in place. The procession was concluded, and the priests and the ark had arrived up front. There was a pause for the orchestra to begin, and then the choir sang a "new song," a new anthem commissioned for the occasion. It was a new anthem because the claim that the choir would verbalize would not have been made or have been appropriate at any time before in the tradition of Israel. It is probable that the temple choir sang the lines that the text has in Solomon's mouth:

> Then Solomon said,
> "The LORD has said that he would dwell in thick darkness.
> I have built you an exalted house,
>   a place for you to dwell in forever."
>   8:12–13

As the choir sang, a cloud filled the temple; all those present understood that it was the descent of the glory of God—the real, palpable divine presence that filled the house (see Exod. 40:34–38). The anthem asserted that Solomon's God, YHWH the Lord of the exodus, would dwell in "thick darkness" in the holy of holies at the back of the temple where only the priest could enter, the priest who was a functionary of the king who acted on behalf of the king. Solomon, so the choir sang, had built for YHWH "an exalted house." Anyone present who knew the tradition would have remembered the play on the word "house" in 2 Samuel 7 in the Nathan oracle. YHWH had said there that he needed no "house" (temple) from David but would build David a "house" (dynasty). But things have changed. And now the house-temple wrought by Solomon offers YHWH a permanent residence. YHWH, so the choir sings, agrees to "dwell" ("sit"; *yasav*) there forever and ever. The wording is astonishing. The verb *yasav* means to occupy permanently in a sedentary way. The earlier verb in the parallel line of verse 12 is *shakan*, to bivouac, but by verse 13 the verb is intensified. And the adverb "forever" is plural, that is, for all thinkable futures.

YHWH has now become fully, permanently, irrevocably present in Jerusalem. As patron of the king and guarantor of the regime, he assures certitude to Solomon and his entourage; the city and the dynasty will be protected from all historical threats. This liturgical claim, as high as it can get in the Old Testament, means the "end of history." After the Soviet Union fell in 1989, Francis Fukuyama published *The End of History*.[3] He made the claim that liberal capitalist democracy had won and would have no more major threat from challengers in the historical process. All that remained was wipe up action. So it was in Jerusalem on that day of dedication; king and people had arrived at full certitude, guaranteeing that the city and the king were immune from threat. What a day! What a liturgy! What certitude!

That certitude is not atypical among us. Religious traditions often are tied to political visions. As with Solomon, it is always tempting to imagine that we have arrived at an ultimacy beyond challenge. The religious temptation is to wrap truth in a package of liturgy or doctrine or piety that now will be permanently beyond criticism and immune from threat or challenge. It is a good day's work when religious symbol, tied to political commitment, can foreclose the future. Solomon had done nothing less than end history in a sweeping liturgical claim without irony or misgiving. A good day's work—mission accomplished!

Except, of course, that the ultimate certitude of the temple could not be sustained. Already amid the extravagant procession itself, the narrative reports a sly note of doubt: "There was nothing in the ark except the two tablets of stone that Moses had placed there at Horeb, where the LORD made a covenant with the Israelites, when they came out of the land of Egypt" (1 Kgs. 8:9). The whole pageant was about getting the *ark* of old tradition into the new *temple*, for the ark was the throne upon which sat the ancient invisible God—except somebody peeked, likely a custodian. It was noted that the ark was empty. There was no God there! There were only the two tablets of commandments from Sinai. If you want divine presence, the mode of presence is the rigor of obedience and not the intimacy of liturgy. This subtle protest amid the loud procession constitutes an awareness that the entire claim of the dedicatory process was something of a sham, because the God of Sinai, as Nathan had told David, will not be domesticated into a pageant of certitude. Immediately after the anthem in verses 12–13, Solomon put the searing question: "But will God indeed dwell on the earth? Even heaven and the highest heaven cannot contain you, much less this house that I have built!" (8:27). Likely it is a question in a theological seminar in the afternoon when some critical scholar raised the issue of ultimate certitude. The creator of heaven and earth is too big, too free, and too noble to obey the anthem that imagines permanent residence. The Holy One cannot do it and will not do it! The claim is immediately placed in jeopardy.

And if the observation of the janitor in verse 9 and the critical assertion of the scholar in verse 27 were not enough, we may read the history. The temple did not last. The city and the king were overrun. The signs of certitude were erased (see Pss. 74, 79). For a time the certitude gave the kind of assurance that the regime craved, but it would not hold. The certitude would not hold because

> Our little systems have their day;
> they have their day and cease to be.[4]

The totems of religious certitude-cum-political-interest are sooner or later swept away.

II.

When we turn the page of the Bible from 1 Kings 8 to 1 Kings 9, we meet a second wave of certitude. It is a more basic, older one, well grounded behind the temple. There have been hints of this more-sober certitude earlier in the narrative, but neither Solomon nor we as readers have paid much attention to it. Already in 1 Kings 3:14, at the end of the dream where the dream God had promised everything to Solomon, the assurance was concluded: "If you will walk in my ways, keeping my statutes and my commandments, as your father David walked, then I will lengthen your life" (1 Kgs. 3:14). The "if" of obedience was a proviso for everything royal in this tradition.[5] That proviso, moreover, was reiterated amid temple preparations in 1 Kings 6:

> Now the word of the LORD came to Solomon, "Concerning this house that you are building, if you will walk in my statutes, obey my ordinances, and keep all my commandments by walking in them, then I will establish my promise with you, which I made to your father David. I will dwell among the children of Israel, and will not forsake my people Israel." (6:11–13)

There is a promise that YHWH would "dwell" in Israel, though the verb is not the hard verb of 8:13. This promise, moreover, is not that YHWH would dwell in the temple, but that YHWH would dwell "in the midst of the children of Israel," a dwelling that does not require a temple.

But the "if" of 1 Kings 3:14 and 6:12, the "if" of covenantal obedience, is only an anticipation of the full statement of what I will term "the second certitude." In these texts and more fully in 1 Kings 9:1–9 there now speaks a different voice. This voice is not intimidated by or implicated in the religious-symbol-cum-political interest; it pushes back behind son Solomon and father David, behind Jerusalem, to Sinai and the forbidding voice of Moses. When all else fails, certitude becomes the stringent voice of obedience:

> Now therefore, if you obey my voice and keep my covenant, you shall be my treasured possession out of all the peoples. Indeed, the whole earth is mine, but you shall be for me a priestly kingdom and a holy nation. These are the words that you shall speak to the Israelites. (Exod. 19:5–6)

The temple had acted out and mediated certitude as a free gift, given through this unprecedented family. But now the tradition recognizes that there is in fact no free lunch. If you want certitude, it will be merited and deserved by keeping the commandments, a distinctly un-Lutheran kind of Pelagianism that goes back to the "if" of Moses.

The particular statement in 1 Kings 9:1–9, the day after the temple dedication, is given in a "second dream." The narrative of the second dream is designed as a match to the dream narrative in 1 Kings 3, except that in substance it contradicts and overrides the first dream. Now the dream God (or perhaps the narrator) is sobered to the risks of kingship and the self-indulgence of Jerusalem, and offers instead a certitude that is lacking in fancy aesthetic decor but comes simply and directly back to commandment. Moses had uttered an "if," but the "if" of Exodus 19:5–6 that was given as a positive invitation at Sinai has now been hardened into a foolproof statement of logical syllogism by which there are only two options, obedience or disobedience, and only two outcomes, life or death.

The invitation "if" of Exodus 19 has now been jelled through the tradition of Deuteronomy into a rigorous theory of historical well-being, a theory given classical and familiar expression in Psalm 1 that is placed as the interpretive key of the Psalter. In that preface to the Psalter, the hymnal committee draws right out of the book of Deuteronomy. It is all about Torah obedience:

> Happy are those
>   who do not follow the advice of the wicked,
> or take the path that sinners tread,
>   or sit in the seat of scoffers;
> but their delight is in the law of the LORD,
>   and on his law they meditate day and night.
>   Ps. 1:1–2

The Torah keepers prosper and live well:

They are like trees
      planted by streams of water,
which yield their fruit in its season,
      and their leaves do not wither.
In all that they do, they prosper.
                              1:3

The wicked, the ones who do not keep Torah commandments, the sinners, and the scoffers do not fare well but are in fact excommunicated from the community of well-being:

The wicked are not so,
      but are like chaff that the wind drives away.
Therefore the wicked will not stand in the judgment,
      nor sinners in the congregation of the righteous.
                              1:4–5

There is no middle ground. You are with God or not. You are with Torah or not. You are with us or not:

For the LORD watches over the way of the righteous,
      but the way of the wicked will perish.
                              1:6

The psalm is not an isolated piece or an occasional opinion. It is a clear expression of Deuteronomic theology that dominates much of the Old Testament, much of the church tradition, and even more, much of popular religion in Christendom.[6] The articulation of this certitude allows no slippage, no forgiveness, and surely no second chance.

In the making of the Solomon tradition, when the narrators began to detect the inadequacy of the claims of the choir in 1 Kings 8:12–13, it was a credible move to report a second dream in 1 Kings 9:1–9. Passionate interpreters are like that. They can readily run roughshod over previous claims, violate aesthetic considerations, commit ready contradictions, and move on without blinking. That is what happens in 1 Kings 9. Either the dream God, without blinking, made a huge interpretive leap back from temple in chapter 8 to Torah in chapter 9, or the narrator did it on behalf of the God of Sinai. Either way, the second certitude of ethical conformity trumps the more aesthetic certitude of the religious symbol. Now it comes down to visible, discernible, public action that can be tested by old command.

Obedience is possible:

As for you, if you will walk before me, as David your father walked, with integrity of heart and uprightness, doing according to all that I have commanded you, and keeping my statutes and my ordinances . . . (9:4)

That is the claim from ancient Deuteronomy. The Torah is doable, and the Torah keepers do not understand why others do not obey the commandments:

Surely, this commandment that I am commanding you today is not too hard for you, nor is it too far away. It is not in heaven, that you should say, "Who will go up to heaven for us, and get it for us so that we may hear it and observe it?" No, the word is very near to you; it is in your mouth and in your heart for you to observe. (Deut. 30:11–14)

The keeping of Torah guarantees well-being, even in Jerusalem:

. . . then I will establish your royal throne over Israel forever, as I promised your father David, saying, "There shall not fail you a successor on the throne of Israel." (1 Kgs. 9:5)

The Torah will guarantee what the temple manifestly cannot.

These good promises are balanced, even more than balanced, by the dangers of Torah violation:

If you turn aside from following me, you or your children, and do not keep my commandments and my statutes that I have set before you, but go and serve other gods and worship them . . . (9:6)

This language is as old as Deuteronomy. The reference to Torah stays lean, with only a mention of the First Commandment, the same one that was cited to indict Solomon in 1 Kings 11:1–8. But, of course, the First Commandment is to be understood in the tradition of Deuteronomy in a systems approach. The commandment covers everything economic and political and military and cultural; in the horizon of Deuteronomy, an entire life of obedience is reduced to a single religious duty. The outcomes of systemic Torah violation are harsh and intense:

. . . then I will cut Israel off from the land that I have given them; and the house that I have consecrated for my name I will cast out of my sight; and Israel will become a proverb and a taunt among all peoples. (9:7)

Torah violation will lead to loss of land and loss of temple. It is likely that the text derives from the sixth-century exile when all had in fact been lost. Given this ideology, however, the implementation of loss was not needed in order for this syllogism to be offered. The tradition knows ahead of time what will happen in the face of Torah violation. It does not know about the failed reform of Josiah or the coming of the Babylonians or the blinding of Zedekiah, but it knows that the Lord of the Torah will not be mocked, not even in Jerusalem, not even by the beloved son of the beloved David, not even in the temple by the temple builder. You can count on the commandments, for the world depends on them.

The "if" of Sinai is now a tight syllogism. It is the work of Deuteronomy, enacted as well with great variation in the prophetic speeches of judgment.[7] The logic is laid over the public domain of Jerusalem, and it yields direct, uncomplicated, manageable moral sense. You can lay the grid of certitude over any social phenomenon, over war and consumerism and greed with liberals, over sex and self-indulgence with conservatives, over any behavior that jeopardizes power arrangements and status quo assurances that bespeak security. The substance of Torah is not to be taken lightly, but that does not blind us to its ideological convenience. The world works the way the Creator has put it together. Nowhere is the Deuteronomic claim clearer than in the simple speech of judgment in the tradition of Hosea. The indictment concerns the commandments:

> Hear the word of the LORD, O people of Israel;
>   for the LORD has an indictment against the inhabitants of the land.
> There is no faithfulness or loyalty,
>   and no knowledge of God in the land.
> Swearing, lying, and murder,
>   and stealing and adultery break out;
>   bloodshed follows bloodshed.
>
> Hos. 4:1–2

The sentence, introduced by a characteristic "therefore," is about drought and loss. Torah violation leads to the undoing of creation. Certitude rests on an undoubted claim for the moral coherence of the world. When that moral coherence is violated, trouble comes. This testimony of Deuteronomy in the prophets is paralleled in commonsense fashion and sapiential teaching:

> Depart from evil, and do good;
>   so you shall abide forever.
> For the LORD loves justice;
>   he will not forsake his faithful ones.
> Ps. 37:27–28

This certitude pervades Scripture—Deuteronomy, Prophets, Wisdom—even as it pervades popular religion among zealous, activist leftists and anxious, eager rightists. It is across-the-spectrum mainstream certitude.

But, of course, the Bible itself knows better. It knows better on two grounds even though it cannot easily overthrow the logic of such certitude. It knows better, first, because there is the slippage of forgiveness and grace that is palpable in the life of Israel. Already in the narrative of 1 Kings itself, the slippage is acknowledged even though not much is made of it. In the final verdict on Solomon, the punishment is sure and deep, as sure and deep as is the warning in 1 Kings 9:7. In that warning, the text says, "If you turn aside . . . I will cut off Israel from the land." The verdict of 1 Kings 11:11 echoes the warning:

> Therefore the LORD said to Solomon, "Since this has been your mind and you have not kept my covenant and my statutes that I have commanded you, I will surely tear the kingdom from you and give it to your servant."

The verbs are different, "cut off" (*karat*) and "tear out" (*qara'*), but the point is the same. The punishment follows the affront. No slippage, no doubt—complete certitude!

Save for one textual reality: verse 11, which announces the punishment, is followed by verse 12, which begins "yet"—in Hebrew *'ak*, a particle that turns against the preceding:

> Yet for the sake of your father David I will not do it in your lifetime; I will tear it out of the hand of your son. I will not, however, tear away the entire kingdom; I will give one tribe to your son, for the sake of my servant David and for the sake of Jerusalem, which I have chosen. (11:12–13)

The wonder of YHWH's commitment to David is that in this text it overrides the logic of reward and punishment. No doubt the narrator had to deal with the hard reality of the continuing divided kingdom. But the point, required by historical reality, is nonetheless a theological point. The syllogism does not hold. The moral certitude so grandly voiced does not account for reality. Not only is there more than this. There is other than this. The motif of divine generosity, divine forbearance, and flat out divine forgiveness surges even in the midst of harsh certitude. The point is voiced as the ground of newness, even in the tradition of Jeremiah, that most terminating of Deuteronomic voices:

> No longer shall they teach one another, or say to each other, "Know the LORD," for they shall all know me, from the least of them to the greatest, says the LORD; for I will forgive their iniquity, and remember their sin no more. (Jer. 31:34; see also 33:8)

And, of course, the slippage beyond the syllogism, the basis for so much of our pastoral work, permeates Israel's best songs:

> The LORD is merciful and gracious,
> > slow to anger and abounding in steadfast love.
> He will not always accuse,
> > nor will he keep his anger forever.
> He does not deal with us according to our sins,
> > nor repay us according to our iniquities.
> For as the heavens are high above the earth,
> > so great is his steadfast love toward those who fear him;
> as far as the east is from the west,
> > so far he removes our transgressions from us.
> As a father has compassion for his children,
> > so the LORD has compassion for those who fear him.
> For he knows how we were made;
> > he remembers that we are dust.
> > > > Ps. 103:8–14

The assurance is sometimes galling for pastors, as it was for Jonah, as the slippage

of grace in the face of savage certitude is to be extended to those who most militantly rely on the syllogism. Such folk militantly rely on the syllogism

> until the world of pain catches up with us,

> until the silence must be broken,

> until the denial cannot be contained,

> until the dissonance of claim and experience can no longer be sustained.

Then, and not till then, the certitude cracks, and there can be newness.

This persistent reality leads to a second point. The Bible knows experientially
that the claim of the syllogism, so boldly proclaimed in Psalm 1, does not hold.
Thus, Jeremiah most vigorously can ask why the wicked, who should suffer, in
fact prosper:

> You will be in the right, O LORD,
>   when I lay charges against you;
>   but let me put my case to you.
> Why does the way of the guilty prosper?
>   Why do all who are treacherous thrive?
> You plant them, and they take root;
>   they grow and bring forth fruit;
> you are near in their mouths
>   yet far from their hearts.
>   Jer. 12:1–2

The point for Jeremiah is picked up and extended in the ruminations of the
poem of Job:

> Why do the wicked live on,
>   reach old age, and grow mighty in power?
> Their children are established in their presence,
>   and their offspring before their eyes.
> Their houses are safe from fear,
>   and no rod of God is upon them.
> Their bull breeds without fail;
>   their cow calves and never miscarries.
> They send out their little ones like a flock,
>   and their children dance around.
> They sing to the tambourine and the lyre,
>   and rejoice to the sound of the pipe.
> They spend their days in prosperity,
>   and in peace they go down to Sheol.
> They say to God, "Leave us alone!
>   We do not desire to know your ways.
> What is the Almighty, that we should serve him?
>   And what profit do we get if we pray to him?"

> Is not their prosperity indeed their own achievement?
>> The plans of the wicked are repugnant to me.
>>> Job 21:7–16

Job, of course, shares confidence in the syllogism. The problem is that his experience tells him otherwise. And so it goes with our life in the world. Just when we commit to a tight, convinced moral coherence, we find our life otherwise, outside the syllogism. For a moment the writer of 1 Kings 9:1–9 had trumped the pretense of the temple and its religious symbolism, but only for a moment. Very soon the narrative had to move on to the "yet" of 1 Kings 11:12 that celebrates and counts on the exception. That exception, of course, is at the heart of pastoral reality. For all of our shrill moral conviction, we are always grateful when our own hurt and loss and pain evoke an exception from the Holy Enforcer. Moral coherence is a treasure, but it will not hold. We are pushed out of that second certitude only a few verses after the exhaustion of temple certitude.

III.

It is a big leap from Solomon to Job, from the book of Kings to the book of Job. It is a big leap from one wave of certitude to get to a third wave of certitude. But we are prepared for it on two counts. First, the big "yet" of 1 Kings 11:12 indicates that the syllogism does not hold. Second, there are some hints, only hints, that Israel did not fully accept the syllogism as an adequate theological explanation for the destruction of Jerusalem; to some, the punishment was disproportionate to the crime. Thus, in Lamentations 3, a poem of grief over the loss of Jerusalem, the poet can say of Babylon, "Those who were my enemies without cause have hunted me like a bird" (Lam. 3:52). The phrase "without cause" is, to be sure, a minority report, for in the same chapter there is a confession of sin: "We have transgressed and rebelled, and you have not forgiven" (3:42). Nonetheless, the minority report is there. It is there in the middle of the lament, suggesting the daring notion that the harsh fate of Jerusalem is outside the syllogism and not adequately explained by a tight moral theory.

That issue is then picked up in the book of Job, though without explicit reference to the crisis of Jerusalem. Job's three friends have become a hardened echo of the certitude of the Deuteronomic syllogism. They have no doubt that Job's intense suffering is matched by his sin; as a consequence, the only wise course of action for Job is to admit guilt, repent, and submit to God's punishment:

> Think now, who that was innocent ever perished?
>> Or where were the upright cut off?
>>> Job 4:7

> As for me, I would seek God,
>> and to God I would commit my cause.
>>> 5:8

Does God pervert justice?
 Or does the Almighty pervert the right?
If your children sinned against him,
 he delivered them into the power of their transgression.
If you will seek God
 and make supplication to the Almighty,
if you are pure and upright,
 surely then he will rouse himself for you
 and restore to you your rightful place.
Though your beginning was small,
 your latter days will be very great.

8:3–7

If iniquity is in your hand, put it far away,
 and do not let wickedness reside in your tents.
Surely then you will lift up your face without blemish;
 you will be secure, and will not fear.

11:14–15

The scandal of the book of Job is not that the old certitude of moral coherence has defenders. The scandal is that Job shares this view with his friends and perceives himself, at least for a time, within the "deeds-consequence" framework.[8] That, however, is no surprise to a pastor. Every pastor knows those who accept such a conviction concerning their own life, a conviction that often requires denial of one's own sense of self.

For a very long time, Job does not step outside the syllogism; even in his last major statement of innocence in chapter 31, what he wants more than anything is a judicial hearing, a bill of charge in order that he can defend himself and gain acquittal:

Oh, that I had one to hear me!
 (Here is my signature! let the Almighty answer me!)
Oh, that I had the indictment written by my adversary!
Surely I would carry it on my shoulder;
 I would bind it on me like a crown;
I would give him an account of all my steps;
 like a prince I would approach him.

31:35–37

Job is not prepared to participate in a Kafka-like trial but believes that a bill of charges will clarify the situation and permit his acquittal. And then Job waits. He waits a very long time, in silence, all through the many words of Elihu (Job 32–37).

It is very late in the book of Job when Job receives an answer for which he has been long waiting. It is very late in the history of pain and the story of certitude when he gains a hearing, and even then the book of Job is notorious, because what he receives in fact is no answer, and what he is offered is in fact no hearing. However we may interpret the profound ambiguity of the divine speeches in the whirlwind, it is clear that the God who speaks here will not participate with Job—or with Solomon or with Israel—in any certitude that proceeds from moral coherence.[9] The God who speaks here is willing to engage with Job. Only now the subject of engagement, the subject determined not by Job's certitude or Job's need but by YHWH's holy awesomeness, is the wonder of creation that transcends and supersedes any moral claim. The subject is changed away from Job's certitude in a massive discrediting and dismissal of this pervasive brand of theology.

Job who has questioned God is now questioned. Job is questioned about mystery, about vastness and awesomeness, about inscrutability and majesty, enough that with Job we would rather break out in "How Great Thou Art"! The issue put on the table by the God of the whirlwind is not guilt or innocence, reward or punishment; now it is about darkness and light, snow and rain and wind and stars, and lions and periods of gestation for mountain goats and deer, and the meandering of wild asses and wild oxen and ostriches and horses and hawks. The recital on the lips of the creator God is thick, so thick that it takes Job's breath away—and ours as well. When the Holy One comes up for air, Job is invited to answer this awesome inventory (40:1–2). But Job cannot think of anything to say. He sees unmistakably that the discussion has not lingered over the question that conservative and liberal ideologues love to fight over. So Job concedes:

> See, I am of small account; what shall I answer you?
>   I lay my hand on my mouth.
> I have spoken once, and I will not answer;
>   twice, but will proceed no further.
>   40:3–5

Even though Job has been silenced of his moral rectitude, the Almighty is not finished. Perhaps God wants to press Job more. But I rather think that the Almighty enjoys his own voice, is something of a show-off, and wants to be celebrated in categories so large that Job as "adversary" cannot participate or respond.

The exhibition of the creator God becomes more specific in Job 40:15–24 as God describes and admires a principal creature: Behemoth (hippopotamus), a creature of strength and power, inscrutability—a champion creature:

> It is the first of the great acts of God—
>   only its Maker can approach it
>   with the sword.
>   40:19

This is followed by an even larger exhibit of Leviathan (crocodile), before whose powerful beauty and beautiful power the Creator cannot keep silent. As Sam Balentine has seen so well, in this powerful exhibit, Job is very much in purview of the Creator.[10] For in the discussion of Behemoth, God can say:

Look at Behemoth,
which I made just as I made you;
it eats grass like an ox.

40:15

Behemoth is made "like you"—that is, like Job. Balentine suggests that in the celebration of Behemoth, the Creator also celebrates Job—that free, powerful, ferocious creature who is summoned in powerful freedom out beyond old, stale certitudes into a life of freedom and courage and exultant self-regard. Everything claimed for Behemoth and Leviathan is claimed for Job as well, who is crowned as king of creation:

Yet you have made them a little lower than God,
and crowned them with glory and honor.
You have given them dominion over the works of your hands;
you have put all things under their feet,
all sheep and oxen,
and also the beasts of the field,
the birds of the air, and the fish of the sea,
whatever passes along the paths of the seas.

Ps. 8:5–8; see also Job 7:17–21

In these utterances, there is a new certitude, a certitude that moves beyond confessional and sectarian modes of reality into a large, cosmic, generic vision of humanity as lead creature. The comparison to Behemoth in the poetry of Job 40:15 is reinforced by the prose of Job 42:7–8 in which Job is celebrated for speaking "what is right," for daring to push the syllogism of moral certitude to its very edge and then summoning God to a fresh response. The certitude offered here, beyond the moral syllogism of Deuteronomy, is that of a Promethean figure, albeit a Promethean figure who is accountable to a Promethean God, universal in scope and out beyond the thinkable categories of explanation. It is no wonder that this certitude can evoke only doxology, even if the doxology must be on the Creator's own lips.

But this is, in a very different way, still a certitude. It is a certitude cherished by sophisticated intellectuals who turn out to be affluent and well coiffed, who are impatient with all of the others and who function with a kind of grand autonomy that can trust in its own wisdom. The text would seem to celebrate urbane courage and is glad for the rare reader of Job who "gets it," who no longer lingers over the petty syllogism of the Deuteronomist. There is God and God's grandeur on such a large scale that it will appeal to "the cultured despisers"[11] of religion, the sort of ordered grandeur that shows up among sophisticates concerning "science and religion," a religion of order and freedom without interventions from God and without excessive moral restraints.

IV.

There are, nonetheless, hints that even this third wave of certitude, the one that counts on moral freedom and a provisional autonomy in the large world of creation, is also a certitude that cannot fully stand. As elsewhere, the text moves beyond its most recently voiced certitude, pressing the faithful to regroup yet again in a new way. The text offers at least two hints that the certitude of cosmic bravado is not the last word, for one cannot practice for very long a kind of generic certitude. Such an open certitude is bound to lead to hubris or to despair, because without concrete reference it becomes free falling space. Given this, I propose that after this third eloquent certitude, the text finishes by summoning Job and his ilk to concrete historical community of moral specificity.

The first extended hint is the final prose paragraph of Job 42:10–17. Job cannot continue in the exalted thin air of cosmic bravado. At the outset it is important to notice that Job is commended by God for speaking "what is right" (42:7–8). Job's disputatious speech, contrasted with the settled truth of the friends, is celebrated by God as though God wants a disputatious partner, as though Job wants the settled syllogism of "these consequences" challenged and upset. It is as though the God of the whirlwind knows full well that that tight moral calculus is inadequate for a world in which ostriches and Leviathans are running loose. Thus, disputatious speech is a welcome match for YHWH's grandeur in which Job is not unlike Behemoth in a fierce splendor of his own.

But it is the final paragraph of verses 10–17 that concerns us, a report in which Job is restored to family and fortune, a recovery of wealth and honor that he had lost. Carol Newsom has seen that this paragraph, after the tragic drama of the poetry, is a "posttragic" response to the poetry. She concludes that taken innocently in isolation, the epilogue depicts a renewal that "was a triumphal expression of its confidence in the possibility of a moral and a material wholeness in life."[12]

When read in relation to the poetry, however, the purpose of the epilogue is not so simple. Rather, in that dialogic frame of reference, says Newsom, the epilogue is "one in which the goodness of life in all its fragility is embraced."[13] I take it that the key accent for Newsom is "fragility." The makers of the book, the character of Job, and we who read all know now that "the goodness of life" is not guaranteed (a) by an absolute religious totem of building, doctrine, or liturgy; (b) by a tight moral calculus; or (c) by a sublime God who exhibits no interest in the goodness of human life. Rather, in this paragraph an episode of such goodness is made available, but the offer is terse and given only after the trauma. There is in this offer of life now no deep certitude, and thus it is "fragile." I want to add to Newsom's "fragility," however, the terms of "concrete" and "community embedded." In the poem of Job, the lead character is void of historical particularity and functions as "every person." But one cannot, in serious drama, remain outside history. Thus, the restoration of Job to new life granted in the final paragraph "descends" from exotic exchange with the holy to the mundane concreteness of life in a specific community. Job, who had been treated like an outsider (Job 30), is now reincorporated into a specific community, the only environment that makes life fully human. Through that reincorporation, even if marked by inescapable fragility, Job is in recovery:

- He is welcomed back into his larger family, who eats together with him (v. 11).
- He receives "sympathy and comfort" for what he has suffered, as only a familiar family can do (v. 11).
- He receives material gifts from them as a sign of their valorization of him (v. 11).
- He receives wealth of 14,000 sheep, 6,000 camels, 1,000 yoke of oxen, and 1,000 donkeys (v. 12).
- He is restored to family with sons and daughters, the daughters the most beautiful in the land, daughters who receive inheritance along with the sons (vv. 13–15).
- He lived a full scope of a hundred and twenty years, "old and full of days" (vv. 16–17; see also Isa. 65:20).

This is indeed restoration! Job is now beyond the tight moral calculus of his friends, though perhaps he is vindicated in their eyes. The issues posed by Job and the friends together are not reiterated here. Job is beyond the "shock and awe" encounter with the holy Lord of Behemoth, the ostrich, and Leviathan. He is, as he was, settled in a prosperous pastoral community, so gifted that he need not dispute or even utter a word about certitude. The large vista of the Job in the argument is as remote now as is the temple claim or the moral syllogism. Job abides now in grace and generosity that make his quarrelsome certitude irrelevant and uninteresting.

But he is fragile and may be tempted again to pursue such certitudes. He is fragile, because he now knows that what is given can be taken away, that what is treasured can be lost. In writing of Rachel's weeping in Jeremiah 31, Emil Fackenheim notes that Rachel refuses to be comforted because of the loss of six million of her children in the Shoah. He rightly sees that "no lost child can be replaced." Commentators mostly have not noticed that when Job recovered everything, he received new sons and daughters—but not the ones who were lost in chapter 1. He is restored and recovered, surrounded by family, property, wealth, and honor—but with lost children. Perhaps it is the case that in the *fragility of loss*, the pursuit of certitude is no longer so compelling. Loss now is in a context of what has been given—grateful, no doubt still sad, and "full of days." Newsom is right:

> Because the prose conclusion does not "belong" to the dialogue between Job and God in chapters 29–31 and 38:1–42:6 but to its own vision of the Job tale, its voice will not merge without remainder into what has preceded. It remains another consciousness, perceiving from another perspective. That irreducible resistance means that there can be no end to the book, no end to its dialogue, and no end to the dialogue it provokes.[14]

There is no end now to this account. But there need not be. There is only living in the presence, amid many gifts and much pain. Where pain lingers, certitude is not on offer.

In Job 28, there is a pondering of wisdom, surely wisdom kept hidden from the human process and not readily transposed into certitude. Indeed, the unavailability of wisdom militates frontally against certitude. But my interest here is only in verse 28, recognized by Newsom along with many other commentators as a "pietistic twist."[15] That twist, however, is exactly the capacity, as Newsom judged, to live "from within the coherency of wisdom":[16]

> And he said to humankind,
> "Truly, the fear of the Lord, that is wisdom;
>   and to depart from evil is understanding."
>   28:28

If we read Job 28:28 alongside the restitution of Job 42:7–17, then it is clear that after the large vista of the whirlwind dispute, Job must return to the immediacy of life in his community. In that concrete community, religious-moral expectations are basic and few: "Fear YHWH, depart from evil." Nothing grandiose, nothing quarrelsome, just a return to the simple, commonsense trusting daily faith of Proverbs (see Prov. 3:7). "Evil" is known without argument as that which disturbs community. YHWH is to be feared as the good savior of the exodus and the high commander of Sinai. Job not only returns home; he returns to the faith that had nurtured him. Now fragile in ways not to be forgotten, with pain honored and taken seriously, he is indeed home, "old and full of days."

V.

The Bible is a meditation upon holy truth and the way we distort holy truth so that it is transposed into certitude. When we transpose holy truth into certitude, it tends always to bear the marks of idolatry and ideology. Idolatry produces gods who are made in our image; ideology is resistant to the pastoral processes of dialogue and transformation.

All of these practices of certitude that I have lined out are present in the life of the congregation:

- *temple absoluteness* that wants to terminate the historical process and end the messiness by our favorite totem, whether building or liturgy or doctrine;
- *tight moral calculus* that reduces the human drama to the syllogism of "deeds and consequences"; and
- escape into a *cosmic mystery* that transcends the costly demands of the concrete.

I have traced uses in Scripture to show that in each case the certitude stands briefly—but then is taken away by the ongoing drama of God's rule in the historical process:

- The temple certitude lasted one chapter in the book of Kings, until the second dream that reminded Solomon of Torah conditionality.
- The certitude of Torah conditionality lasted only until the shrillness of the first lament psalm that declared that the system of moral calculation does not work.
- The grandeur of divine mystery in the book of Job will last, but only until Job must once again be embedded in concrete, fragile social reality.

The certitudes are not sustainable for long. They are undone by the concrete painfulness of the human project.

It is the glory of pastoral work to conduct a dialogic, transformative conversation among many certitudes. It does not surprise that such work is difficult and sure to be contested. The pastor seeks always to reinitiate the dialogue after certitude tries to reduce to monologue. The apparent winners all prefer a monologue that they can control. But what we keep rediscovering is that monologue offers no adequate cadence for the embrace and healing of pain. The pastor stands in the midst of folk who deny pain and despair of healing. The pastor invites them to an openness that is not certain but abidingly faithful, a faithfulness deeper than our deepest fragility.

Chapter 5

Crisis as a Mode of Public Faith

We cannot adequately pray that "God's kingdom should come on earth," that "God's will should be done on earth as in heaven," unless we consider at the same time how we faithfully practice citizenship in that God-intended political economy. It is an urgent as well as complex time to consider public dimensions of evangelical faith. My reflection will be in three parts:

1. Our problematic context for consideration of faith and public policy
2. Biblical resources for public faith
3. Some reflections on congregational practice

I.

It is evident that consideration of public dimensions of faith is now profoundly difficult in many of our congregations. It is equally evident that we have a long history whereby we have arrived at this problem. I could think of six factors producing our current problem.

1. We are, for all our Reformation rhetoric, nonetheless inheritors of a medieval sacramental system that defines theological matters in terms of sin and salvation, with the church as the healthcare provider to deliver "the medicine of immortality." While that sacramental system concerns the well-being of the "catholic world," it became in practice a highly individualized offer. That individualization, moreover, was intensified by Luther's famous misreading of Paul, together with a doctrine of "two swords" that left the public dimension to the princes. Here I am not raising questions about Luther's intention, but only the popular force of an offer of grace that had to do with the redress of personal default. The outcome is privatism.

2. That privatism through a sacramental system was taken up in new ways in the Treaty of Westphalia, which removed contentious religious claims from the public domain and left for religion private affairs of family that invited the public to go secular.[1] Beyond that desperate settlement of the religious wars, the soon-to-follow Enlightenment championed autonomous reason that defeated any thick theological claims of faith that might have impacted public life. Thus medieval sacramentalism, an intense personal-pastoral concern in the Reformation, and Enlightenment autonomy all converged to exempt public life from any legitimate summons from faith.

3. The U.S. settlement of the matter was not so easy. While deism of a benign kind may have dominated the founding fathers, alongside that deism there was and continues to be a powerful Puritan insistence upon a theological dimension to public life. There was and is no easy settlement between a passion for the secular and a commitment to religious claims. But the practical effect, so it seems to me, is the equation of "the American dream" with the gospel narrative. Thus, across the political spectrum, I believe, there is a readiness to believe that the U.S. political economy with its religious ingredient is the best available representation of God's intention for public life and an accompanying passion for justice and liberty. (So Niebuhr could claim that Christian faith has its best ally in a democratic ordering.) And as the American dream has increasingly become marked by global competition and military adventurism in the pursuit of empire, the unquestioned assumption is the convergence of that vision and the gospel narrative. Every pastor knows the risk of suggesting open critical space between the American *vision* and the gospel *narrative*.

4. That convergence of American vision and gospel narrative has, from very early days, produced a notion of U.S. "exceptionalism," that the United States is a special people that is not subject to the normal rule of the nations.[2] The ground for this claim is that the U.S. political economy is the best carrier of God's intention for creation. The outcome is that the United States does not need to play by the rules of other nations and is not subject to the restraints or sanctions of any "world order." Thus, for example, by its power the United States can arbitrarily exempt its citizens from the rulings of the World Court, set its own rules for military trials, and even as a primary polluter need not acknowledge the summons of the Kyoto Treaty, or a dozen other acts of common restraint.

The ground for such exceptionalism is a coziness with God who is no longer transcendent or over against this historical dynamism. And as Niebuhr often wrote, the United States assumes a kind of moral innocence that is incapable of self-criticism or irony. As a result, the military and economic adventurism of the United States goes uncriticized and unrestrained, using up resources that might otherwise contribute to a humane infrastructure.

5. One outcome of this immunity from restraint and this exceptionalism from the requirements of history is that our practices and policies proceed by default on two large matters:

- There is a default on world political economy, for immunity suggests that we are not bound in a common destiny with all our neighbors in terms of war or healthcare policy.
- There is default about creation as an ecosystem of health, because we do not see our own practices and policies as related to a system larger than ourselves, we having opted out of that system as an exception.

6. Finally, from the perspective of an exegete, the narrative of exceptionalism is a totalizing narrative. It manages to co-opt everything before it. Specifically, practitioners of this totalizing narrative delight to take specific biblical verses out of context, fit them to the narrative of exceptionalism-cum-pietism, and give new totalizing meanings that are alien to a text itself. A case in point: I read in *Christianity Today* of a report that CIA operatives were studying the book of Joshua in order to learn more about the legitimacy of spying. Or alternatively, the famous quote from Deuteronomy 15 by way of Jesus, "The poor you will always have with you," is used against the meaning of the text in Deuteronomy as an invitation to indifference about the social crisis of poverty. The outcome of such practice is a total loss of the biblical narrative on its own terms, a narrative that of course dramatically and forcefully breaks the connection of the gospel to U.S. exceptionalism.

On all counts, our subject requires great and informed intentionality to reclaim a more-or-less biblical understanding of reality that stands in deepest tension with the self-justifying narrative of exceptionalism that occupies much of the imagination of both liberals and conservatives in our society.

II.

Given that read of our societal setting, I will devote my energy to the resources in the Old Testament to which we may appeal in our address of public faith.

At the outset, it is important to recognize that public ethics in ancient Israel was in every generation upstream, always "in the shadow of an empire," an empire that characteristically appealed to a totalizing narrative that sought to silence any particularized ethical claim.[3] (It is not different in the New Testament church; witness the book of Acts.) Thus, one can trace the *imperial reality* amid which ancient Israel practiced its peculiar narrative in times both of resistance and alternative. I mean to suggest that one cannot open the Old Testament anywhere without seeing an intention of *resistance and alternative*, even though there were always those who sought to collude with totalizing narratives at the expense of a peculiar moral summons. Thus:

- At the outset, the narrative concerns Egypt and its slave labor policy.
- Solomon and his slave labor policy with a sense of entitlement permeate the entire history of that monarchy.
- The Assyrian empire displays uncommon brutality.
- Babylon terminates Jerusalem and deports its leading citizens.
- Persia, though more benign than Assyria or Babylon, has insistent tax policies that reduce Jews to slavery.
- In a later period, Hellenism came to forcible dramatic contempt by the remarkable act of a pig sacrificed on the Jerusalem altar, a quintessential mocking of Jewish particularity.

In every season, Israelites and then the Jews had to sort out a peculiar God-given identity, had to find ways to cooperate with empire without being co-opted, had to participate in the general political economy but with one eye on distinctiveness.[4]

Did you notice in my listing of the empires that I included Solomon, a home-grown totalizer that in his policies of indifference and exploitation was quite like all the others?[5] For good reason Solomon is singled out by Jesus as the quintessential model of self-sufficiency permeated by anxiety: "Not even Solomon in all his glory . . ." (Matt. 6:29).

I begin with imperial environment, because I believe that a public ethic in the U.S. church now must make the case that our evangelical *vision* and our baptismal *version* of public reality are from the ground up at deep odds with dominant culture. This stance of "deep odds" that we mostly resist in our sense of exceptionalism might be an invitation to a retreating sectarianism. But it need not. It can also be a sustained insistent alternative proposal to the empire, rooted deep but wide and sophisticated in its word that seeks to impinge upon, modify, and correct the dominant narrative that is now almost everywhere seen to be inadequate. In what follows, I trace out four rootages of *resistance and alternative* where the church may take its stand. These will be obvious to you, but there is, I take it, merit in our reflection upon them.

The beginning point in the Bible for resistance and alternative can hardly be anywhere except the Sinai covenant of Exodus 19–24, a text that Jesus understands to be the center of the Torah. Frank Crüsemann has made the point that because the Sinai covenant cannot be located chronologically or geographically, it is given in the tradition as a *utopian* claim outside of time, always there, always alternative, always making demand.[6]

The God who speaks at Sinai is the one "who brought you out of the land of Egypt, out of the house of bondage." Israel arrives at Sinai with the scars, scabs, and echoes of Egypt still in its body. The Israelites could still hear the primal command of Pharaoh to "make more bricks," to give your life over to the imperial enterprise of gratification and self-sufficiency. And when the Israelites arrived at Sinai, the first thing they said to Moses was, "Whatever the commands of Sinai, we will obey them" (Exod. 19:8). We will take them as alternative to Pharaoh's brick quota.

The liberator of the slaves—still in an emancipatory position—gave ten intransigent guidelines for public policy, ten alternatives to Pharaoh's royal commands of productivity. Of course, the Ten Commandments are not offered as a totem for empire-obeying right-wingers. But we have defaulted in interpretation, have exempted these resources from public policy, and have permitted the commands to be co-opted to fit imperial requirement.

I comment on only two of the commandments. The Third Commandment is "Do not take the name of the LORD in vain" (Exod. 20:7). The commandment is not a prohibition against bad language. It is a warning that the name and presence of YHWH cannot be preempted to serve as a legitimating support for pet projects—not war, not stewardship, not church programs—because the Holy God stands apart from and over against our best enterprises.

The Fourth Commandment, placed at the center of the Decalogue, is a curb on defining life in terms of productivity (Exod. 20:8–11). The public act of Sabbath is a declaration to our children that the rat race of getting ahead is not the story of our life. Jews must regularly and visibly disengage from the brick quota of the consumer economy to give evidence that life consists in being and not in getting or having or eating. The command is of course echoed in the Tenth Commandment, on coveting, itself a curb on acquisitiveness (Exod. 20:17).

What if we take the Ten Commandments as an antidote to anxiety? There is anxiety in the empire because we will never have enough bricks. And Jesus said, "Do not be anxious about getting ahead in the world, for the Father God knows and provides what you need" (Matt. 6:25, 32; my paraphrase). Israel resists the anxiety of the empire and offers an alternative of covenantal freedom that has peaceable rest at its center.

Empires proceed by euphemism, characteristically toxic euphemisms. Empires proceed by denying what is happening, by pretending it is something else, characteristically by religious or moral legitimization. In that practice the alternative community of covenant—since Sinai—requires the question that was eventually asked by the Roman governor, "What is truth?" (John 18:38).[7]

In ancient Israel, the ones who ask the truth question are the prophets. They are, in a general way, informed by the claims of Sinai. But mainly they are freelance poets who, by their artistry, turn the language, rich with image and metaphor, this way and that so that we may see reality differently. They are engaged in acts of imagination that stand outside the normative imagination of the empire.[8] The practice of image and metaphor leaves them deeply elusive, but they must be elusive in order not to be "apprehended" by the rulers of this age.

We may, in an act of interpretive reductionism, suggest that the prophets have two primary accents. The first, best known to us, is that they pronounce judgment upon dominant culture because dominant culture has violated the gifts of God's will and therefore will evoke trouble from God. While the prophets use the language of supernaturalism concerning direct divine intervention, they are in fact poets. They do not describe what God will do. They anticipate how the world will feel.

Their utterances of judgment, I suggest, are designed to counter the dominant pathology of the empire—namely *denial*, the refusal to see honestly and clearly what is going on. So Amos can narrate a characteristic picture of self-indulgence even though that picture pales before our own contemporary self-indulgence:

> Alas for those who lie on beds of ivory,
>   and lounge on their couches,
> and eat lambs from the flock,
>   and calves from the stall;
> who sing idle songs to the sound of the harp,
>   and like David improvise on instruments of music;
> who drink wine from bowls,
>   and anoint themselves with the finest oils,
>   but are not grieved over the ruin of Joseph!
>
> Amos 6:4–6

The first word of the oracle, "alas," is a grief word, anticipating a funeral. Those who live as the poet describes will face a deathliness. The portrayal of self-indulgence, of which the self-indulgent themselves are rarely aware, ends in a characteristic and savage "therefore":

> Therefore they shall now be the first to go into exile,
>   and the revelry of the loungers shall pass away.
>
> 6:7

Notice that in this poetry God is not mentioned. There is no supernatural agent. It will simply happen. It will happen among those who do not notice, who refuse to notice, who are unwilling to notice. The tricky word "therefore" connects in the rhetoric a savage practice of the political economy and an outcome that, except for prophetic imagination, has no connection to the foregoing. The denial is that "this" will not lead to "that." The prophetic insistence made by daring rhetoric is the connection. The connection breaks the denial, not unlike the connection that Jesus makes concerning the *Messiah* who must *suffer and die*, a connection that was unthinkable to the disciples even as exile from Samaria was unthinkable in the ancient Israel of Amos (Mark 8:31).

The second theme of prophetic imagination, found everywhere in the great prophetic books of Isaiah, Jeremiah, and Ezekiel, is hope for God's full restoration of a community that has been radically displaced. The announcement of divine promise does not arise *de novo*. It arises from the seedbed of candor birthed through suffering and loss and displacement. So the prophets speak out of deep need in a context where many are in despair that God has forgotten, that God does not notice, that God's arm is too short to save. But despair is routed by these originary affirmations:

> Comfort, comfort my people.
> Behold the days are surely coming . . .
> In that day . . .

And the poets line out comfort, homecoming, new temple, new covenant, new land, new possibility—all things new! As the poets *refuse denial* and *speak judgment*, so they *refuse despair* and *speak possibility*. They speak such inexplicable possibility as they anticipate restored Jerusalem, even as they anticipate in later reference, "He is risen, he is risen indeed." Risen from the dead, risen from exile, and risen from humiliation and displacement (Ezek. 37:1–14). Such utterance is *against denial* that the Messiah must not die. Such utterance is *against despair* that he has risen. I have no doubt that the beginning of a public ethic is to break *the denial in truth-telling* that goes behind euphemism, to break *the despair in hope-telling*, because new obedience has to do with what is made newly possible.

The third canon of the Old Testament concerns wisdom. That literature, as in the book of Proverbs, articulates steady-state order in the world, while the books of Job and Ecclesiastes dispute that order. The entire discussion, however, is about a given order that is inscrutable but intransigent, in order to be probed but while probed, respected. It may be that wisdom is the best entry into public policy, because this teaching entails no appeal to the particular confessional traditions of Israel. Rather, it is an observation-based judgment about the nature of lived reality that is generated and guaranteed by the creator God who makes no concessions or compromises. Wisdom teaching makes connections that are intransigent even if we cannot trace them, connections like these:

- Smoke long enough and you get lung cancer.
- Destroy the rainforests and have global warming.

Those connections require no explicit divine intervention. They are the way the world works. The connections may later be lined out by scientific specificity, but short of such specificity the connection is observable to the discerning. The world works that way. It is guaranteed, and one cannot circumvent it. Wisdom is the capacity to recognize and accept limits that will not be violated.

- "Mock the poor . . . insult their Maker" (Prov. 17:5).

There is an intrinsic connection between the creator God and poor people, and the connection cannot be broken by the willful action of the powerful.

- "The horse is made ready for the day of battle, but victory belongs to the LORD" (Prov. 21:31).

There are not enough bombs in Vietnam or enough brutal force in Iraq to ensure military victory for the empire, if the gods are allied with homegrown land-loving soldiers.

- Avoid debt like a hole in the head.

Everywhere in Proverbs the warning is that if you get into debt, you will eventually belong to somebody else, and eventually China or Saudi Arabia will wind up having leverage on your economy.

The foolish, the ones Gerhard von Rad calls "practical atheists," are those who refuse to recognize such limits, and imagine that by power and shrewdness they can outflank those inscrutable, God-given limits.[9] But wisdom is aimed especially against such technical reason that proceeds as if there were no givens. Nonetheless, every empire imagines that it can make new givens, a new world order, as in "We don't respond to events—we create new events to which others must respond." The wisdom teachers eventually assert that *arrogance* is the decisive violation of the creation that is ordered by God. The wisdom teachers, perhaps with due gender distinctions, can therefore conclude:

> Three things are stately in their stride;
>   four are stately in their gait:
> the lion, which is mightiest among wild animals
>   and does not turn back before any;
> the strutting rooster, the he-goat,
>   and a king striding before his people.
>   Prov. 30:29–31

That is *stateliness*. But this is preceded by the wisdom sayings about trembling:

> Under three things the earth trembles;
>   under four it cannot bear up:
> a slave when he becomes king,
>   and a fool when glutted with food;
> an unloved woman when she gets a husband,
>   and a maid when she succeeds her mistress.
>   30:21–23

New power seduces, and the earth trembles.

We make the claim that it is the wisdom of the cross that contradicts the sureness of the world:

> For since, in the wisdom of God, the world did not know God through
> wisdom, God decided, through the foolishness of our proclamation, to save

those who believe. For Jews demand signs and Greeks desire wisdom, but we proclaim Christ crucified, a stumbling block to Jews and foolishness to Gentiles, but to those who are the called, both Jews and Greeks, Christ the power of God and the wisdom of God. For God's foolishness is wiser than human wisdom, and God's weakness is stronger than human strength. (1 Cor. 1:21–25)

The gospel is the awareness that the best certitudes of the world are always placed in jeopardy by the truth of God. Paul has seen this clearly in Jesus of Nazareth. But even before that, the poem of Job ponders the settled conclusions of the book of Proverbs and comes to see that the best absolutes of human imagination are known to be penultimate. The voice of God speaks from the whirlwind, not even acknowledging the absolutes handed back and forth between Job and his friends. In the end, says the poem, there is inscrutable mystery behind our best claims. We are invited by the poet to pause with our deepest convictions and then to wait. In the end, Job may return to the simplicities of the book of Proverbs, but he relearns them now sobered away from his arrogance. He receives everything back even with new children, but he does not receive back his lost children (Job 42:10–17). Now he must live with that unrecoverable loss and find new ways to obey. The conclusion drawn is one of deep simplicity:

And he said to humankind,
"Truly, the fear of the Lord, that is wisdom;
    and to depart from evil is understanding."
                    Job 28:28

"Fear of the Lord" places all else, even our best ideologies, in jeopardy. Both the arrogance of the friends and the deep felt impulse of Job are judged before the God of all wisdom.

The empire wants a monologue, the silencing of every voice except its own. The CEO of Home Depot, in the most recent meeting of stockholders, sets a time clock to limit questions of shareholders to one minute. The United States builds the world's largest embassy in Baghdad, constructed under all-night lights, while the city lacks power. All around—in gender, in class, in race—there is silencing power, and silent people can only conform in resignation or seethe in resentment, but they cannot act as free agents in their own history.

The book of Psalms is Israel's instrument and practice of speech, designed to counter the imposed silence of all monitoring librarians. Imagine ancient Israel, gathered regularly in the face of the relentless empire, ranging through its repertoire, refusing techno-speech that comes from the Pentagon and the psychobabble that comes from Dr. Phil, and engaging in speech that is truth-telling, the self-in-community a daring, demanding exhibit, refusing safer silence. I have no doubt that bringing the self fully to speech is the first act of public ethics to notice how a voice of advocacy and insistence sounds in the corridors of power.

Israel sings and speaks and prays, refusing every silence. *Israel claims self.* The voice of the lament psalms is the break made by the depleted self willing to declare self a worthwhile agent, even at the throne of God. Such speech is first of all the *I, I* in my need, *I* in my insistence and my resistance and my expectation and my sadness and my readiness to wait, but not too long:

> I cry aloud to God,
>> aloud to God, that he may hear me.
> In the day of my trouble I seek the Lord;
>> in the night my hand is stretched out without wearying;
>> my soul refuses to be comforted.
> I think of God, and I moan;
>> I meditate, and my spirit faints.
> You keep my eyelids from closing;
>> I am so troubled that I cannot speak.
> I consider the days of old,
>> and remember the years of long ago.
> I commune with my heart in the night;
>> I meditate and search my spirit:
> "Will the Lord spurn forever,
>> and never again be favorable?
> Has his steadfast love ceased forever?
>> Are his promises at an end for all time?
> Has God forgotten to be gracious?
>> Has he in anger shut up his compassion?"
> And I say, "It is my grief
>> that the right hand of the Most High has changed."
>> Ps. 77:1–10

The laments, without conceding anything, are about the self. Too long the church, in its fascination with guilt, has diminished self, urged self to deference and default, and effaced self until finally there is a disappearance of the self.

But if the laments risk too much self-assertion, they are checked in the rich repertoire by a change of posture. For lament will most often move to *hymn* in which the *claimed self* is gladly transposed into the *abandoned self*, abandoned in exuberance to the wondrous reality of God who is worthy of all praise:

> The LORD sets the prisoners free;
>> the LORD opens the eyes of the blind.
> The LORD lifts up those who are bowed down;
>> the LORD loves the righteous.
> The LORD watches over the strangers;
>> he upholds the orphan and the widow,
>> but the way of the wicked he brings to ruin.
> The LORD will reign forever,
>> your God, O Zion, for all generations.
> Praise the LORD!
>> Ps. 146:7b–10

Praise the LORD!
How good it is to sing praises to our God;
    for he is gracious, and a song of praise is fitting.
The LORD builds up Jerusalem;
    he gathers the outcasts of Israel.
He heals the brokenhearted,
    and binds up their wounds.
He determines the number of the stars;
    he gives to all of them their names.
Great is our Lord, and abundant in power;
    his understanding is beyond measure.
The LORD lifts up the downtrodden;
    he casts the wicked to the ground.

147:1–6

Now the world is peopled by the extravagant power and the overwhelming generosity of God. The self is on the receiving end and glad to be so.

The wonder of the Psalter is that these genres of claimed self and abandoned self are in close and easy proximity to each other. Israel finds no awkwardness or contradiction in its capacity *to claim self* in demanding entitlement and *to yield self* in buoyant theological affirmation. It is the capacity to praise and to lament, to yield and to claim, to be exuberant and then indignant, that is the supple emancipated practice whereby the self can be fully free and fully grateful, fully demanding in the world. The wonder of the book of Psalms is that the God of Israel is willing to be the responding partner for Israel in all these dialogical transactions, ready to be addressed in lament in order to respond, ready to be praised by Israel and therefore magnified above all the other gods, ready to ascend in large rule and to descend into unbearable mystery, ready to be a party to the fluid, open dialogue that constitutes the covenantal existence promised at Sinai and practiced by Moses.[10] One cannot go easily to public policy unless there is a people prepared, schooled, and equipped for the open extremities of human existence. Capacity to live to the edges of wonder and dismay creates a large arena in which we are able to move beyond ourselves, bold before intransigent reality and buoyant alongside people in need. It is this large arena of human possibility that makes a faithful life sustainable:

> We are afflicted in every way, but not crushed; perplexed, but not driven to despair; persecuted, but not forsaken; struck down, but not destroyed; always carrying in the body the death of Jesus, so that the life of Jesus may also be made visible in our bodies. (2 Cor. 4:8–10)

The life of Jesus is a life of suffering that requires lament. The life of Jesus is a life of resurrection that requires doxology. We carry that whole life in our bodies, lament and doxology, suffering and resurrection, and we are unafraid!

Thus, I suggest ample resources in the text for faith enacted in the public domain:

1. *The Torah*, which offers an alternative to the endless productivity of Pharaoh, and *Jesus*, who offers discipleship as an antidote to anxiety;
2. *Prophetic truth-telling* that exposes the euphemisms of exploitation among the rulers of this age; that speaks judgment to open denial, even as we confess that the Messiah must suffer and die; that speaks *hope to penetrate despair*, even as we confess, "*He is risen*," against all conventional expectations.
3. *Wisdom* reflection is acknowledgment of a given order of *shalom* that contradicts our technological arrogance, an order that gives life but not on our own terms, a protest that makes all our absolutes penultimate even as we ponder the one whose foolishness is wisdom, whose weakness is strength, whose poverty is wealth.
4. *The Psalms* are an invitation to extremity—the extremity of the claimed self, the extremity of the abandoned self, the nurture of a free self who proceeds in dialogue that leads to a self open and free and with energy, against all our silencing in conformity and collusion.

Each of these literatures invites us to *an either/or*:

- Either Sabbath rest or the anxiety of productivity
- Either truth-telling or life hidden in denial and despair
- Either all before a life-given order or arrogance too much in love with our own absolutes
- Either the rhetoric of extremity or a safe life of silence

That either/or can perhaps be thematized into large narrative claims:

- Either: a life from creation through obedience to peace at the last
- Or: a life of self-invention through anxiety to death

Thus, we are confronted with a *narrative of hope* versus a *narrative of fear*. And we may choose. The two narratives have been lined out by Jeremiah:

> Thus says the LORD: Do not let the wise boast in their wisdom, do not let the mighty boast in their might, do not let the wealthy boast in their wealth; but let those who boast boast in this, that they understand and know me, that I am the LORD; I act with steadfast love, justice, and righteousness in the earth, for in these things I delight, says the LORD. (Jer. 9:23–24)

Jeremiah uttered these words just as his world was collapsing. He understood the *trajectory of disaster* marked by wisdom, might, and wealth, and the *trajectory of possibility* marked by steadfast love, justice, and righteousness—and he never confused the two. It is worth noticing that Paul, in his great rendition of the wisdom of the cross, quotes this text from Jeremiah:

> He is the source of your life in Christ Jesus, who became for us wisdom from
> God, and righteousness and sanctification and redemption, in order that, as
> it is written, "Let the one who boasts, boast in the Lord." (1 Cor. 1:30–31)

Paul asserts that those who are chosen by God have subversive work to do:

> God chose what is low and despised in the world, things that are not, to
> reduce to nothing things that are, so that no one might boast in the pres-
> ence of God. (1 Cor. 1:28–29)

"Bringing to nought" creates space for that new kingdom ruled by the one who
"calls into existence the things that do not exist." (Rom. 4:17)

III.

I am obligated, even if ill-equipped, to conclude with some comments on congregational practice. I am not a pastor, though I am the son of a pastor, but I
think I do not underestimate the difficulty of these issues in the life of a congregation. First, I offer six observations about the congregation:

1. It is important to reconstrue the congregation, in all its aspects, as an
   arena in which we practice *evangelical imagination*, that is, in which we
   conjure the world through the claims of the gospel. This means that we
   do something very different "in here" from what happens "out there"; it
   means that we engage in deep contestation of a healing kind. I believe
   that most congregations are not construed as places where we do something different from our culture, which means to work at distinguishing
   the gospel from the American dream.
2. It is important to recognize that we have so much to *unlearn*, both fearful conservatives and shrill liberals. Partly we have to unlearn because we
   have learned poorly. But more important, we have to unlearn because
   what we have learned is not now adequate. As per the model of Thomas
   Kuhn, it is as though we are working with Ptolemaic assumptions in a
   Copernican universe.[11]
3. The beginning point for reconstrual is *baptism*, and we must now learn from
   the Anabaptist traditions. Baptism is the marking of an alternative identity
   wherein "we renounce Satan and all his works," wherein we declare that
   God's promises are definitional for us and for God's whole creation.
4. The *Eucharist* as an act of alternative imagination needs to be reconstrued away from the older "sin-salvation" model into the obedience of
   creation with twelve baskets of bread left over. Loaves abound!
5. The *sacraments* are reconstrued because of the *word*. My exposition has
   been an argument that everything needful for our work is in the text of
   Scripture and the great ecumenical tradition of interpretation of that

Scripture. But we have been lazy and compliant about the text; we have been content to take bits of the text and fit it into another narrative. I have no doubt that the beginning point of public policy is text, text, text. That is not because the Bible tells us what to do about abortion or immigration, but because the Bible places us in an alternative world where the God of the gospel is clearly enacted.

6. So much depends upon pastors and teachers of the church being *faithful witnesses*, not to pet projects that are liberal or conservative, but to the deep claims that invite us to Easter. I call your attention, if you get frightened like I do, to the words of Jesus to his disciples about the dangers of testimony:

> But before all this occurs, they will arrest you and persecute you; they will hand you over to synagogues and prisons, and you will be brought before kings and governors because of my name. This will give you an opportunity to testify. So make up your minds not to prepare your defense in advance; for I will give you words and a wisdom that none of your opponents will be able to withstand or contradict. (Luke 21:12–15)

Jesus promises to give his witnesses "mouth."

I conclude with four comments about the congregation:

1. The work of congregational ministry is to help people *find themselves in crisis* so that the ambivalence between old and new can be felt and named. I believe the crisis is already felt, but it mostly remains unnamed. I believe people, if alive at all, are wistfully in crisis that cannot be dealt with unless it is named.

2. The crisis is to be conducted visibly and overtly in *a mood of pluralism*, so that the pastor cannot very far urge specific outcomes but people are led by the Spirit in ways beyond even us.

3. The context of congregation as arena for evangelical imagination is so that people can *re-decide* against a false story; such re-deciding gives energy and freedom for obedience to new possibility.

4. *The truth makes free.* Nothing else does. We have some truthfulness entrusted to us. The rest is given by the Spirit through our practice. The promise is that we may be free:

> Free at last,
> Free at last,
> Thank God almighty, free at last!

See the doxology of Miriam in Exodus 15:21 that anticipates this later song of freedom.

Chapter 6

"It's the Economy, Beloved"

Texts in Neighborly Materiality

It is conventional to say that modern Western theology, from the seventeenth century onward, developed in three competing and perhaps complementary trajectories:

Orthodoxy in both Lutheran and Calvinist forms developed through scholastic exposition of the church's dogmatic tradition. It constructed a more-or-less complete system of certitude that was articulated in deeply coded propositions that allowed little or no variance. In context such orthodoxy functioned to resist "modernism" and offered certitudes unimpacted by the intellectual power of modernism. Such orthodoxy, in the face of the rise of science in the seventeenth century and the emergence of historicism in the nineteenth century, came to function in ways parallel to the First Vatican Council in Roman Catholicism— that is, as a claim of "infallibility."

Rationalism was an alternative development that intended to counter fideistic orthodoxy and to appeal to the critical categories of the best academic thought available in context. This propensity sought to articulate a way of faith that was culturally self-conscious and that eschewed the more intellectually embarrassing dimensions of faith such as miracles and resurrection. It tilted toward ethical accent and assigned to categories as "myth" whatever violated reason. This tendency was of immense importance in the generation of the critical study of Scripture in a way that insisted that the Bible must be studied like any other book.

Pietism, contrasted to orthodoxy as a church movement and to rationalism as an academic movement, was a folk movement that found both orthodoxy in its sterility and rationalism in its reasonableness inadequate. Pietism, my own tradition, sought to overcome the "coldness" of theological thought by celebrating intimacy with God—or with Jesus—and in a kind of spiritual innocence imagined direct communication with God that did not linger over correct ideas but that treasured an intimacy marked by emotional engagement that was rich and direct.

It is clear in retrospect that these three trajectories of interpretation continued to feed and mark the church even in our own contemporary cultural setting:

1. What has been termed *orthodoxy* now passes for theological *conservatism*. It is a mode of thinking and believing that thrives on absolutism; this perspective yearns for certitude and so rejects any notion of the impingement of context or any notion of dynamism that would cause ambiguity in the truth that has been received.
2. What has been termed *rationalism* now passes for theological *liberalism*. This is a mode of thinking and believing that thrives on relevance; this practice yearns for connection to cultural forms and cultural assumptions and is embarrassed by what is old-fashioned, traditional, or supernatural, a stance nicely exemplified in the so-called Jesus Seminar and more generally in historical criticism. This stance, as much as possible, wants to make a common cause with what Schleiermacher called the "cultured despisers" of religion.
3. What has been termed *pietism* now appears among us in the form of *spirituality* that eschews both the certitudes of orthodoxy and the relevance of rationalism. Pietism seeks rather a connectedness that is intimate and experiential, and it resists any attempt to sophistication that seeks to move past the simplicity of directness into anything more remote, more complex, or more cognitive.

It will be clear that these three trajectories, into which most of us can readily situate ourselves, go in quite distinct directions; one may, moreover, judge that many of the tensions in the church today arise from these tensions in perspective. Given all of that, I begin with a quite different point—namely, that these three trajectories have roughly in common that they have all misunderstood the *neighborly materiality* of biblical faith. That is, they have, in different forms, transposed the claims of biblical faith into propositions, ideas, feelings, or relationships, all of which in different ways flee from the earthiness and the earthly grounding of biblical faith. I begin with this observation because the distortion or neglect of neighborly materiality, in the end, makes stewardship deeply problematic and endlessly marginal to the faith and practice of the church. My judgment then is that good stewardship must redirect and summon the church back to a neighborly materiality that has to do with the generous, community-creating management of earthly commodities that begins neither with proposition, idea, nor feelings but with the creator God who has been "fleshed" among us and who mandates neighborly love as the primal mode of the love of God. Or as Jeremiah puts it:

> He judged the cause of the poor and needy;
>   then it was well.
> Is not this to know me? says the LORD.
> Jer. 22:16

Or as 1 John has it:

> Those who say, "I love God," and hate their brothers or sisters, are liars; for those who do not love a brother or sister whom they have seen, cannot love God whom they have not seen. The commandment we have from him is this: those who love God must love their brothers and sisters also. (1 John 4:20–21)

This neighborly materiality is grounded in at least three primal claims of faith:

First, the God we confess is *the creator God*, and the world we inhabit is God's creation; we live here as God's beloved, free, responsible, summoned creatures. It is the earth in all of its wonder that God has called "good." It is the earth that our primal ancestors—and we after them—have been mandated to "till and keep" in order to enhance the neighborhood (Gen. 2:15).

Second, the God we confess has come *bodied among us* (John 1:14). The category of "incarnation" is an awkward one, the church's mumbling way to speak of Jesus, our humanness, and the rule of God all at once. It cannot be doubted in any case that the one who embodied God among us cared most about creation and the human role in creation, about the defeat of the powers of death so that there may be abundant life:

> And he answered them, "Go and tell John what you have seen and heard: the blind receive their sight, the lame walk, the lepers are cleansed, the deaf hear, the dead are raised, the poor have good news brought to them." (Luke 7:22)

Third, the God who creates and has come fleshed is the God who will make all things new, will create yet again *a new creation*. That new creation, finally, is about the rule of God on earth as in heaven, the rule of God—as in Isaiah 65:17–25—about houses and vineyards, about infant mortality and wolves and lambs—all things neighborly, all things material!

Thus, I propose as we take up this special season of stewardship[1] that we who are orthodox, we who are rationalists, and we who are pietists take as our task the reengagement of the large themes of our faith that pivot around neighborly materiality. We do so in order to discover that our particular trajectory of interpretation has readily led us away from the core of our faith, and now we return to our faith in the new freedom to be the managing, caring, enhancing creatures we are called to be, ensuring that the neighborhood can eventually be called "very good."

II.

In that context of neighborly materiality, I will identify and exposit ten texts. These I intend to be representative texts, not necessarily the "best texts."

Genesis 28:20–22

Jacob has fled for his life from his brother Esau and encamps en route to Haran. He finds as he sleeps that "this is none other than the house of God, and this is the gate of heaven" (v. 17). On that night, he sees in his dream a ladder filled with angels, and he knows God's presence; in that context, he is addressed by a divine voice that offers him the definitive promises in the Bible made to him and beyond him to Israel:

> And the LORD stood beside him and said, "I am the LORD, the God of Abraham your father and the God of Isaac; the land on which you lie I will give to you and to your offspring; and your offspring shall be like the dust of the earth, and you shall spread abroad to the west and to the east and to the north and to the south; and all the families of the earth shall be blessed in you and in your offspring. Know that I am with you and will keep you wherever you go, and will bring you back to this land; for I will not leave you until I have done what I have promised you." (Gen. 28:13–15)

With these verses our reading usually stops. But Jacob must respond to the promise; he—and we—must respond to the faithful, self-giving of God who makes futures for us. And Jacob does respond, in a way characteristic of his irascibly demanding character:

> Then Jacob made a vow, saying, "If God will be with me, and will keep me in this way that I go, and will give me bread to eat and clothing to wear, so that I come again to my father's house in peace, then the LORD shall be my God, and this stone, which I have set up for a pillar, shall be God's house; and of all that you give me I will surely give one tenth to you." (28:20–22)

Jacob's response is an "if-then" formulation. The "if" appeals back to God's promise that Jacob now roughly reiterates:

If God be with me

If God keep me in the way I go

If God give me bread to eat and clothing to wear,

so that I return home in peace . . .

then YHWH will be my God

then this pillar will be God's house

then of all you give me, I will surely give one-tenth to you

If factored out in this way, there are three "ifs" and three "thens." Jacob's response depends completely upon YHWH's initial fidelity that is to be tested in concrete ways.

The "thens" mean that Jacob will accept this God as God (a theological decision), will recognize the pillar as a place of presence (a cultic decision), and will tithe (a stewardship decision). The tithe, of course, signifies acknowledgments of YHWH's proprietary right to the land; thus, it is a tenant rental agreement.

I cite this text because of the "if-then" status of the speech. At worst, Jacob is bargaining. At best, Jacob is acknowledging that the economic transaction of stewardship is not a disinterested act but is in the "interest" of both parties. That interest, moreover, is roughly spelled out. I suggest that honest stewardship from the outset is about a win-win transaction. Thus, most of our conventional rhetoric concerning payment of vows—church pledges—is recurrent in this mode in the Bible:

Then my soul shall rejoice in the LORD,
    exulting in his deliverance.
                        Ps. 35:9

How long, O LORD, will you look on?
    Rescue me from their ravages,
    my life from the lions!
Then I will thank you in the great congregation;
    in the mighty throng I will praise you.
                        35:17–18

Then my tongue shall tell of your righteousness
    and of your praise all day long.
                        35:28 (au. emph.)

With a freewill offering I will sacrifice to you;
    I will give thanks to your name, O LORD, for it is good.
For he has delivered me from every trouble,
    and my eye has looked in triumph on my enemies.
                        54:6–7

My vows to you I must perform, O God;
    I will render thank offerings to you.
For you have delivered my soul from death,
    and my feet from falling,

so that I may walk before God
in the light of life.
56:12–13

For you have delivered my soul from death,
my eyes from tears,
my feet from stumbling.
. . . .
What shall I return to the LORD
for all his bounty to me?
I will lift up the cup of salvation
and call on the name of the LORD,
I will pay my vows to the LORD
in the presence of all his people.
116:8, 12–14

In all these cases, the payment of vows and tithes is on condition and in response to God's action in their life.

The question that Satan puts to God concerning Job is this: "Does Job fear God for nothing?" (Job 1:9). That question, however, was not on the mind of Israel for the most part. For the most part, it was clear that Israel did not fear and trust and obey God "for nothing," but in response to and on condition of God's goodness. I cite this text from Jacob because at the outset it should be clear that stewardship is not a disinterested activity. It is the completion of a transaction that involves the initiative, intervention, and fidelity of YHWH in concrete ways, to which Israel makes concrete response. Israel is not at all embarrassed to assert that stewardship—the offer of tithes and vows to YHWH—as part of a covenantal transaction in which YHWH is generous and faithful, from which Israel benefits in nameable, identifiable ways.

Exodus 31:12–17

This is an oddly positioned, always neglected text. It comes at the end of Exodus 25–31, the dreary commands of YHWH to Moses concerning the construction of the tabernacle. That long section issues in seven addresses from YHWH to Moses that scholars correlate to the seven days of creation in Genesis 1.[2] Exodus 31:12–17 is the seventh speech of YHWH to Moses, correlating to the seventh day of creation, the Sabbath. The command to Israel is this:

> You shall keep the sabbath, because it is holy for you; everyone who pro-
> fanes it shall be put to death; whoever does any work on it shall be cut off
> from among the people. Six days shall work be done, but the seventh day is
> a sabbath of solemn rest, holy to the LORD; whoever does any work on the
> sabbath day shall be put to death. (Exod. 31:14–15)

Sabbath here is work stoppage; work stoppage is crucial and is a mark of Israel, so serious that it is to be enforced on pain of death. But consider, Sabbath is not about blue laws or puritanical requirements. Rather, it is disengagement from the rat race of production, acquisitiveness, and consumption that eventually undermines our humanness. Thus, stewardship inescapably begins in the disengagement of Sabbath, a regularized disruption that reminds us that life is given, given in the generosity of the Creator for whom in turn we may be generous. Sabbath is a disciplined, regular enactment of the conviction that our life is pure gift and not achievement, that our identity consists in who we are before God and not what we do in the world.

It is simply astonishing that Israel took Sabbath to be the quintessential mark of being God's covenant people in the world. That seventh day is a sign in the world that Israel depends upon YHWH and not upon self, that Israel's identity in the world is through a relationship and not a commodity or a possession. Personal identity in this community toward this God consists in a disengagement, a yielding of commodities and possessions. The stance of this community in the world, as Paul later wrote, is for "those who deal with the world as though they had no dealings with it. For the present form of this world is passing away" (1 Cor. 7:31).

In the commandment in Exodus 31, there is a most remarkable conclusion in verse 17: "In six days the LORD made heaven and earth, and on the seventh day he rested, and was refreshed." Now this rendering "refreshed" is astonishing. The noun *nephesh* means "self" or "soul." But the verb "to be *nepheshed*" only occurs three times, once for David (2 Sam. 16:14), once for Sabbath concerns that the *nephesh* of the sojourner slave may be recovered (Exod. 23:12), and once in this text that signals the *recovery of God's* nephesh. Note two things. First, YHWH's *nephesh* can be and is depleted by six days of hard work as creator. God can be diminished! Second, God's *nephesh* can be restored and rehabilitated by Sabbath. This is not an immutable God, but one subject to the vagaries of life and to the rhythms of work and rest.

The summons of the text is that we, alongside YHWH, are to do Sabbath, because Sabbath is for the restoration and rehabilitation of depleted, diminished selves. Entertain this thought on stewardship: Most pastors minister to depleted selves, self-depleted by the pressures and anxieties of the rat race of the consumer economy. More than that, many ministers are depleted selves because of the rat race of catering to a consumer economy that mostly is never satisfied.

The truth is that exhausted, spent, diminished selves can rarely be generous or gracious toward others. In our depletion, we tend to become driven, compulsive, short-tempered, angry, and eventually violent. The first act of stewardship is to break the vicious cycle of production and consumption. A way in which that vicious cycle is to be broken is not recreation or sports or entertainment. It is disciplined work stoppage in order to let life *come to us* as pure gift from the Creator. There is no limit, I suspect, to the generosity and graciousness of selves that have been re-*nepheshed*. YHWH and Moses and Israel have known that since the Sinai. It is plausible that such a break in the cycle of viciousness is the most crucial pastoral act in stewardship. Marva Dawn writes of the Sabbath:

> All the great motifs of our Christian faith are underscored in our Sabbath keeping. Its Ceasing deepens our repentance for the many ways that we

fail to trust God and try to create our own future. Its Resting strengthens our faith in the totality of his grace. Its Embracing invites us to take the truths of our faith and apply them practically in our values and lifestyles. Its Feasting heightens our sense of eschatological hope—the Joy of our present experience of God's love and its foretaste of the Joy to come. . . . Shabbat ritual is designed to disconnect us from our normal attitude of making, doing, changing material existence, and to connect us to the realm of time [Resting]. To experience the world free from the need to interfere with it is a transformative and liberating experience. But it can't be achieved in the midst of a day filled with getting, spending, and making. . . . When Sabbath is finally fulfilled, our divisions and weaknesses will *cease* forever. We will *rest* eternally in God's grace and love. We will *embrace* his kingdom and sovereignty ultimately and perfectly. We will *feast* unceasingly in his presence.[3]

Sabbath is a mystery of which we are stewards. In the practice of the mystery, we become more able stewards.

Exodus 36:3–7

This third text also comes from the dreary, neglected texts wherein YHWH instructs Moses on the construction of the tabernacle. As we have just considered, in Exodus 25–31 we have a long instruction, culminating in Exodus 31:12–17, on Sabbath. After a narrative break in Exodus 32–34, Exodus 35–40 tells of Moses' obedience to YHWH's commands as he constructs the tabernacle. Thus, Exodus 25–31 is reiterated almost word for word in Exodus 35–40. Our text in Exodus 36:2–7, however, is not paralleled in the earlier commands. In this text, Bezalel and Oholiab are appointed the master craftsmen for the tabernacle. But of course the craftsmen need materials with which to work, or money with which to buy materials:

> And they received from Moses all the freewill offerings that the Israelites had brought for doing the work on the sanctuary. They still kept bringing him freewill offerings every morning. (Exod. 36:3)

This is one of the most dramatic acts of stewardship of which I know—people who bring "freewill offerings," a technical term that refers to extra offerings outside of the normal calendar of required and expected gifts. This is indeed second-mile giving, giving that lasted all day, given by those whose hearts were stirred. In fact, the Hebrew is "whose hearts were lifted up," which brings to mind "Lift up your hearts. . . . We lift them to the Lord." People with hearts lifted above self turn out to be grateful and generous to God:

> So that all the artisans who were doing every sort of task on the sanctuary came, each from the task being performed, and said to Moses, "The people are bringing much more than enough for doing the work that the LORD has commanded us to do." (36:4–5)

This is a remarkable crisis: Too many offerings, more than enough, campaign oversubscribed! In response to this remarkable crisis, Moses issues a restraining order against generosity:

> So Moses gave command, and word was proclaimed throughout the camp: "No man or woman is to make anything else as an offering for the sanctuary." So the people were restrained from bringing; for what they had already brought was more than enough to do all the work. (36:6–7)

The report takes our breath away. A wave of generosity swept over Israel that threatened to overwhelm the plans and the workmen who requested the restraining order.

One could of course imagine a freewill offering for a building project that appeals to those whose hearts were not stirred, whose hearts were not lifted up. Such hearts in such potential givers are not stirred by God's spirit or lifted up by God's promise. Such people—who are not mentioned in this budget report in the book of Exodus—are characteristically mired in self-preoccupation and cannot get beyond themselves. Such potential givers, absent in this report, may be in the grip of fearfulness or self-indulgence, cut off from any engagement with the generous God. And those cut off from the generous God are unable themselves to be generous.

But not here! We are not told how the hearts of these givers were stirred, or why the offerings were overwhelming. But we can surmise. The money and the contributions in kind were for the tabernacle. The Israelites were building, at YHWH's command and at Moses' behest, an access point to the holy presence of God. This was a people who had observed the enslaving idolatries of the gods of the Egyptian empire. They had in turn danced their way into the new freedom given by this God. They had endured wilderness scarcity because of the bread of heaven given by this God. They had come to see that this disturbing, life-giving, revolutionary God made new life possible, and they did not want to revert to absence, either to the brick quotas of the imperial system or the shriveling scarcity of the wilderness. They had come to see that this holy presence was a life-or-death, a slavery-or-freedom, a bread-or-hunger question. Their decision was on that count an easy one.

And then they learned, through the speech of Moses, that this intruding God was prepared to be an abiding God. But the quality of that holy abiding still trembled with the marks of holy disruptiveness. The usual critical judgment about these texts is that there is no connection between the exodus narrative and the sanctuary provisions of the Priestly tradition—except that Moses hears YHWH's assurance:

> I will dwell among the Israelites, and I will be their God. And they shall know that I am the LORD their God, who brought them out of the land of Egypt that I might dwell among them; I am the LORD their God. (29:45–46)

It is the same God. In this text, Israel recognizes that the God known regularly in the cult is the God of revolutionary transformation out in the world. The money given is not just to maintain the punctiliousness of the priests. It is to make possible the life-giving presence of God in the sanctuary and in the world, to keep the world from closing in on us by either exploitation or by scarcity. Stewardship as is practiced here is immensely pragmatic. They invested in the presence of God's holiness that will keep life open. They invested subsequently in bringing goats and lambs without blemish, the best without flaw, because they reasoned that the best is not to be siphoned off for self-preoccupation or self-indulgence. This stewardship is an act that submits to the wonder of divine presence. And when they had finished, by Exodus 40, we are told that in this place funded by willing hearts, God's own glory was beheld, "the glory as of a father's only son, full of grace and truth" (John 1:14). In the Exodus report, the summary conclusion goes like this:

> Then the cloud covered the tent of meeting, and the glory of the LORD filled the tabernacle. Moses was not able to enter the tent of meeting because the cloud settled upon it, and the glory of the LORD filled the tabernacle. (40:34–35)

Finally, it should not be missed that the contributions "in kind" were artistic in character:

> All those with skill among the workers made the tabernacle with ten curtains; they were made of fine twisted linen, and blue, purple, and crimson yarns, with cherubim skillfully worked into them. (36:8)

The Israelites exulted in color. They adorned the place with presence in uncommon beauty. This is indeed the beauty of holiness, the awareness of the holy hospitality of beauty. In doing this aesthetically compelling construction, they affirmed (a) that the God of holy presence is not a starchy moralistic agent, but one whose life is set down in the joy of beauty, and (b) that life in YHWH's presence, unlike the violent contested world beyond, is full of eye-pleasing, sense-enhancing loveliness. This is articulated in a classic call to worship from Psalm 29:

> Ascribe to the LORD, O heavenly beings,
>   ascribe to the LORD glory and strength.
> Ascribe to the LORD the glory of his name;
>   worship the LORD in holy splendor.
>   Ps. 29:1–2

Deuteronomy 14:22–29

When we move from the Priestly tradition to the book of Deuteronomy, we enter a quite different world. This text also enjoins an annual tithe, indicating YHWH's entitlement as owner of the land. What interests us here is the intention of the tithe:

> With the money secure in hand, go to the place that the LORD your God
> will choose; spend the money for whatever you wish—oxen, sheep, wine,
> strong drink, or whatever you desire. And you shall eat there in the pres-
> ence of the LORD your God, you and your household rejoicing together.
> (Deut. 14:25b–26)

The tithe is to be brought to YHWH's place. But once there, the offering is to
be used for the contributors themselves. The verse is a doublet:

> . . . whatever your heart desires
> . . . whatever your life asks

This may strike you as odd, as it strikes me. The command is an invitation for
self-satisfaction of highly desired consumer commodities—oxen, sheep, wine,
strong drink. These are cited as examples of an unremunerated list of other commodities one might like. And the Israelite can have them all, once the money is
brought to YHWH's shrine.

The point is that worship of YHWH, in the horizon of Deuteronomy, is a
highly contested matter with other gods competing for offerings, with other
gods claiming entitlement to the land and so entitlement to the tithe. The
implicit prohibition in this license for self-satisfaction is that tithes acknowledging entitlement must not be given to any other loyalty or claim, because every
other claim is false. Thus, the command of the tithe is a function and echo of
the First Commandment—no other gods, no offerings to any other would-be
landowner. The offering is to be brought publicly, openly, dramatically down
Main Street so that everyone can see a confessional act. Everyone can see that
it is the creator God who owns and governs the land, who is the redeemer God
from Egypt, who is the single legitimate claimant to the land. One can imagine
that in Deuteronomy this is a quite hard-nosed, uncompromising requirement
that allows no gesture toward racism, sexism, militarism, nationalism, consumerism, or a dozen other isms that seduce and seem to be sources of security and
well-being. This is the theological tradition of stewardship that takes its stand
on Deuteronomy 6:4: "Hear, O Israel: The LORD is our God, the LORD alone."
YHWH alone! YHWH as sole source of security and well-being. Of course, such
a public acknowledgment of the single source of blessing and well-being carries
with it Sinai-sized mandates.

The mandates in Deuteronomy, however, are of another kind. For in Deuteronomy 14:28–29, perhaps an addendum but now in the text, a typical provision
is given by Moses:

> Every third year you shall bring out the full tithe of your produce for that
> year, and store it within your towns; the Levites, because they have no allot-
> ment or inheritance with you, as well as the resident aliens, the orphans,
> and the widows in your towns, may come and eat their fill so that the LORD
> your God may bless you in all the work that you undertake.

Every third year—that means one-third of all offerings of the tithe. That also means, does it not, that two-thirds of the tithe are to be spent on communal maintenance and well-being for the land-using donors. But one-third is for the neighbors. They are enumerated in typical Deuteronomic fashion: Levites, who have no land, home mission pastors, resident aliens, orphans, and widows. Nicholas Wolterstorff terms these latter three, along with the poor, "the quadrilateral of vulnerability."[4] They are the ones in a patriarchal society who have no male advocates. And so the tithe that YHWH has deployed for the vulnerable who are YHWH's special friends is deployed even away from the donor community itself.

The company of the vulnerable, now to be the special recipients of the land tax, are to eat and be satiated—not grudgingly, not parsimoniously, not with calculation, but in abundance. Indeed, in the following chapter, concerning the year of release, the donor community is urged to be generous with an infinite absolute in the Hebrew (i.e., the Hebrew intensifies the verb in a way not visible in English translation):

> If there is among you anyone in need, a member of your community in any of your towns within the land that the LORD your God is giving you, do not be hard-hearted or tight-fisted toward your needy neighbor. . . . Give liberally and be ungrudging when you do so, for on this account the LORD your God will bless you in all your work and in all that you undertake. (Deut. 15:7, 10)

The care for the poor is not minimal maintenance but generosity for a full life. Frank Crüsemann terms this provision the first social safety net in the history of political economy.[5] And, adds Moses, do this "so that the LORD your God may bless you in all the work of your hands" (Deut. 14:29).

This notion of stewardship is typical of Deuteronomic reciprocity. Generosity evokes the generosity of God. That of course is the lived experience of every generous steward. A life of generosity toward God via the neighbor sets in motion the juices of blessing that flow by the will of the Creator. One cannot overestimate the outcome of blessing that flows from a life of generosity. Indeed, in chapter 15, at the end of the provision on the year of release, Moses comments:

> Do not consider it a hardship when you send them [debtors] out from you free persons, because for six years they have given you services worth the wages of hired laborers; and the LORD your God will bless you in all that you do. (15:18)

1 Chronicles 29:14–17

This great text in the mouth of David comes in the final chapter of 1 Chronicles just before the report of David's death in verses 26–30. The long Davidic narrative in 1 Chronicles is mostly about preparation for the building of the temple that his son Solomon will implement in 2 Chronicles. After David's financial and administrative planning, David's last act is a prayer that is clearly designed to portray the king as a man of immense piety. The prayer begins in verses 10–13 with doxology and thanksgiving. And then in verse 14, the beginning of our textual unit, David responds to the wonder of YHWH just stated with a self-deprecating act of deference that is characteristic of such royal prayers. Kings may be powerful and full of themselves, posturing and strutting, but before the Holy Creator, all such royal posturing is impertinent.

Thus David begins: "Who am I? And what is my people?" Answer: "I am nobody before you. My people is no people before you." Consequently this thank offering now to be given in a quite public way is offered by an unworthy king. The offering, as in the other texts we have cited, is a *freewill offering*, beyond any specific requirements, an act of generosity rooted in gratitude. David's offering is grounded in amazement that this nobody king who presides over this no people should have come to this awesome moment of grandeur at the threshold of building the temple. That of course is the proper stance for stewardship—awe at God's fidelity and generosity that, when properly reflected upon, can be overwhelming.

But there is more to come of royal deference:

> All things come from you,
> and of your own have we given you.
> 1 Chr. 29:14

This verse is a cliché for presenting church offerings in many worship services. It is unfortunate that the phrase has become so jaded, because it articulates the central truth of stewardship. It is all of God! It all belongs to God! Our offering to God is simply a return to God in gratitude. We stewards are indeed like the slaves in Matthew 25 entrusted by the master with different measures of wealth. Some of us invest and grow the trust from God. Some of us, in distrust, covet and save and return only the initial gift. But all of us, sooner or later, must report back to the owner on the status of the trust.

Here David acknowledges that there is only one giver, the Creator who has settled in awesome generosity on this no people presided over by this no king. David's prayer continues with two other accents that voice the incommensurate relationship between God and God's donor people. First, concerning us: "For we are aliens and transients before you, as were all our ancestors; our days on the earth are like a shadow, and there is no hope" (1 Chr. 29:15). What a characterization of the true status of all donors before God! All of us are aliens and transient residents without any rights or entitlements. All of us are like fleeting shadows, as have been our mothers and fathers who in mortality soon pass away. All of us with no land, no wealth, no resources—all of us without hope. Second, concerning the creator donor of life: "O LORD our God, all this abundance that we have provided for building you a house for your holy name comes from your hand and is all your own" (29:16). It is all yours! None of it is ours! This steward-ship transaction is a moment of truth-telling between the fully possessing God and this king who is truthfully unpossessing and unprepossessing.

This transaction between unequals, nonetheless, can delight the one creator donor. The condition of divine pleasure is that the human donor community must be "upright in heart," without guile or calculation, motivated by simple gratitude rooted in awe. That is the condition of a genuine offering that is authentically *freewill*, that is, without requirement or expectation—second-mile giving, third-mile giving, sixtieth-mile giving! Only in such a context of prayer and deference does David's prayer finally move in verses 18–19 to petitions con-cerning Solomon's future. Such petitions are not acts of bargaining but are the appropriate outcome of genuine gratitude. The one who gives and prays is of himself without hope. And so the prayer turns to the single source of all hope. Thus, stewardship is an honest reckoning of our true status in the world, our true status before the creator God who wills abundance. The culmination of the transaction is *new hope*, whereby the king expects his petitions to be heard and answered. No wonder that David, when he ended his prayer, said to his congregation, "Bless the LORD." And they did! They moved in gratitude from hopelessness to hope, the perfect outcome of authentic stewardship.

Micah 6:6–8

We now enter prophetic texts, where the matter of stewardship becomes more elemental and acute. This familiar text in Micah comes at the end of a pro-phetic speech of judgment in verses 1–8. It begins as YHWH announces a "case" against Israel. YHWH asserts that things are skewed between the two parties of the covenant. In verses 3–5, YHWH expresses exasperation with Israel and articulates YHWH's own generous fidelity to Israel over a long period of time:

> O my people, what have I done to you?
>   In what have I wearied you? Answer me!
> For I brought you up from the land of Egypt,
>   and redeemed you from the house of slavery;
> and I sent before you Moses, Aaron, and Miriam.
> O my people, remember now what King Balak of Moab devised,
>   what Balaam son of Beor answered him,
> and what happened from Shittim to Gilgal,
>   that you may know the saving acts of the LORD.
>   Mic. 6:3–5

Good stewardship is rooted in a memory of miracles of radical acts of rescue and transformation. Israel lives by such a recital of miracles, a recital that is par-alleled by Christians in the miracle stories of Jesus. Such a powerful memory of inexplicable gifts is the ground for genuine stewardship. But here something is amiss. Apparently Israel has forgotten that recital and so has forgotten the God who is the subject of the recital. We may formulate the matter this way: amnesia is an inadequate ground for good stewardship, because forgetting divine miracles invites us to imagine that we are self-made and can be self-secured. The speech of judgment on YHWH's lips is because Israel in its self-sufficiency has a deeply distorted notion of the true relationship of miracle worker and miracle receiver out of which no good stewardship can come.

Consequently, the summons to stewardship is a summons to move back into memory, to notice that life is gifted and sustained by divine miracle. It is on that basis that the poem can begin to think about a response to the case brought by YHWH, an answer probed in this familiar text.

The text begins its answer in a query that sounds like a puzzlement:

> With what shall I come before the LORD,
>   and bow myself before God on high?
>   6:6a

The puzzlement receives a series of possible answers that are entertained and found to be less than adequate:

> Shall I come before him with burnt offerings,
>   with calves a year old?
> Will the LORD be pleased with thousands of rams,
>   with ten thousands of rivers of oil?
> Shall I give my firstborn for my transgression,
>   the fruit of my body for the sin of my soul?
>   6:6b–7

The series of rhetorical questions requires a series of negative answers:

No, not burnt offerings.

No, not year-old calves.

No, not a thousand rams.

No, not a myriad of rivers of oil.

No, not the fruit of the body, not a son.

It is regularly observed that this inventory of possible offerings to YHWH moves from the least valuable to the most valuable, from a burnt offering to child sacrifice by way of a large herd of male sheep and precious oil. The list in total is rejected. It should, however, be taken seriously. It is an inventory of the most precious commodities that could possibly have been offered to the creator God.

But the text reverses field in verse 8. Now the speaker who has been musing over his or her own rhetorical questions is the one addressed. The voice that addresses is not YHWH, for YHWH is cited as "he." The voice is that of the prophetic poet, who knows the most about covenant and about broken covenant. The question now asked is not rhetorical:

> He has told you, O mortal, what is good;
>   and what does the LORD require of you . . . ?
>   6:8a–b

The answer has been "revealed." Our usual rendering of the term "require" is not quite right. It refers to what is good and what is beautiful. It asks what will restore and enhance the relationship that has become broken and distorted. The answer is this:

> . . . but to do justice, and to love kindness,
>   and to walk humbly with your God?
>   6:8c–d

The first of the three elements that are commended sounds Israel's most core claims of covenant: do *mispat*, do *hesed*. Thus, the true act of stewardship is *mispat*: covenant solidarity, which brings us immediately to neighborliness. The term *mispat* is used in many places, but surely it is best voiced in Deuteronomy and then derivatively is taken up in the Psalter:

> You must not distort justice; you must not show partiality; and you must not accept bribes, for a bribe blinds the eyes of the wise and subverts the cause of those who are in the right. Justice, and only justice, you shall pursue, so that you may live and occupy the land that the LORD your God is giving you. (Deut. 16:19–20)

> Those who walk blamelessly, and do what is right,
>   and speak the truth from their heart;
> who do not slander with their tongue,
>   and do no evil to their friends,
>   nor take up a reproach against their neighbors;
> in whose eyes the wicked are despised,
>   but who honor those who fear the LORD;
> who stand by their oath even to their hurt;
> who do not lend money at interest,
>   and do not take a bribe against the innocent.
> Those who do these things shall never be moved.
>   Ps. 15:2–5

Stewardship is the enhancement of the community to make sure that all the neighbors are included in well-being.

Hesed is a rough synonym for *mispat*, except that it bespeaks covenantal solidarity that is not simply formal, external, and contractual; rather, it is a practice of fidelity that takes the well-being of the neighbor as one's own well-being— that is, to love one's neighbor as one's own life.

The third element is less critical—to walk in meekness before God. But the term "meek" or "humble" does not suggest self-effacement. Rather, it means to live out of a connectedness that knows that one's status is derivative and penultimate and in a posture of submission. Thus, the first two members of this famous triad concern neighborly love, and the third member is about love of God—thus love of God and love of neighbor. Stewardship is to situate one's life in the network of defining relationships of solidarity and reliability. See as well Deuteronomy 10:12–22, which focuses eventually upon love of the stranger:

> So now, O Israel, what does the LORD your God require of you? Only to fear the LORD your God, to walk in all his ways, to love him, to serve the LORD your God with all your heart and with all your soul. . . . You shall also love the stranger, for you were strangers in the land of Egypt. (Deut. 10:12, 19)

Isaiah 58:6–9

This text emerges in a postexilic dispute. There was after the exile a raging controversy over who was in and who was out, over what constituted a legitimate mode of Judaism in an imperial context. There was the powerful Torah party to culminate in Ezra, and there was the punctilious Priestly tradition of Leviticus articulated by Ezekiel. This text in Isaiah is the countervoice of the inclusivists, who assert in 56:3–8 that the God who gathers outcasts is willing to gather even the eunuchs and foreigners who keep covenant.

Chapter 58 includes an argument about authentic worship. The normative tradition of worship featured a regularized calendar of festivals and a rota of proper sacrifices. Whoever kept the calendar and the rota could anticipate communal legitimacy and access to the holy presence. Here, however, in Isaiah 58, there is a dissent from such confidence in liturgic routine. The poet observes that that deeply valued practice which was wonderfully satisfying to its practitioners in its aesthetic dimension was too often left unconnected to real life. This worship, it is here insisted, only calls attention to the contradiction between worship and real life. The real life of the worshiping community is shabby and incongruent with the justice-demanding God of covenant: "Look, you serve your own interest on your fast day, and oppress all your workers" (Isa. 58:3c–d).

That indictment cuts close for us treasured, privileged, mainline stewards. For the ways in which our market practice oppresses workers is kept well hidden by the complexity of the economy. Nonetheless, such an economic practice is incongruent with the God Israel is said to worship, for even the God settled in temple and tabernacle is still the God attentive to the cries of the vulnerable, the exploited, and the poor. The ambience of worship must resonate finally with the God worshiped. We cannot have nice worship inside surrounded by cries of wretchedness outside.

The indictment of verses 1–5 is sharp. I can imagine that the ones under assault for their worship immediately became defensive. They probably said,

"Well, the economy is complex. Do you have a better idea?" And then more boldness, the "Yes, this is a better idea" of verses 6-7:

> Is not this the fast that I choose:
>   to loose the bonds of injustice,
>   to undo the thongs of the yoke,
> to let the oppressed go free,
> and to break every yoke?
> Is it not to share your bread with the hungry,
>   and bring the homeless poor into your house;
> when you see the naked, to cover them,
>   and not to hide yourself from your own kin?
>   Isa. 58:6–7

The poetry commits an inventive interpretive maneuver. The term "fast," of course, concerns a religious discipline of self-denial in the interest of empowerment. The new content of "fast" given here, however, now concerns the neighborly economy. The alternative concerns the big theme of *mispat* and emancipation. But then in verse 7 the big theme comes down to specificity: *bread, house, clothing*. But then, biblical faith always trades in concrete materiality. We cannot live without food, clothing, shelter—all outcomes of a functioning economy. But then, neither can our neighbors live without these—that is, our "neighbors in need." They also require dignity and security, but they do not have those through the normal workings of an economy of greed. In an economy of greed, the food, clothing, and shelter intended for the oppressed and poor is taken over as surplus by those who are agents of injustice. The poor and vulnerable can have dignity and security only from those who have some deep religious neighborly passion. Thus bread, clothing, and shelter become the substance of worship, whereby the deep solidarity of life is made sacramental when it draws near to needy neighbors.

The outcome of such disciplined liturgical intention is that God will be available and palpably present in a society that cares materially for the neighbor:

> *Then* you shall call, and the LORD will answer;
>   you shall cry for help, and he will say, Here I am.
>   58:9a–b (au. emph.)

> *Then* you shall take delight in the LORD,
>   and I will make you ride upon the heights of the earth;
> I will feed you with the heritage of your ancestor Jacob,
>   for the mouth of the LORD has spoken.
>   58:14 (au. emph.)

It is affirmed that the full functioning of neighborly materiality evokes the blessing of God. It may be asked whether matters are so connected between God and the neighbor. It may be asked whether worship really does spin off in this way when we worship the food-gathering, clothing-providing, house-making

Creator. And of course we are bound to answer yes, yes, yes. This is indeed stewardship to be practiced in the church and in public policy even where we have emptied stewardship of its neighborly focus.

Psalms 50:8–14, 51:17–19

Psalm 51 is a familiar psalm, the deepest of the psalms confessing sin. It is a favorite of Calvinist seminarians who have a propensity to guilt. The psalm culminates with a stewardship instruction:

> The sacrifice acceptable to God is a broken spirit;
> a broken and contrite heart, O God, you will not despise.
>
> Ps. 51:17

The only offering YHWH wants is a broken and contrite heart, one ready to submit to YHWH. The psalm is placed on the lips of David after his adultery and violence and his return to life with God. The psalmist acknowledges that God is not interested in commodity offerings, not interested in material pledges:

> For you have no delight in sacrifice;
> if I were to give a burnt offering,
> you would not be pleased.
>
> 51:16

While we know Psalm 51 well, we mostly neglect Psalm 50. In Psalm 50, matters are distorted between YHWH and Israel. Apparently Israel has tried to overcome the distortion by much stewardship, many offerings that in fact constitute a bribe to YHWH. But such bribery stewardship leaves YHWH cold and unimpressed:

> Not for your sacrifices do I rebuke you;
> your burnt offerings are continually before me.
> I will not accept a bull from your house,
> or goats from your folds.
> . . . .
> For every wild animal of the forest is mine,
> the cattle on a thousand hills.
> I know all the birds of the air,
> and all that moves in the field is mine.
> If I were hungry, I would not tell you,
> for the world and all that is in it is mine.
> Do I eat the flesh of bulls,
> or drink the blood of goats?
>
> 50:8–13

That marvelous verse 9 in the Revised Standard Version has it, "I will accept no bull from your house." God is not hoodwinked by extravagance that lives at the cusp of manipulation.

Indeed, God is not needy and never begs for stewardship. God has no need of goats or cattle or birds or stocks or bonds or cash. God is not needy, and so we do not imagine that we can do anything for God. And besides not being needy, God owns everything and has ample supply of all creaturely commodities because the Creator continues to possess all that has been created.

Should we then desist from stewardship offerings? No, because in verse 14 the psalm—after negating manipulative offerings, circles back:

> Offer to God a sacrifice of thanksgiving,
>   and pay your vows to the Most High.
>   50:14

There is another kind of offering, a thank offering—in Hebrew, a *todah*. A *todah* included *a material gift* of gratitude brought to YHWH along with *a verbal acknowledgment* of that for which there is gratitude. Bring that offering, pay that vow, honor your pledges, and call upon YHWH in the day of trouble. The offering, the pledge, and the cry of petition all bespeak a very different relationship that is no longer calculating, cunning, or manipulative. Notice that to an outside observer the manipulative offering and the gift of gratitude look exactly the same. But they are not. They bespeak and enact very different relationships, one grounded in the agenda of the giver, the other focused upon the goodness of God toward whom gratitude is a deeply felt, guileless submission of dependence. Need is not on the part of God, which has already been precluded, but it is on the part of the petitioner, who is needy and grateful to God. This thanksgiving is so rare in our contemporary world for those who imagine themselves to be self-sufficient. In the big themes of covenant and creation, there is no human self-sufficiency. There is indeed healthy need for a dramatic acknowledgment of insufficiency that submits to the all-sufficient God.

As proper modes of stewardship, Psalm 50 summons to give a thank offering, and Psalm 51 calls for a broken and contrite heart. That is the gift YHWH will surely receive. Having said that, we are astonished to return to Psalm 51 and notice its conclusion. After verse 17 indicating that the right offering is a broken and contrite heart, the psalm ends this way:

> Do good to Zion in your good pleasure;
>   rebuild the walls of Jerusalem,
> then you will delight in right sacrifices,
>   in burnt offerings;
> then bulls will be offered on your altar.
>   51:18–19

These verses, perhaps an addendum, focus on Jerusalem and surely the temple. They assert that the enhancement of Jerusalem will cause delight in right offerings, in burnt offerings, in whole burnt offerings, and in bulls offered on the altar. Thus, the psalm ends with a brief inventory of appropriate priestly acts of worship.

Notice how odd the sum of it all is:

- Psalm 51:17 specifies only a broken and contrite heart.
- Psalm 50:8–13 asserts that YHWH needs no animal sacrifices.
- Psalm 51:19 authorizes animal sacrifices.

This sequence transfers readily to stewardship. It reflects the recognition that the same offering can mean and function very differently:

- Offerings can be substitutes for serious commitment to God.
- They can be acts of manipulation.
- Or they can be appropriate acts of gratitude when life with God is whole and healthy in terms of trustful submission and obedience.

The distinctions among these different modes of sacrifice are not obvious, but they merit sustained, careful consideration.

Psalm 112:2–9

Psalm 111 is a doxology that gives thanks for YHWH; it recites and reviews YHWH's generous, gracious, merciful ways of acting. That psalm is paired, surely intentionally, with Psalm 112, which is a characterization of a righteous person. No doubt Psalms 111–112 are intended to match the *generous, gracious God* and the *generous, gracious person* who enacts God's character in his own character. This interface of psalms suggests that stewardship is a reflection of God's own way in the life of the human community.

The righteous person is celebrated in Psalm 112, one whom we might think of as a good steward. Whereas the generous God of Psalm 111 is thanked and praised, the generous human agent in Psalm 112 is *happy, lucky, blessed,* the term meaning to be made materially prosperous through obedience to YHWH's Torah commands:

> Praise the LORD!
>> Happy are those who fear the LORD,
>> who greatly delight in his commandments.
>> Ps. 112:1

Then follows a portrait of what prosperous, obedient persons look like.

They are wealthy, and their wealth is matched to acts of community enhancement. They own a lot of land and benefit from family stability:

> Their descendants will be mighty in the land;
>> the generation of the upright will be blessed.
> Wealth and riches are in their houses,
>> and their righteousness endures forever.
>> 112:2–3

The psalm does not think one must take a vow of poverty in order to be a good steward, but one's wealth must be well integrated into the neighborly fabric of the community.

The righteous get up early in order to enhance the community:

> They rise in the darkness as a light for the upright;
>   they are gracious, merciful, and righteous.
>   112:4

What they do is marked by the great covenantal triad, "gracious, merciful, righteous," all rough synonyms that concern sustained involvement in the community.

They manage their affairs justly:

> It is well with those who deal generously and lend,
>   who conduct their affairs with justice.
>   112:5

This means they do not leverage the community for private gain. They do not live as though autonomous, but manage their money as members of the community. Justice means taking into account the reality of the neighbor. No doubt this concern reflects *oblige majesté*, the strong caring for the weak, perhaps with some paternalism, but a paternalism that is marked by generosity. The recognition of making loans does not say so, but we may judge that it consists in loans *without interest*, putting one's resources to use for others in the community. Long ago, before Calvin worked it otherwise, Moses had limited the charge of interest on loans, a limit that is designed to make the community workable:

> You shall not charge interest on loans to another Israelite, interest on money, interest on provisions, interest on anything that is lent. On loans to a foreigner you may charge interest, but on loans to another Israelite you may not charge interest, so that the LORD your God may bless you in all your undertakings in the land that you are about to enter and possess. (Deut. 23:19–20)

A good steward has staying power:

> For the righteous will never be moved;
>   they will be remembered forever.
> They are not afraid of evil tidings;
>   their hearts are firm, secure in the LORD.
> Their hearts are steady, they will not be afraid;
>   in the end they will look in triumph on their foes.
>   Ps. 112:6–8

The righteous do not totter or flutter. They are not upset at bad news. In context, bad news may be about the collapse of the economy. It is clear that what gives constancy to such persons is not wealth but good stewardship. What yields staying power is not good luck but the long-term capacity to turn one's life to the well-being of the community. In times of adversity, then, one has colleagues and neighbors and is not—as a modern individualist might be—left without resources beyond one's own sufficiency.

The portrayal concludes with the most direct matter concerning stewardship:

> They have distributed freely, they have given to the poor;
>> their righteousness endures forever;
>> their horn is exalted in honor.
>
> 112:9

The hallmark of righteousness is generosity, and the object of generosity is the poor. Now of course such generosity might be nothing more than occasional acts of charity. In context, however, it is more likely that the generosity is a sustained, long-term habit with immense policy implications. It is clear in this context—as in Job 31—that righteousness is not a moralistic category. It is rather a responsible way to position oneself in the community for the sake of the community. In doing so, the righteous person replicates the righteous God, for God so *loved* that God *gave*. The recipient of that giving love—the world, the community, the neighbor, the poor neighbor—has life. A good steward acts just like YHWH, for it is said of YHWH in his power,

> The LORD your God is God of gods and Lord of lords, the great God, mighty and awesome, who is not partial and takes no bribe, who executes justice for the orphan and the widow, and who loves the strangers, providing them food and clothing. (Deut. 10:17–18)

Power is deployed in concrete, material ways for the neighbor. As with YHWH, so with YHWH's loyal partners.

Proverbs 15:31; 17:5

Finally, I cite two verses from the book of Proverbs. These sayings are the outcome of slow, steady affirmation about the governance and the connectedness that make a life of well-being possible in the world. These two proverbs are among many that concern the management of the economy. Some proverbs are quite conventional about property and individual privilege. But these two bespeak an alternative kind of wisdom:

> Those who oppress the poor insult their Maker,
>> but those who are kind to the needy honor him.
>
> Prov. 14:31

> Those who mock the poor insult their Maker;
>> those who are glad at calamity will not go unpunished.
>
> 17:5

The focus is upon the poor, who in other texts are to receive the benefit of the offerings given to YHWH. These proverbs articulate a remarkable connection between YHWH and the poor, clearly an anticipation of the later teaching of "God's preferential option for the poor."

We might imagine that *insulting the Creator* could take place through blasphemy, heresy, bad doctrine, bad liturgy, or bad morality. That is what we might expect in the Priestly traditions. But no, not here. Here it is the way in which the poor are treated that honors or mocks YHWH. Thus, stewardship revolves around the awareness that *love of God* and *love of neighbor* (the one in need) are intimately connected to each other. It is clear that this old wisdom teaching is an anticipation of the eloquent connection of the later epistle:

> There is no fear in love, but perfect love casts out fear; for fear has to do with punishment, and whoever fears has not reached perfection in love. We love because he first loved us. Those who say, "I love God," and hate their brothers or sisters, are liars; for those who do not love a brother or sister whom they have seen, cannot love God whom they have not seen. The commandment we have from him is this: those who love God must love their brothers and sisters also. (1 John 4:18–21)

The only qualifying mark in the proverb that does not show up in the teaching of the epistle, one that would have been accepted in the early church, is that here it is not just love God and love neighbor, but love God and love *poor neighbor*. It is clear here, as in many of these texts, that the embodied form of God in the Old Testament—as in the New—is in the human community that pays attention to resource and need, to wealth and poverty, to care and misery. Proverbs focuses upon stewarding goods for the sake of the poor. But our first attention in these proverbs is not to the poor but to God who stands at the center of Proverbs, the one who from the outset has social differentiations and who commands that faith is an act of attending to those differentiations and, where appropriate, redressing them.

III.

Many conclusions derive from this battery of texts. These five occur to me:

1. Our life consists in love of God who is constant, reliable, and generous. The catechism has it "Glorify God and enjoy God forever"; our mode of glorifying and enjoying God is via gratitude.
2. Because this God never comes alone but always with friends—in the Old Testament, widow, orphan, alien, poor; in the New Testament, publicans and sinners—we enact gratitude to God through generosity toward the neighbor.

3. The act of gratitude consists in enhancing the social fabric for the benefit of all, each in a particular circumstance. It is insisted, of course, that our economic practice must be subordinate to and made to serve the human fabric of society. Stewardship is community enhancement that begins in materiality.

4. There is no split between the cultic and the civic, even if the Deuteronomic and Priestly traditions offer different accents. The practice of liturgical holiness is twinned with the practice of communal justice; no liberal or conservative, moreover, is free to rend them asunder, because God has joined them together.

5. Every dimension of this vocation of gratitude is deeply countercultural, counterintuitive, and subversive. Only deep rootage in "the good news of the gospel" makes such practice sustainable and defining in our lives.

So here is the conclusion: It's the economy! I do not say, "It's the economy, stupid," for we Christians are not stupid, but we have been sadly miseducated:

- The orthodox among us—now conservatives—have imagined that our faith is about certitude. Well, it's about the economy.
- The rationalists among us—now liberals—have imagined it's about reasoned social analysis. Well, it's about the economy.
- The pietists among us—now into spirituality—have imagined it's about feelings of intimacy. Well, it's about the economy.

It's about the economy, beloved—not stupid . . . beloved.

It has been about the economy since God called the world "very good," since the word became flesh, since the wind infused the body. Soon and very soon the Messiah is coming, who will make all things new, God's will done on earth as it is in heaven. In the meantime, it's the economy, beloved!

Chapter 7

Full of Truth and Hope

The matter of bold, visible, courageous public faith—and its derivative as a confession—is as unnerving as it is urgent. My comments are in four unequal parts.

I.

This consultation of the Wisconsin Council of Churches[1] has focused on three great confessions from many that might have been chosen: Barmen, Kairos, and Birmingham. All three were risky and decidedly uphill assertions, even if to a belated observer the issues seem clear and unambiguous. Each constituted a summons beyond the status quo:

- Barmen was a summons to "German Christians" (*Deutsche Christi*) who saw no conflict between the gospel and National Socialism and did not want to choose.[2]
- Kairos was addressed to particularly well-meaning liberals in South Africa who agreed that apartheid was evil but who passively colluded in its continuation.

- Birmingham was Martin Luther King's address to pastors who were "fence sitters" and who did not want to face the ominous matters of race.

Many of us think that our general situation is amid a national security state that is propelled by market ideology. This situation reduces all of life to commodity and is an issue of parallel urgency on which matters are equally ambiguous. It occurs to me that much of the anxiety and wise fear (or reluctance) felt by many of us are grounded in two complicating factors.

First, the issues facing us, even if I have not used the right words—national security state, market ideology, commodity—are complex and multifaceted. That is, they concern variously unrestricted militarism in the pursuit of empire, unrestrained market ideology that assaults the human infrastructure, unregulated abuse of the environment in the interest of money-making, and disregard of justice concerning gays, immigrants, race, and any "others." All of this has created a political environment that bespeaks the collapse of a free press and the elimination of an independent judiciary. The issues are so complex that it is not very easy to voice a clear, uncompromising moral imperative. Perhaps it was the same in Germany, but with Kairos and Birmingham, it appears now that matters in these circumstances could be more readily focused in moral urgency. Concerning the many facets of our contemporary crisis, we have not yet been led by the Spirit to great clarity.

Second, the force of civil religion that sustains U.S. exceptionalism permits some measure of "moral cover" for our current policies and social commitments, so that much can be done in the interest of "democracy" and "freedom" that variously excuses military aggression and free market exploitation. This historical reality too easily takes the edge off of our moral suasion; whether in good faith or not, it is relatively easy for defenders of our system to credit it with moral legitimacy. Reinhold Niebuhr's stricture against the claims of "the children of light" continues to be a faithful exposé of our cultural context.

Our opportunity for confession, then, must take into account the enormous complexity of our lethal ideology, and the resources available for a "moral defense" of that ideology, even if a like defense was available in the earlier confessional contexts.

It is my judgment that before we get very far toward a confession, we have an enormous task of preaching, teaching, witness, and interpretation in order to show that the urgency of confession is powerfully intrinsic to our faith and not an "extra" about which there is an option. Thus, our thinking about confession, so it seems to me, does not fit our concern about "being prophetic" in any conventional way. It concerns core matters. But such a claim would be an immense surprise to many of our church people, precisely because we have, for the most part, cast our preaching and teaching and witnessing in other categories.

II.

I thought that from my limited capacity and focus I might best line out *four claims of faith* that may help focus on the preaching, teaching, witnessing, and interpreting that may evoke confession.

First, there is no doubt that the concrete, history-transforming, world-redefining happenings of Friday and Sunday constitute the core of our faith and of our preaching. Paul has familiarly summarized for us, "of first importance what I too had received"—namely, the core proclamation of the church (1 Cor. 15:3), all of this "in accordance with the scriptures." The church, in its mumbling, unthinking fashion, regularly recites the creedal formulation, and even after that it "proclaims the mystery of faith," that "Christ has died, Christ is risen, Christ will come again."

We are entrusted to *preach Christ crucified*. That Friday turn of the world was the exposure of the vulnerability of God to the violence of the empire. Jesus' trial before Pilate—which turned out to be a trial of the empire before Jesus—and his subsequent conviction and execution is the best show of power and authority that the world can muster. In that exhibit of power and authority, the world is exposed as fraudulent in its claim of ultimacy, a papier-mâché practitioner of violence and good intention. That effort by the world to eliminate him did not work. However one lines out the claim that we are "saved by the cross"—without the niceties of a theory of atonement—something decisive happened there in which God's vulnerability was exhibited as ultimate truth. It is for good reason that Jürgen Moltmann terms the cross not only the "foundation" of Christian theology, but also the "criticism" of Christian theology. The cross, in its raw, abrupt, quotidian fleshliness, testifies against our smoother theological truth that gives false assurances and that makes easy alliances in the world. Luther's famous phrase "the crucified God" calls us always back to the raw claim that it is the utter self-giving of God in weakness that is the true exhibit of holiness that eludes the control of the world. That has been entrusted to us.

We are empowered to *preach Christ risen*. From the beginning, the church has struggled and mumbled about this miracle. In any case, what has been entrusted to us is the news that the death systems of the world lack staying power and authority and do not merit our loyalty. They do not merit our loyalty because they disappear after two days, driven from the field by the overflowing power of new life invested in the body of the risen Christ. While the church has mumbled about the particular way of Easter, it has been forthright in God's gift of energy and freedom and joy that comes when our lives depart the death systems and move in a myriad of ways into the uncharted territory of well-being given as the gift of the Spirit.

The church and its preachers are instructed to attest to the saving *vulnerability of Friday*, even while we are citizens of a society that wants no vulnerability at all. The church is invited to witness to the intense *surprise of Easter*, even though we live in a society that by technological anxiety wants to reduce and overcome all surprise, to make it a world in which no gifts are given and no compassion enacted that makes all things new. The church is invited to *the great violent festival of vulnerability* and to *the great exuberance of surprise.*

The dramatic movement from *Friday vulnerability* through *Saturday dread* to *Sunday surprise* is only made by narrative particularity, not by scientific proof, not by universal truth, not by logical discourse. It is done, rather, by narrative acknowledgment that subverts *a world of power* by vulnerability that exposes *a world of dread* through brooding absence that rejects *a world of control* through surprise. All of that is entrusted to the preacher, to be lined out each time we meet, along with a little imagination, a little cleverness, a few gimmicks, but mostly as a stark alternative to a world that has failed in its extravagant claims that lack any life-giving power.

The second claim of faith is the particularity of Friday-Sunday, crucifixion-resurrection, vulnerability-surprise—rooted deeply in Israel's lived experience—which constitutes the shaping memory and abiding reality for Jews and Christians. That shaping experience has been stylized by liturgy and tradition that mediates and makes available the raw bodily reality, the scars of which continue to be carried in the community of faith. It is the truth of our narrative that Jewish life *led to an abyss* that foreshadowed the Friday crucifixion. The crisis is singularly the dislocation of the holy city of Jerusalem, the loss of a temple, monarchy, and political identity, and the deportation of leading citizens at the behest of the empire. Whatever may be the historical detail of destruction and deportation, that abyss is seared into the imagination of God's people, an abyss before which faith is powerless and silent. The raw reality is the crude imposition of force that culminates in the capture of "the last king" in Jerusalem. It is reported that Zedekiah watched his sons, the princes, being executed, and then his eyes were put out (2 Kgs. 25:6). Many others suffered, but Zedekiah's suffering is Jerusalem's epitome of helplessness, vulnerability, and humiliation; he is representative of his people that had lost their way in the process of geopolitics. His blinding and execution signify the roughshod termination of the lead figure in the Davidic line, a humiliation for the God who had made promises. The Old Testament does not flinch from the geopolitical reality of imperial power, the sort of imperial power enacted by Rome on a later Friday. Empires produce abysses, and faith cannot resist or counter that reality.

It is the truth of our narrative, moreover, that life in displacement eventuated in a *restoration*, albeit a modest, even feeble restoration. The leading Jews of Babylon did indeed return to Jerusalem and recover some semblance of Jewish identity and social reality. There apparently was a modest return of Jews to Jerusalem just after 537 BCE, just after Cyrus the Persian had come to imperial authority. After that feeble effort, there was a more visible effort in the years 520–516 BCE, noted by Haggai and Zechariah, at the modest accomplishment of the "Second Temple." These returnees, however, were not very significant, for we learn, with reference to Nehemiah, the continuing sorry state of the city: "They replied, 'The survivors there in the province who escaped captivity are in great trouble and shame; the wall of Jerusalem is broken down, and its gates have been destroyed by fire.'" (Neh. 1:3). Out of that report, with deep and trouble-some sadness and with cunning negotiations with the Persians, Nehemiah leads a more effective effort at restoration in Jerusalem. In the wake of Nehemiah came the Torah-enterprise of Ezra that is commonly regarded as the reconstitu-tion of Judaism.

This experience of being *led into abyss* and *led out in restoration* proved to be the defining marks of Jewishness and surely the large truth of the Old Testament. The reality is a geopolitical one: Israel found itself as exposed and vulnerable to the vagaries of the empire, as did the body of Jesus in the Christian narrative.

The reason I take this much time with historical detail (that will not preach well in most of our congregations) is that there surely is an interpretive connec-tion between the *core tradition of the church* and the *core memory of Israel*:

- Behind Friday vulnerability lies the stamp of the Jewish abyss.
- Behind the Sunday surprise, the church remembers the wonder of res-toration of Jerusalem, even on a small scale.
- Behind the dread silence of Saturday lies the long years of displacement wherein we were coerced into "songs of Zion" in a strange land, in order that we should be mocked for our faith and scorned for its failure (see Ps. 137:1–3).

It belongs to the church to make the trek from Friday vulnerability through Saturday dread absence to Sunday surprise. Before that trek made by the com-munity around Jesus, it belongs to Jews—and continues to belong to Jews—to make the journey into the *abyss of displacement* through the mocking of *humili-ation in historical absence* to the *miracle of restoration*. It belongs to the truth of history and to the truth of faith. At the center of faith, for Christians as for Jews, is the *gap of discontinuity*, where we are led into the dismantling power of the world; this gap of discontinuity arises in a way and in a depth that is beyond our construction or imagination. The truth of lived faith is engagement with that lived experience that is given liturgical articulation. It is, however, a lived expe-rience that defies stylized articulation, about which every pastor knows. Every pastor walks the walk with folk into that journey of vulnerability, dread, and surprise. And every pastor is compelled to talk the talk of vulnerability, dread, and surprise, a task that we rightly call "prophetic."

The third claim of faith is that we do not want to go. Jews did not want to go, in that ancient world. And Christians with whom we minister do not want to go; nor do we ourselves much want to go. We do not want to walk the walk.

There is huge resistance to being led into the abyss. It is called *denial*. I believe that denial is now a major pathology in our society, as it was in that ancient Jew-ish society. It is, rather, a "Don't ask, don't tell" policy in which if one does not know and is not told, one need not have to go.

In that ancient world of Jerusalem, as they walked closer and closer to the abyss that had the fingerprints of empire all over it, the Jews pretended that it was not happening and that they could manage their future without walking that dread journey. I will cite three texts that exhibit the vigorous denial of the coming abyss.

1. In Jeremiah 6:13–15, Jeremiah issues one of his many poems of sad truthfulness. He begins with a standard indictment:

> For from the least to the greatest of them,
>   everyone is greedy for unjust gain;
> and from prophet to priest,
>   everyone deals falsely.
>
> Jer. 6:13

He describes an acquisitive society in which everyone is on the make with the kind of deception that makes neighborliness impossible. That acquisitiveness, moreover, is rooted in a sense that acquisitiveness is possible and legitimate because "everything is coming up roses":

> They have treated the wound of my people carelessly,
>   saying, "Peace, peace,"
> when there is no peace.
>
> 6:14

There was a wound in Jerusalem society. That was the wound of external threat and internal alienation. It was, so Jeremiah concludes, a lethal wound—but his contemporaries had managed by easy words to "heal" the wound, to cover it over, to make it invisible, to remove it from the screen by smooth talk. The word is *shalom*, "All is well and all manner of things will be well." It was the cant of the temple liturgy sustained by political ideology:

> God is our refuge and strength,
>   a very present help in trouble.
>
> Ps. 46:1

Jeremiah follows his assault on deceptive words with the most acute indictment: "They do not know how to blush." They have no more shame. They are incapable of being embarrassed at their true situation. Abraham Heschel remarks that the loss of embarrassment is the quintessential loss of human capability. And so Jeremiah issues a massive "therefore," a consequence of such denial:

> *Therefore* they shall fall among those who fall;
>   at the time that I punish them, they shall be overthrown,
> says the LORD.
>
> Jer. 6:15b (au. emph.)

And just in case the oracle was not noticed, the tradition of Jeremiah permits the prophet to say it yet again in chapter 8:

> Therefore I will give their wives to others
>   and their fields to conquerors,

because from the least to the greatest
    everyone is greedy for unjust gain;
from prophet to priest
    everyone deals falsely.
They have treated the wound of my people carelessly,
    saying, "Peace, peace," when there is no peace.
They acted shamefully, they committed abomination;
    yet they were not at all ashamed,
    they did not know how to blush.
Therefore they shall fall among those who fall;
    at the time when I punish them, they shall be overthrown,
says the LORD.

Jer. 8:10–12

Here the poem reverses matters and begins with anticipation that wives and fields will be taken over by conquerors (Babylon). The juxtaposition of wives and fields surely echoes the Tenth Commandment: "Neither shall you covet your neighbor's wife. Neither shall you desire your neighbor's house, or field" (Deut. 5:21). The empire covets and will have its way, so says the prophet, because of Jerusalem's denial.

2. The second exemplar of denial is the narrative transaction between Hananiah and Jeremiah in chapter 28. The latter prophet's name means "YHWH is gracious," and Hananiah expected YHWH to be gracious enough to save the city in its current crisis. Indeed, Hananiah had meditated on the rescue of Jerusalem a century earlier from the hand of the Assyrians at the time of Hezekiah and Isaiah, and he reckoned that the same rescue would happen again. Jeremiah has just announced the coming onslaught of Babylon against Jerusalem, and Hananiah refutes his words:

> Thus says the LORD of hosts, the God of Israel: I have broken the yoke of the king of Babylon. Within two years I will bring back to this place all the vessels of the LORD's house, which King Nebuchadnezzar of Babylon took away from this place and carried to Babylon. I will also bring back to this place King Jeconiah son of Jehoiakim of Judah, and all the exiles from Judah who went to Babylon, says the LORD, for I will break the yoke of the king of Babylon. (Jer. 28:2–4)

Hananiah anticipates, according to YHWH's promises, that the little deportation of 597 BCE will be ended; everyone will come home, including the boy king Jehoiachin. The yoke of the empire will be broken, and there will be return to normalcy—within two years. The two prophets argue the point, and Jeremiah is put on trial for his life. In the end, the narrative dismisses Hananiah tersely as a false prophet whom YHWH has not sent: "In that same year, in the seventh month, the prophet Hananiah died" (28:17).

Though Hananiah died, his message is an important one, because denial of the coming abyss is a major establishment enterprise. We may imagine that Hananiah, unlike Jeremiah, enjoyed good access to the establishment and that his patter of cheap grace was welcomed as free grace: God is good all the time, and all will be well. Just pretend.

3. A third pertinent text is Ezekiel 13, in which the prophets (who oppose Ezekiel) are accused of falsehood: "Because, in truth, because they have misled my people, saying, 'Peace,' when there is no peace; and because, when the people build a wall, these prophets smear whitewash on it" (Ezek. 13:10). The political leaders may have been at fault, but the religious leaders are the ones who put a good face on their fault and enacted a cover-up. The outcome, of course, is that members of the community do not need to face reality. It is as though it were not happening! And therefore one need only pretend.[3]

Just pretend:

- that the economy has bottomed out;
- that the war has turned and we are making great progress;
- that the addiction can be controlled with discipline;
- that the index of teenage suicides is societally insignificant;
- that date rape is just boys who will be boys;
- that generous gun laws will make us safer;
- that if people work harder they will prosper like us.

There is also a huge resistance about life eventuating in restoration; it is called *despair*. It is the mood of those who have looked clearly into the abyss, who have gone reluctantly but necessarily into it, and who have come to regard the abyss as bottomless and perpetual, a world without end. Despair is the conclusion that we reach in the pit of our stomachs that we are trapped here forever and we had best make the most of it. In the end, there will be no well-being, so get what you can now. Eat and drink and own all that you can, because there are no new gifts to be given. There are no dreams, no visions, no possibilities, only this—the worst kind of eschatology, sadly "realized." Here are five texts on despair in ancient Israel in the midst of the abyss.

1. The book of Lamentations, sad poems of grief, concludes with a stunning realization:

> Why have you forgotten us completely?
>   Why have you forsaken us these many days?
>   Lam. 5:20

The verse assumes that God has forgotten and God has forsaken. The poem does not debate that claim, but accepts and asks "Why?" To be sure, the verse is followed in the penultimate verse of the book by a petition, indicating that hope is not completely voided. But the final verse leaves us with a notion of rejection and divine anger:

> . . . unless you have utterly rejected us,
>   and are angry with us beyond measure.
>   5:22

The poem cannot make a move toward restoration because the abyss is all-defining. The use of the word "forsaken," of course, anticipates the Friday lament of

Jesus in which he replicates the pain of Jerusalem in his own body (Matt. 27:46; Mark 15:34). In the abyss there is only rejection!

2. In Isaiah 40:27, the lyrical poet of hope begins by quoting Israel's utterance of despair, perhaps a liturgical formulation of despair:

> Why do you say, O Jacob,
>   and speak, O Israel,
> "My way is hidden from the LORD,
>   and my right is disregarded by my God"?

In its abyss, Israel could only conclude that YHWH did not know and did not care.

3. Isaiah 49:14, in what appears to be a quote from the liturgical formulation of Lamentations 5:20 that I have already cited, again uses the double terminology of forsake:

> But Zion said, "The LORD has forsaken me,
>   my Lord has forgotten me."

That is what Zion said. That is what they said in shabby, shattered Jerusalem. That is what they said in Babylon where they had been taken against their will. The big defining terms again are "forsake" and "forget."

4. In Isaiah 50:2, YHWH asks in indignation:

> Is my hand shortened, that it cannot redeem?
>   Or have I no power to deliver?
> By my rebuke I dry up the sea,
>   I make the rivers a desert;
> their fish stink for lack of water,
>   and die of thirst.

YHWH is indignant because when YHWH comes to rescue, God finds no takers. When God called, there were no respondents. And why did Israel not respond? Because they had drawn the conclusion that YHWH's hand was short. They remembered when YHWH had delivered them from Egypt with "a strong hand and an outstretched arm." But now, by contrast, there was no evidence of a strong divine hand, no show of a divine outstretched arm. All the evidence suggested that YHWH's arm, a vehicle of divine power, had shriveled to uselessness. It is as though YHWH had become disabled. All around, the Israelites could see the geopolitical outcomes of an empire no longer kept in check by divine restraint. They had drawn the only conclusion that the evidence permitted. There was no reason to answer YHWH, no motivation to receive or welcome the coming of YHWH, no ground for any hope at all. They were, they judged, alone in the world, without an advocate or a strong intervener.

5. We can see, from Isaiah 59:1, that this way of voicing despair must have been prevalent in displaced Israel. An affirmative voice answers the doubt of 50:2:

> See, the LORD's hand is not too short to save,
>   nor his ear too dull to hear.

The Israelites concluded that YHWH did not save because YHWH could not save. The world is beyond YHWH's recovery, and the news is not good.

Jeremiah had dealt with denial among those who could not see the disaster coming. The tradition of Isaiah, somewhat later, deals with despair among those who are caught in the abyss. The denial is among those who refuse to see and so imagine that Israel will not be destroyed—that the Messiah will not die. The despair is among those who know but cannot imagine a future, cannot discern a way out of no way; they could not believe that the Messiah will be raised from the dead to new life. Denial resists abyss—and so crucifixion. Denial fends off vulnerability. Despair resists homecoming—and so resurrection. Despair fends off surprise. Faith is to walk that walk, but denial and despair refuse the walk.

The fourth claim of faith is that our ministry is among those who refuse the walk. The wonder of faith is that the talk sometimes authorizes, empowers, and emboldens the walk. Ministry is *talk the talk* that the community may *walk the walk* of faith into the abyss and *walk the walk* of faith out of the abyss into restoration. Urgent ministry now is to talk in ways that *move past denial* into the walk of vulnerability and that *move past despair* into the walk of surprise, there to find the gift of God and the possibility of genuine humanness. Because the deniers and the despairers do not want to go, evangelical talk is characteristically upstream against great resistance. I shall insist in what follows that in the reality of abyss and restoration, in the practice of vulnerability and surprise, in the face of denial and despair, the task has a twofold accent about the shape of reality in a world where the living God is on exhibit.

The walk into the abyss is fended off by denial. The evangelical antidote to denial is *truth-telling*. It is the task of truth-telling that belongs to prophetic ministry, an act that is sure to provoke resistance and hostility among those in denial, because it requires seeing and knowing and engaging with that which we have refused to see, know, or engage. The truth that is to be told is that the world is out of sync, that we live against the grain of God's holiness, and that such living has immense negative consequences because the sync and the grain are God-given and cannot be outflanked. Such talk of "out of sync" and "against the grain," put theologically, is the truth that the world is under divine judgment. That is the primal burden of truth-telling among these ancient prophets in the face of the abyss enacted—at the behest of YHWH—by Babylon. The rhetorical tradition of the prophets suggests that there are two modes of such truth-telling as divine judgment; a "hot mode" that imagines the intrusive agency of YHWH as punisher, and a "cool mode" that makes connections between cause and effect and so traces the consequences of actions, consequences that belong intrinsically with the choices and the policies.

The truth-telling is an insistence that we live, by the goodness of the creator God, in a morally coherent creation. For that reason, matters are connected in terms of present choices and future outcomes. It is to be noticed that prophetic

truth-telling—whether hot or cold—is characteristically poetic. It is not excessively confrontive, unless, of course, there is objection to subversive poetry that
is not especially issue-oriented. Such poetry aims, characteristically, below social
specificities to the brooding anguish and dismay of the God who will not be
mocked. It is always the propensity of the powerful to imagine that with enough
technology or shrewdness, the holy intransigence of creation can be outflanked.
The poets arise to bear witness to the deep conviction that God is not mocked
and that the moral coherence of the creation will hold.

I have selected a series of occasions of truth-telling in the prophetic tradition.
As I pondered them, it struck me that these ancient utterances require almost
no interpretive imagination, so contemporary are they. And therefore as belated
prophetic voices, we ourselves can appeal to the ones who uttered before us and
trade on their imagination and courage.

Isaiah 5:20. This verse is among a series of "woes." "Woe" means big trouble
coming that cannot now be averted. (In the NRSV, the "woe" is translated as "ah.")

> *Ah*, you who call evil good
>   and good evil,
> who put darkness for light
>   and light for darkness,
> who put bitter for sweet
>   and sweet for bitter!
>   (au. emph.)

The verse asserts that big trouble that cannot be averted will come to those who
engage in euphemism, who call things by their wrong names and so disguise the
truth of social reality. Prophetic ministry consists in calling things by their right
names and so summoning folk to face the social reality of being out of sync.
Consider, for example, "friendly fire," "collateral damage," "welfare reform,"
"outsourcing," "downsizing," to name a few; and perhaps the most shameless
usage, to term a lethal missile "peacekeeper." Ancient Jerusalem, in its liturgies
of complacency, disguised reality, as do we. The church is the place for naming
things faithfully, because euphemism is a tool for denial.

Amos 6:4–7. Amos offers another "woe," though the term is not in the Hebrew
and must be borrowed from verse 1. Amos describes the indulgent entitlement
of his contemporaries in Samaria with their exotic ivories; their at-ease lounging;
their killing of young animals for veal, which only the affluent can do; their idle
entertainment; and their self-indulgent society out of control:

> *Alas* for those who lie on beds of ivory,
>   and lounge on their couches,
> and eat lambs from the flock,
>   and calves from the stall;
> who sing idle songs to the sound of the harp,
>   and like David improvise on instruments of music;
> who drink wine from bowls,
>   and anoint themselves with the finest oils . . .
>   Amos 6:4–6a (au. emph.)

The poem moves inescapably to the "but" of verse 6b:

> . . . *but* are not grieved over the ruin of Joseph!
> 6:6b (au. emph.)

Not grieved! Not upset! Not in touch with reality! This is consumerism gone amok—without notice. And there comes the big prophetic "therefore" of verse 7:

> *Therefore* they shall now be the first to go into exile,
>   and the revelry of the loungers shall pass away.
> 6:7 (au. emph.)

They had not noticed at all and were not worried; they surely could not have extrapolated the deportation into exile, for "exile" was nowhere on the screen of the folks at the club, as it was not on the screen with the Shah or with the Tsar or with any who are narcotized in power. When they heard the poem of Amos, they must have wondered: Perhaps "exile" does not follow from self-indulgent entitlement; that is a connection only in the rash thrust of the poem and, besides, it is only a poem.

I know that such poetry, if made contemporary, cannot be uttered in most of our venues of ministry. But here it is, a text inviting other texts, a poem inviting other poems, an act of imagination authorizing other acts of imagination that seek to do truth-telling.

Hosea 4:1–3. YHWH has an "indictment" against Israel. The poem announces YHWH to be a litigator who is suing God's people. The bill of particulars is the Decalogue that has been violated:

> There is no faithfulness or loyalty,
>   and no knowledge of God in the land.
> Swearing, lying, and murder,
>   and stealing and adultery break out;
>   bloodshed follows bloodshed.
> Hos. 4:1b–2

This is a clever poetic utilization of the Ten Commandments, for who would have thought to turn the Sinai charter into subversive poetry? There is an edginess to the rhetoric when command becomes poetry.

And then comes the big "therefore" of verse 3:

> *Therefore* the land mourns,
>   and all who live in it languish;
> together with the wild animals
>   and the birds of the air,
>   even the fish of the sea are perishing.
> 4:3 (au. emph.)

"Land mourns" means there is a drought. Violation of commandment, in poetic construal, causes drought. Violation of Sinai impinges upon the ordered fruitfulness of creation. Talk about environmental crisis! Such talk makes no sense unless it is *creation* behind which sits *the Creator*, who is not to be mocked. Hosea can use the triad "beasts, birds, fish" because he has studied Genesis 1. He takes old liturgy and makes poetry. Prophetic talk is not explanation and rational argument. It is, rather, poetic declaration that is outrageous in its performance. And when once performed in utterance, the poetry lingers with its own force and cannot be recalled. Technical achievements in our contemporary world require us to imagine our autonomy, but Hosea, long before Al Gore, knew that such autonomy is a joke. The divine commands are ways in which we answer for creation to the Creator. (See also Mic. 2:1–4; Jer. 5:23–29; 9:17–19; 18:14–17.)

The walk out of the abyss into newness is fended off by despair. The prophetic antidote to despair is *hope-telling*. It is the task of *hope-telling* that belongs to prophetic ministry, an act that is sure to evoke doubt and resistance among those in despair, because hope-telling requires risk and venture that we characteristically do not want to undertake. When an alternative is possible, it requires us to leave present circumstance, even if that present circumstance is debilitating, and to move out to new gifts that we thought would not be given. The hope to be told is that the abyss will not defeat God or deter God from bringing creation to full *shalom*. The news of prophetic utterance is that the world is under promise. That is the primal burden of hope-telling among these ancient prophets who spoke right in the midst of the abyss. That hope takes a modest political form about the recovery of Jewish society in Jerusalem. But it also takes a larger, lyrical form in grand doxological exuberance that does not doubt that the world is on its way to well-being. That doxological exuberance invites us to be the vanguard of newness that will arise among the bold, exactly in the abyss. One of the great wonders is that the exile is precisely the venue for hope, a venue out of which comes the promises of God upon which we continue to count.

I have selected a series of occasions of hope-telling in the prophets. As I pondered these promissory texts, it struck me that they are now very difficult to enunciate in a world that knows too much and that is largely emptied of the mystery of God. But then it struck me as well that they must have been very difficult to enunciate in ancient times, for they are in defiance of facts on the ground. But then, in this tradition of faith, the future will be given by God to those who act in defiance of the apparent facts on the ground.

I imagine that all of these texts (and many others) are summarized by God who has on God's lips, "I have a dream." It is a dream that rushes beyond present circumstance in which God, like Martin Luther King, has no strategy for getting from here to there. But the dream and the utterance of the dream keep the abyss from being absolutized. The news is that there is more and there is other. It is on offer to those who refuse to abide in despair, the despair of defeat or the despair of entitled affluence. It is on offer to those who move out according to the God who has one more trek to make across the wilderness.

Amos 5:14–15. Amos is not much of a hoper, fixed as he is on the coming abyss in Samaria. Nonetheless, in these verses there is a series of imperatives that culminate in this way:

> Seek good and not evil,
>> that you may live;
> and so the LORD, the God of hosts, will be with you,
>> just as you have said.
> Hate evil and love good,
>> and establish justice in the gate;
> it may be that the LORD, the God of hosts,
>> will be gracious to the remnant of Joseph.

Such imperatives are acts of hope. They assert that things may still be turned but that such a renewing turn will require radically altered conduct. The new conduct is "good" (not evil), hate of evil and love of good, good finally equated with social justice, that is, economic reform. It is an act of hope to perform in this way, because "it may be"—the prophetic "perhaps"—that YHWH will be gracious. Hope is active, transformative conduct.

Hosea 2:18–23. The crisis is deeper in Hosea. In Hosea 2:2–13, the prophet has announced divorce and termination of the covenantal relationship. At the end of verse 13 comes the abyss. The remarkable fact is that the poem does not end in verse 13. There is a very long pause after verse 13, long enough to inhale the reality of abyss, of being abandoned by God. But then God says more. In verses 14–23, YHWH speaks Israel out of abyss and into renewed covenant. It is a covenant that renews creation and that rescues the environment from a meltdown:

> I will make for you a covenant on that day with the wild animals, the birds of the air, and the creeping things of the ground; and I will abolish the bow, the sword, and war from the land; and I will make you lie down in safety. (Hos. 2:18)

It is a covenant that reaches to God's forsaken people. The people divorced will be re-embraced, reloved, and remarried:

> And I will take you for my wife forever; I will take you for my wife in righteousness and in justice, in steadfast love, and in mercy. I will take you for my wife in faithfulness; and you shall know the LORD. (2:19–20)

All the great words of Israel's covenantal faith are mobilized to bespeak YHWH's renewal of faithfulness. Beyond abyss lies passionate, divine fidelity. Along with the *restitution of covenant,* comes full, glad *restoration of fruitful creation,* the very creation that had been plunged into the abyss:

> On that day I will answer, says the LORD,
>> I will answer the heavens

and they shall answer the earth;
and the earth shall answer the grain, the wine, and the oil,
and they shall answer Jezreel;
and I will sow him for myself in the land.
And I will have pity on Loruhamah,
and I will say to Loammi, "You are my people";
and he shall say, "You are my God."

2:21–23

The earth will answer in fruitfulness. Israel will luxuriate in its new status: "You are my people." It is never so in the abyss. The poet, however, refuses despair and asks his listeners to move beyond abyss into glad expectation.

Micah 4:1–5. There will be days to come! The abyss is not the last day. The description of exile (and Friday) does not disrupt YHWH's rule. The poet imagines, as does every prophet, a world out beyond despair. In this case, it is the scenario of all nations and peoples on the road together:

In the days to come
the mountain of the LORD's house
shall be established as the highest of the mountains,
and shall be raised up above the hills.
Peoples shall stream to it,
and many nations shall come and say:
"Come, let us go up to the mountain of the LORD,
to the house of the God of Jacob."

Mic. 4:1–2a

The nations will refuse to sink in mutual deterrence and destruction. They will gather together peaceably to make a trip into YHWH's future. The reason they will go to the house of the God of Jacob—going joyously and peaceably—is in order to learn what they do not yet know:

. . . that he may teach us his ways
and that we may walk in his paths.
For out of Zion shall go forth instruction,
and the word of the LORD from Jerusalem.
He shall judge between many peoples,
and shall arbitrate between strong nations far away.

4:2–3a

From Zion comes "instruction," that is, Torah. From the temple come commandments for all, commandments of discernment and disarmament and peace. There are days coming when wars will end. The weapons will be overcome; they will be transposed by Torah. Nations will eventually decide that obedience beats oppression:

They shall beat their swords into plowshares,
and their spears into pruning hooks;

nation shall not lift up sword against nation,
   neither shall they learn war any more;
but they shall all sit under their own vines
   and under their own fig trees,
and no one shall make them afraid;
   for the mouth of the LORD of hosts has spoken.
                        4:3b–4

It is only a poem, a vision, a hunch, a hope. But that is all you get in the abyss. Such a hunch on the lips of a bold poet, however, is enough. It asserts, without explanation or apology, that it will be otherwise. Listeners are to be ready for otherwise, because God's world will not remain in the abyss, not more than three days' worth. (See also Jer. 31:34; 33:10–11; Isa. 65:17–25.)

Isaiah 43:1–5. The ultimate defeat of despair is delivered by this remarkable poem that contains the quintessential overthrow of despair. It begins and ends the same way:

But now thus says the LORD,
he who created you, O Jacob,
   he who formed you, O Israel:
Do not fear, for I have redeemed you;
   I have called you by name, you are mine.
                 Isa. 43:1 (au. emph.)

Do not fear, for I am with you;
   I will bring your offspring from the east,
   and from the west I will gather you.
                 43:5 (au. emph.)

The beginning and the end are the same: Do not fear! It is an assurance in the form of a command. It is an imperative requiring moving out of the abyss, out of a world defined by imperial cynicism, out of a world of abuse that discounts the displaced.

The ground for such assurance-as-imperative is twofold. First, "I am with you." You thought I had abandoned you; you thought that because you accepted imperial definitions of reality that are not true (see Isa. 54:7–8). Second, "You are mine." You had forgotten that, because you accepted the definitions of the empire that identified you as subjects of the empire. Thus, the assurance is a vigorous contestation of the reality accepted too easily in the abyss. I am with you—not absent, not negligent, not indifferent. You are mine—not theirs! This *assurance-as-imperative* is the rock-bottom assurance of hope, that the world— and our particular context—is inhabited by the Holy One who will prevail in the same way that the same Holy One has prevailed over the powers of death when he descended into Saturday hell.

Do not fear:

- It is the word of the angels to the shepherds in Bethlehem (Luke 2:10).

- It is the word to the visitors of the tomb on Easter morning, because "Do not fear" is the substance of Easter power (Matt. 28:5, 10).
- It is the word every parent speaks to every child in the midst of a nightmare: "Do not fear. I am right here." That utterance ends the child's nightmare, and in the abyss of Israel that divine utterance ended the long nightmare of displacement and transformed exile into home.
- It was the primal utterance of John Paul II when he first came back to Poland as pope, a word uttered to Solidarity leaders who had much to fear.

The word from empire in all of its manifestations—and its various colors of red/orange/yellow alert—is "Be very afraid."

- Be very afraid of not conforming to social authority and social expectation.
- Be very afraid of peer pressure.
- Be very afraid for your life, your food, your home, your future.

And then, "Do not fear." The world waits for hope-filled truth. But the word must not be spoken too soon, or the word of hope will only reinforce denial. It is a word among those who despair, not among those who deny.

III.

The claims of faith that I have lined out here are central for us and familiar to us and are shared, mutatis mutandis, by Jews and Christians:

crucifixion—resurrection

exile—homecoming

denial—despair

truth-telling—hope-telling

This cluster of terms, in broad stretch, indicates both the crisis in which we find ourselves and the work to which we are called.

The twin pathologies of denial and despair, I submit, indicate the context of our work. Despair arises when we discover how it is with us. But behind despair lies denial, which in some large part is produced by the forces of empire that find narcotized people easier to manage and manipulate.

The outcome of denial and despair is *passivity and acquiescence*, whether it is the passivity of our illusion of moral superiority and assured triumph, or the acquiescence of fatalism that cowers before an inescapable despair. Either way, the consequence of such acquiescence is *abdication*, a refusal to engage issues, an inability to think or act outside the box of dominant power arrangements and consensus plausibility systems. The empire does not require agreement or need approval. It requires only passive conformity among those who believe that there is no alternative.

Since the beginning, it has been the work of preaching, teaching, witnessing, and interpreting in the biblical tradition to create time, space, energy, will, and imagination for a break with the narcotic of acquiescence and the exercise of an alternative—all the way from Moses' initial "Let my people go" to Billy Graham's most recent altar call. The work has been to evidence that life is choosable beyond the closed system of empire—whether Egypt, or Babylon, or Rome, or "Satan, sin, and death," or the American system of totalism.

I submit that it is now the work of the church in the United States, in a society narcotized by denial and despair, to tell *truth and hope* in a way that makes new, evangelical decisions possible. Such a responsibility on the part of the church is risky, because no one easily foregoes the safety of denial, and no one readily relinquishes despair for the demanding possibility of hope.

The act of creating space for alternative decisions, of course, includes advocacy for a particular alternative decision. But behind particular advocacy is the more elemental insistence that *there are indeed choices, options, and alternatives.* It is the totalizing intent of the dominant system (empire) to assert that there are no alternatives but that the choices have already been made and matters foreclosed. Every person in despair has concluded that. And every person in denial takes that option—whether about addiction, a bad marriage, an unworkable job, or whatever. It was not different in ancient Israel as it found the Egyptian-Canaanite religion-economic-political system completely defining and containing all thinkable possibilities. The tradition of Moses, however, would not quit. So I cite five texts that invite decision.

1. The preaching tradition of Deuteronomy insists that enactment of Torah can create a social system that is alternative to the Canaanite social system that we used to call "fertility religion." After all of the particularities of Moses' instruction, the appeal for covenant concludes in Deuteronomy 30:15–20:

> See, I have set before you today life and prosperity, death and adversity. If you obey the commandments of the LORD your God that I am commanding you today, by loving the LORD your God, walking in his ways, and observing his commandments, decrees, and ordinances, then you shall live and become numerous, and the LORD your God will bless you in the land that you are entering to possess. But if your heart turns away and you do not hear, but are led astray to bow down to other gods and serve them, I declare to you today that you shall perish; you shall not live long in the land that you are crossing the Jordan to enter and possess. I call heaven and earth to witness against you today that I have set before you life and death, blessings and curses. Choose life so that you and your descendants may live, loving the LORD your God, obeying him, and holding fast to him; for that means life to you and length of days, so that you may live in the land that the LORD swore to give to your ancestors, to Abraham, to Isaac, and to Jacob.

This is a life-or-death decision. It is a choice that will determine the future for generations to come.

2. The matter is reiterated in the extraordinary encounter of Joshua 24, the covenant renewal at Shechem. Joshua urges a new decision:

> Now therefore revere the LORD, and serve him in sincerity and in faithfulness; put away the gods that your ancestors served beyond the River and in Egypt, and serve the LORD. Now if you are unwilling to serve the LORD, choose this day whom you will serve, whether the gods your ancestors served in the region beyond the River or the gods of the Amorites in whose land you are living. (Josh. 24:14–15a)

He himself models the decision:

> But as for me and my household, we will serve the LORD. (24:15b)

The exchange that follows indicates how freighted the decision for covenant is, for his listeners are ready to embrace YHWH, but Joshua does not make it easy for them:

> Then the people answered, "Far be it from us that we should forsake the LORD to serve other gods; for it is the LORD our God who brought us and our ancestors up from the land of Egypt, out of the house of slavery, and who did those great signs in our sight. He protected us along all the way that we went, and among all the peoples through whom we passed; and the LORD drove out before us all the peoples, the Amorites who lived in the land. Therefore we also will serve the LORD, for he is our God."
> But Joshua said to the people, "You cannot serve the LORD, for he is a holy God. He is a jealous God; he will not forgive your transgressions or your sins. If you forsake the LORD and serve foreign gods, then he will turn and do you harm, and consume you, after having done you good." And the people said to Joshua, "No, we will serve the LORD!" Then Joshua said to the people, "You are witnesses against yourselves that you have chosen the LORD, to serve him." And they said, "We are witnesses." He said, "Then put away the foreign gods that are among you, and incline your hearts to the LORD, the God of Israel." The people said to Joshua, "The LORD our God we will serve, and him we will obey." (24:16–24)

The narrator concludes with the laconic observation that they made a new, *chosen* decision:

> So Joshua made a covenant with the people that day, and made statutes and ordinances for them at Shechem. (24:25)

3. In the polemical narrative at Mount Carmel (1 Kgs. 18), Elijah takes issue with the Canaanite socioeconomic-religious system and summons Israel to a decision:

Elijah then came near to all the people, and said, "How long will you go limping with two different opinions? If the LORD is God, follow him; but if Baal, then follow him." (1 Kgs. 18:21a)

The summons is echoed in every confessional statement, perhaps most dramatically among the "German Christians" who did not want to choose:

The people did not answer him a word. (18:21b)

Of course, that dramatic contest did evoke a decision from Israel:

When all the people saw it, they fell on their faces and said, "The LORD indeed is God; the LORD indeed is God." (18:39)

4. In the later, deeper crisis of Jerusalem in the seventh century, the prophetic tradition of Jeremiah articulates the choices before his contemporaries in Judah:

Thus says the LORD: Do not let the wise boast in their wisdom, do not let the mighty boast in their might, do not let the wealthy boast in their wealth; but let those who boast boast in this, that they understand and know me, that I am the LORD; I act with steadfast love, justice, and righteousness in the earth, for in these things I delight, says the LORD. (Jer. 9:23–24)

This most succinct and remarkable text lays out the options for the city clearly:

Either: wisdom, wealth, and might—the hallmarks of Solomon

Or: steadfast love, justice, and righteousness—the identifying marks for Moses

But Jeremiah's society was completely inured, as is ours, to Solomonic pursuits. In his courageous imagination, Jeremiah asserts that deciding otherwise is possible. Not surprisingly, he advocates the big triad in which YHWH delights. But along with such advocacy, he asserts that choosing, choosing alternatively, choosing outside the box, choosing beyond the consensus, choosing against the establishment, is possible. The ground for such choosing is the reality of YHWH, whom Solomon had long sought to eliminate from the equation of the Jerusalem establishment. Patrick Miller says of such a prophetic summons:

The problem of talking about confession and repentance, therefore, is in direct proportion to the conviction that human life is really grounded in God. Without that operative assumption, all talk of sin and repentance is perceived as anachronistic, a "preacherish" way of talking about our problems. Preaching that evokes repentance is prepared for by preaching that confronts the congregation in inescapable ways with the reality of God and the reality of God as the most important thing to say about the human, about ourselves.[4]

5. The most important text for our topic, I judge, is the remarkable assertion of Jeremiah in the midst of a visit to the potter's house. After he asserts that the potter can "rework" spoiled clay, YHWH seems to depart spectacularly from the metaphor of clay to make this assertion:

> At one moment I may declare concerning a nation or a kingdom, that I will pluck up and break down and destroy it, but if that nation, concerning which I have spoken, turns from its evil, I will change my mind about the disaster that I intended to bring on it. And at another moment I may declare concerning a nation or a kingdom that I will build and plant it, but if it does evil in my sight, not listening to my voice, then I will change my mind about the good that I had intended to do to it. (Jer. 18:7–10)

The assertion is that Israel's fresh decision can cause YHWH to revamp Jerusalem's future. The initiative and possibility are in Israel's hands. Israel, not YHWH, can choose Israel's future. The odd thing is that in context, the implication is that the clay can take the initiative and cause the potter to do differently. Human history, Israelite history with YHWH, is in Israel's hands. Mutatis mutandis, the church in U.S. society can assert that our national community can have a different future, even given the intractable moral passion of YHWH. It is on the basis of that premise that Jeremiah is sent by YHWH to make a bid for Jerusalem's new decision:

> Now, therefore, say to the people of Judah and the inhabitants of Jerusalem: Thus says the LORD: Look, I am a potter shaping evil against you and devising a plan against you. Turn now, all of you from your evil way, and amend your ways and your doings. (18:11)

It takes no imagination to think that the church in this place is dispatched by God to invite our society to "make amends."

If we are honest, we may read verse 12, the verse after the lectionary committee ended the reading, to notice that Jerusalem refused:

> But they say, "It is no use! We will follow our own plans, and each of us will act according to the stubbornness of our evil will." (18:12)

But that verse, in our contemporary reading, need not follow. Otherwise is possible, and the creator of heaven and earth, the responsive potter, is prepared to follow new human decisions.

The news entrusted to the church is that new decisions are possible, the kind asserted by Jesus—good news! "Now after John was arrested, Jesus came to Galilee, proclaiming the good news of God, and saying, 'The time is fulfilled, and the kingdom of God has come near; repent, and believe in the good news.'" (Mark 1:14–15). Not to be able to choose new is very *bad news*. It is the bad news embraced by those in despair. It is the bad news practiced by those in denial. But it need not be so, depending on voices to the contrary.

IV.

I want now to report on seven convictions at which I have arrived that I think are germane to the matrix of confession.

1. The possibility of a confession depends upon a *disengagement* from the coercive practices of the national security state. This is exceedingly difficult for any of us and all of us, for the entitled life we live without "inconvenience" is a rich and reassuring one. I imagine this is not a call for heroic action, but it is a call for a deliberate, sustained mindset that receives concrete enactment. I am mindful of the case of Poland under the Solidarity movement of Lech Walesa and Adam Michnik. They did not fight the communist regime but intentionally ignored it and operated as though it did not exist. They were propelled in this by their moral ground and their deep moral passion that was rooted in old Catholic faith.

When I think about disengagement from common practice, I think first of all about the demands of production and consumption that are defining for the lives of many of us, and the reality of Sabbath as a deep act of resistance and alternative, the refusal to have our lives defined by the lens of the market.

2. The practice of *calling things by their right name* and practicing the exposé of toxic euphemisms is the peculiar work of the church. This does not need to be excessively confrontational, but it is certain that the national security state with its commoditization of everything and everyone depends upon false identifications. For the most part, we are inured in such practice so that we do not notice, an enterprise that can be extended to public life.

3. The church is—or can be—a hospitable place for *hosting the profound ambiguity* many people feel about these matters. On all of the great questions before our society—war, immigration, abortion, sexuality—it is clear that most people are enormously ambivalent. Our society, in its dominant mode, allows no such ambivalence to be voiced; but clearly that widespread ambiguity needs to be honored and processed.

It is only this that gives me pause about confession, for any serious confession may preclude the practice of ambiguity. But I should argue that the church, in our society, must be a safe venue for ambiguity, an arena in which people will not be scolded, judged, coerced, or manipulated, because it belongs to us to be undecided. Indeed, Mark Slouka has argued that such openness on hard decisions is the hallmark of democracy. Where such openness is precluded, he asserts, we are on the way to fascism.

4. More than that, *a safe venue of honest ambiguity is the seedbed for newness*; it is the place where God's spirit can do the work of newness. I would not, of course, suggest that there is any circumstance in which God's spirit cannot work newness. But it is surely evident that newness, as the gift of the Spirit, does not come easily in arenas of completely settled certitude. Thus, I suggest that the church, as a venue for honest ambiguity, is an environment in which newness may be given. It does happen by the work of the Spirit that we are led to places

where we have not thought to go. Thus, the book of Acts is powerful testimony that apostolic preaching and witness created an environment, led by the Spirit, where folk re-decided about Caesar and Christ. The empire is dead set against ambiguity and suspicious of our hints of uncertainty. It is for that reason that the church, led by the Spirit, always creates dis-ease for the empire.

5. The church that would be in a state of confession will need to be a church *responsive to the Spirit* who breaks down walls, opens prisons, and makes all things new. To the extent that we are in thrall to the national security state, we will not and cannot be led by the Spirit. Perhaps it is worth observing that the national security state has "no spirit":

> The Egyptians are human, and not God;
>   their horses are flesh, and *not spirit*.
> When the LORD stretches out his hand,
>   the helper will stumble, and the one who helped will fall,
>   and they will all perish together.
>   Isa. 31:3 (au. emph.)

> Do not put your trust in princes,
>   in mortals, in whom there is *no help*.
> When their breath departs, they return to the earth;
>   on that very day their plans perish.
>   Ps. 146:3–4 (au. emph.)

That is, the empire cannot generate life, cannot provide security, cannot evoke well-being or joy. The empire cannot keep its promises that touch human reality. It is the wonder of the church that it knows the name of the Spirit who creates and sustains life, who makes safe, and who breeds joy.

6. Pastors and church members who cease to meet the expectations of conventional religion and who cease to count on the payouts and gifts of conventional religion are more likely to be *unafraid and filled with energy*. I offer two attestations to this truth. The first is set soon after World War II. There was a group of aging German pastors and their wives who had suffered much at the hands of the German regime. They were getting on a tour bus while a young man scurried to get all their luggage on, working with great zest. Someone asked who he was, prompting another to answer, "That is Martin Niemoeller. He is eighty." Niemoeller long before had decided not to be afraid. I read that when he was a much younger man, he was in a delegation to see Hitler just after Hitler had come to power in 1933. When Niemoeller came home, his wife asked him about the meeting and what he had learned. He answered, "I learned that Herr Hitler is a very frightened man." It was given to Niemoeller, unlike most of us, to be unafraid. And when we are unafraid, energy is given.

The second attestation is on a less dramatic note and involves my participation in a Lilly consultation with pastors at Memphis Theological Seminary. In their reflection on three years in their study groups, the pastors reported that they had learned (a) they did not need to remain hidden in their personal lives of struggle, and (b) they did not need to be loners. The outcome for most of them was new energy for the task of ministry. We have much to unlearn about faith and ministry and fear and what it means to be summoned to "fear not." There are no doubt different strategic questions related to the issue of confession, but this consultation comes to us differently when fear is submitted to the great spirit of newness.

7. This leads me, finally, to reflect on the third article of the Creed, as I imagine a movement of confession to be Spirit led. It occurs to me that in the Spirit and through the Spirit and by the Spirit, we may do what the spiritless national security state can never do:

- The Spirit creates and sustains *the holy catholic church* as a *communion of saints*, as a community of those who have given their lives over to God's newness. The spiritless national security state can never form community. William Cavanaugh, in his exposé of the Pinochet regime in Chile, reports that the intent of state-sponsored torture in Chile was to make community impossible.[5] I submit that it is the work of the national security state—whether intentional or not—to preclude communities of commitment, trust, and generosity.
- The Spirit makes possible *the forgiveness of sins*. The Spirit has the power to break the grip of guilt for the sake of new beginnings. The national security state, and its market ideology, offers no forgiveness, no free lunch, no beginning again; it is all "three strikes and you are out," with nothing ever forgiven or ever forgotten.
- The Spirit makes possible *the resurrection of our bodies and eternal life* in God's promise. The national security state has no hope, but imagines at best the endless perpetuation of the present state of greed and acquisitiveness.

The Creed's third article is the matrix of freedom and courage in the church, and everything depends on yielding to the Spirit. It has always been so. Every confession calls for a decision that is only credible if the world is under the aegis of God's life-giving spirit:

- The Barmen Declaration called "German Christians" to an either/or decision of gospel or National Socialism. It is correct, I believe, that "spirit" is only mentioned once in the Declaration, in Article 4, after quoting Ephesians 4:15–16:

    The Christian Church is the community of brethren in which, in Word and sacrament, through the Holy Spirit, Jesus Christ acts in the present as Lord. With both its faith and its obedience, with both its message and its order, it has to testify in the midst of the sinful world, as the Church of pardoned sinners, that it belongs to him alone and lives and may live by his comfort and under his direction alone, in expectation of his appearing.[6]

- The Kairos Document called Christians to an either/or decision concerning apartheid. The document is not at all based on references to the Spirit. It is asserted that prophetic theology is "deeply spiritual," and the document quotes Luke 4:18–19 concerning "the Spirit of the Lord."[7]
- King's letter from the Birmingham jail called "white moderates" to an either/or decision concerning segregation and integration. It mentions a "sacrificial spirit," but that is all.

And now it is our time and our circumstance. (I add as a belated note that just recently, led by Jim Wallis, a new confession has been issued under the title "Reclaiming Jesus." It is immediately evident that this new confession is deliberately shaped after the manner of Barmen with conviction that "this is our Barmen moment.") What matters is (a) how deeply we ourselves are free from or yet contained by claims of empire, and (b) how we judge wisely about a radical bid for the mind and heart of the church. We are back to Friday and Sunday, to the truth of crucifixion and the hope of resurrection. Our society waits in denial and despair to hear a truth-filled, hope-filled word of healing and newness.

Chapter 8

Purity, Unity, Miracle

Overcoming Divisions

For starters try this: it is the task of preaching to evoke, maintain, sustain, nurture, and guide a faithful community of praise and missional obedience. That is, preaching aims at a self-conscious, intentional community that has a distinctiveness to it in terms of how it thinks and imagines and lives its life. This is congruent with the ecclesial concerns of the epistles in the New Testament, and before that literature it was the concern of prophetic imagination in ancient Israel. The test is to imagine what the world would be like if we agreed that YHWH—creator of heaven and earth, covenant partner of Israel, and father of our Lord Jesus Christ—were a decisive player in the life of the world and in the life of the church.

I.

When we think about the church as such a community of praise and missional obedience, we are drawn quickly to the issue of the *unity* and *purity* of the church. We blithely mouth both terms, but it seems clear, even in the very moment of utterance, that they contain a deep contradiction, or at least an unmanageable tension.

So consider the claim that faithful preaching aims at the unity of the church. It is a truism of the ecumenical movement that the unity of the church is a given in the gospel. It is not something we accomplish, but it is a gift of God given in Jesus Christ, who prays that we may all be one.

But it is also a truism of our lived experience that the way we receive the gift of unity from God is a failure. The ecumenical movement of the twentieth century has rightly understood that our church divisions are themselves an affront to God. Paul asks the question, "Is Christ divided?" He intended the answer, "No, Christ is not divided." But our lived experience tells us otherwise. Christ is indeed divided; we have each taken the part of Christ that we prefer and treasure. But here I do not speak of the big divisions among traditions and denominations. Rather, I speak of the deeply felt divisions at the local level in which the church, propelled by anxiety, divides into red and blue, liberal and conservative, camps that mostly exhibit little openness for unity with those across the divide. I was once in a meeting of Episcopal bishops in which this red and blue issue was rightly viewed with alarm.[1] In any denomination now, we may make a list of red and blue churches and red and blue pastors, and those who try not to fall off of one side or the other. At its most vigorous, the red/blue, conservative/liberal division does not remember much that our vocation is to be a community of praise that exalts the God above all our parties and that missional obedience calls all sorts and conditions of people to perform that obedience in a variety of ways.

Our usual response to such divisions, locally or in larger judicatories, is to win, to control offices and budgets and programs in ways that lead to tacit excommunication of those who think otherwise. The capacity to be so right as to impose unity-cum-excommunication arises from a heavy moral conviction that can be held together by a piety in which the only unity that can be entertained is a unity of like minds. Either that, or the preacher grows mute and timid so as not to offend.[2]

Unity thus continues as a puzzle or as a disappointment among us, because most of our efforts at unity are accomplished in juridical ways that vote and win or lose, a polity that likely reflects Enlightenment rationality. It seems clear enough that our conventional modes of unity will not work, especially in a social environment of acute anxiety where many people are on edge and without any gentle patience.

It is perhaps only another abstract turn to say that the unity of the church that is at all workable among us is a *dialogic unity*. This dialogic unity allows and honors and hears voices quite unlike our own and expects to be impacted and transformed by those other voices. In a society that is on a desperate quest for absoluteness and certitude, dialogic modes of thought and speech seem soft and unreliable and perhaps cowardly. But surely it is true that in our most important and intimate and trusted relationships—those with spouse or parent or child, especially those between parent and teenage child—the only possible way to sustain the relationship is a dialogue in which there is listening and honoring and expecting to be impinged upon and transformed by the exchange.

At a practical level, the dialogic listening that is most crucial is to hear the voice of pain that comes from "the other side."[3] The voice of pain lies beneath the voice of hate and anger and indignation and even guilt. It is the most elemental rendering of humanness, so that even the youngest child knows, as Freud understood, all about pain (and pleasure) before he or she knows anything about transformative dialogic transaction.[4]

That practical reality of hearing and honoring pain is reflected, I have no doubt, in the formation of the biblical canon that is from the ground up pluralistic and that has included within it "voices to the contrary," so that almost nobody is left out and surely nobody wins all the way.[5] Thus, in the Old Testament it is the traditioning presence of J and E and most especially D and P that provide voices that are in deep dispute with each other. That Old Testament reality, moreover, has its counterpart in the New Testament offer of four Gospel narratives because the early church knew from the outset that no single Gospel narrative from no single local congregation could possibly get it right. It takes a village; it takes a series of villages; it takes a cacophony of voices to tell the truth.

My urging is that preaching that concerns the unity of the church must be dialogical preaching. By that I do not mean dialogue sermons or talk-back sessions, but that the preacher should be capable of sounding many voices of truth, bearing witness to a dialogical God who is not readily captured in any treasured formulation.[6] This is not simply a matter of the rhetoric of the preacher; it is, I believe, the hard work of nurturing a dialogic readiness in the church that does not readily seek closure but hears many voices in the text, attends to many stirrings of the Spirit in the church, and recognizes many voices in our own persons that simply refuse closure or silence. It is a primary temptation of church to seek closure; it is a powerful Jewish reminder to Christians that there will always be another rabbi with another reading. The reason rabbis know there will be another one is that Jews have learned repeatedly that "final interpretations" are the likely venue for "final solutions." Thus, I suggest that pastoral ministry and preaching depend upon the internal capacity to hear and honor voices other than the ones we have long preferred. And that means for the church the deep unlearning that the truth of the gospel and the witness of Scripture consist in a seamless package, red or blue. Most of us, moreover, live less than a seamless life. Thus, I imagine that a community of faithful praise and faithful obedience is a dialogic venue for our many feeble attempts to voice the truth—the truth of pain and the truth of hope—for which we care so passionately.

II.

But as we pray for and preach the unity of the church as a dialogical community, we pray at the same time for purity. By *the purity of the church* we have come to mean, for the most part, a moral earnestness that identifies right morality that makes a judgment about contamination caused by folk who think and act otherwise. Just now that moral reductionism is primarily aimed at the issue of sexuality, whereby we come most immediately to the truth of our bodily experience. People on the right (red) specify the purity of the church according to the old purity codes of the Old Testament (especially Leviticus) or the epistolary admonitions of the New Testament. These texts, which are read without any acknowledgment of the deep difference between ancient and contemporary, notice the deep rigor of commandments concerning who is in and who is out.

But it is not different in the blue church. My own denomination is, for now, set happily on a quite blue direction. But such a passion tends to make no room for those who carry a different set of wounds or a different set of hopes. And so in the church we keep voting, hoping to prevail over those who manifestly have it wrong.

It was not always so. There was a time when the "purity" of the church referred to that claim that the church relied only on the saving power of Christ without additional assurances of race or party or ethnicity or whatever. The practice of a "pure faith" must not be distorted by other loyalties or other appeals that can have no saving effect on us. I will return to this.

For now, in considering the purity of the church, let us take the exemplar case of lepers, an uncleanness that would have jeopardized the first-century community as much as any of our current uncleannesses can jeopardize faithful living and true teaching. In the season of Epiphany, one of the lectionary readings concerns Naaman, the Syrian leper (2 Kgs. 5:1–14), and Jesus' remarkable healing of a leper (Mark 1:41–45). The psalm for that day is Psalm 30, which needs to be read in the context of the lepers as the song of "ex-lepers." In this psalm, the speaker identifies an acute personal crisis in his life:

> As for me, I said in my prosperity,
>   "I shall never be moved."
> . . . .
> You hid your face;
>   I was dismayed.
>
> Ps. 30:6, 7b

In the lectionary context, that means, "I became leprous." The psalmist then prays:

> What profit is there in my death,
>   if I go down to the Pit?
> Will the dust praise you?
>   Will it tell of your faithfulness?
> Hear, O LORD, and be gracious to me!
> O LORD, be my helper.
>
> 30:9–10

The prayer is a bid for care in the midst of deep trouble. The next verse reports an answered prayer:

> You have turned my mourning into dancing;
> You have taken off my sackcloth
> and clothed me with joy.
>
> 30:11

The psalm in the context of the lepers is, as Erhard Gerstenberger has suggested, a "drama of rehabilitation" in which the troubled one (here the lepers) have been rehabilitated into their community.[7] So Naaman, the Syrian general, goes home to his military politics, and the leper leaves Jesus and spreads the word about his rehabilitation. The church at its best has always been ready to rehabilitate. What strikes one about the lepers is that there is no blame, no guilt, no condemnation; it is all welcome by the one who can save. This is "purity," pure action from the saving God, unqualified by other commitments of red or blue.

So consider purity as singular gospel that permits restoration. Purity as starchy moralism permits only excommunication from the right or from the left. But the preacher must take a deep look at the common pattern of parties that are now parsed as red and blue, perhaps more voiced by red but deeply felt as well by blue.

Preaching that is partisan, that chooses purity at the expense of unity, is not "pure gospel" that relies only on Christ, but is a manifestation of deep anxiety. I believe that anxiety is now the central characteristic of our society and the central opportunity for the preacher. The anxiety common among us is the dread that something or someone unlike me may sojourn with me in a way that jeopardizes my package of certitudes and my power arrangements whereby I maintain modest measures of control over my complex life. It is exactly the fear of the other that leads to this pathological purity that has no grounding in the gospel, the other being variously gay and lesbian, Muslim, communist, or even conservative. We are, moreover, smart enough now to know that when we work to excommunicate the other in a fit of fearful moral indignation, there lurks in hidden ways and in secret places that which is unsettled and that contradicts our preferred "facts on the ground." Purity of that sort is an attempt to keep the lid on a kind of deep restlessness that stirs beneath our composure. We know enough to anticipate that when that restlessness is not honored in a community of truth and hope, it will likely turn in destructive directions.

Thus, the purity of the church that is to be preached surely is a purity of wheat and tares, of plants and weeds, in the knowledge that there will be a time of accountability—but we are not on that committee.

Thus far it is my purpose to problematize both unity and purity. I seek to make the point that unity that is faithful and trustworthy is *a dialogical unity* that honors voices other than our own, that purity that is faithful and trustworthy is *the capacity to host the other* that comes to us as threat but that turns out to be companion.

None of this is easy in a local congregation. I propose that preachers must move into such issues of *unity as dialogue* and *purity as holy otherness* because it is clear the Bible gives us a God who is engaged in dialogue and who struggles in

God's own life with otherness. If we do not engage these matters, then I think the church, red and blue, simply replicates the frightened society around us. The issues of unity and/or purity are not themselves defining matters for us. They are, rather, a way to be in the world, a more excellent way that is the way of the cross. It is *a Friday summons to foster unity* of a dialogical kind. It is *a Friday summons to practice purity* that hosts the other. And without such demanding Friday work, there is no Sunday of new life.

III.

My third term is *miracle*, the enactment of the impossible by the power of God that violates the reason of this age. Without having used this term, that is how I have understood unity and purity in the church. In most congregations I know, it would be an uphill effort to be dialogic in the interest of unity; it would require *a miracle*. In most congregations I know, the odds would be very long of hosting the other in the interest of purity; it would require *a miracle*. Thus, I propose that after the preacher considers unity and purity, the next theme is the miracle of God that concerns something that emerges anew in the world that is beyond our expectation or our explanation. The wonder is that that new emergent does come about, here and there.

I have waited all my life to attempt an exposition of Romans 4; I think this text is one of the most remarkable expositions of evangelical miracle in the entire Bible. It is an in-between chapter in Romans in which Paul does a midrash on a series of Genesis texts. Although he is not mentioned at all, the real star of this exposition is Isaac, Abraham's son and heir, born to Sarah in her old age. The birth of any baby in any family is a wonder and a miracle, and Jon Levenson has shown that birth is a metaphor for resurrection in the Hebrew Bible.[8] Birth is an even greater wonder if the parents are really old; here the father is described "as good as dead," and the mother is one with a "barren womb." Any birth, especially a birth in old age, is a wonder, but even more of a wonder is a birth that is embedded in a narrative of promise that will propel a people and a land and a book, and then two more peoples. Everything hangs on the thin thread of Isaac, who in any normal "reckoning" should not have been born. Indeed, in the birth announcement in Genesis 18, there is this odd, playful exchange between Abraham and the three visitors who bring the news of the baby to come. The visitor declares, "I will surely return to you in due season, and your wife Sarah shall have a son (v. 10).

The visitor calls her by name, which is more than a bit aggressive on his part. The narrative says that "Sarah laughed" as she replied, "After I have grown old, and my husband is old, shall I have pleasure?" (v. 12).

The visitor counters her laughter: "Why did Sarah laugh, and say, Shall I indeed bear a child now that I am old?" (v. 13).

Sarah denies that she laughed, either in joy or in puzzlement. And the visitor responds before he departs, "Oh yes, you did laugh" (v. 15).

In the middle of this exchange, the visitor says about Sarah's skepticism, "Is anything too wonderful for the LORD?" (v. 14). That of course is the ultimate question of biblical faith, the big issue to which the preacher must give testimony. It can be rendered, "Is anything too difficult for God? Is anything too marvelous? Is anything impossible?" Is anything possible that is beyond the range of our explanation or our anticipation? There is no answer given in this text. But the tradition, over the generations, must give an answer, and every preacher must take a run at it. The preacher faces two temptations. On the one hand, the preacher may settle for a simplistic supernaturalism that makes the claim so glibly that there is no wonder left, for of course God can do anything! On the other hand, the preacher may engage in liberal criticism and conclude that this is a fable or a legend—that is, the biblical writers tell it with a wink and do not quite mean it. Either way is to miss the narrative particularity whereby the teller and the listener are jerked beyond their comfort zone into awesome newness.

Every preacher must try. So here is Paul the preacher making a try in Romans 4. At the beginning of the chapter (v. 3) and at the conclusion (v. 23), Paul reiterates the narrative from Genesis 15:6 that played such a major part in Reformation theology. Abraham's faith is "reckoned" to him as righteousness. The exegetes have worked loud and long over this verb "reckon" and over the question about whose "righteousness" is intended. In any conventional reading, Paul can take the narrative affirmation as justification by grace in trust: "But to one who without works trusts him who justifies the ungodly, such faith is reckoned as righteousness. So also David speaks of the blessedness of those to whom God reckons righteousness apart from works" (vv. 5–6).

The words "it was reckoned to him" were written not for Abraham's sake alone, but for ours also. It will be reckoned to us who believe in him who raised Jesus our Lord from the dead, who was handed over to death for our trespasses and was raised for our justification (vv. 23–25).

While there is new ferment in Pauline study, here I want only to return the formula back into the text from which doctrinal controversy has hijacked it. The verdict of which Paul makes such use is in response to a particular divine promise about Isaac to come: "This man shall not be your heir; no one but your own issue shall be your heir" (Gen. 15:4). And the promise of the son is then multiplied to the peoples: "Look toward the heavens and count the stars, if you are able to count them. . . . So shall your descendants be" (v. 5).

In verse 6 the narrative says tersely, "He believed the LORD." He found the Lord to be reliable, believed that God's promise would open the future. The larger narrative of Genesis exhibits little Isaac as verification of the divine promise. And the inventory in Hebrews 11 adds this:

> By faith he received power of procreation, even though he was too old— and Sarah herself was barren—because he considered him faithful who had promised. Therefore from one person, and this one as good as dead, descendants were born, as many as the stars of heaven and as the innumerable grains of sand by the seashore. (Heb. 11:11–12)

From that testimony, Paul derives his core claim about getting right with and right before God, without reference to the law.[9]

We have become so jaded by the testimony of Paul that we scarcely notice. Except for the most passionate Lutherans, we trot out the teaching on Reformation Sunday and explain it to the folk who never thought much about "the law" anyway. But if this theme of the miraculous is to underpin our passion for unity in dialogue and purity with otherness, then it is an affirmation of our full worth before God without our performance. Most folk with whom we preach are not much worried about the "performance of the law" except as it is the law of my mother, or the law of peer pressure, or the law of the marketplace, or any of the "works of the law" in our sociopolitical system that provides no free lunch for anyone and works on a quid pro quo—and for outsiders it is two quids for one quo. The question of Paul's theme in a flattened, fatigued society like ours is whether there are promises that can be trusted, promises that will open new futures, promises stirring through old tired bodies and old weary spirits and old fatigued institutions. Such a question will drive the preacher back to the promise maker who is the promise keeper who does not conform to any of our rules or schedules about birth, who repudiates our passion for a system of production and consumption and any of the qualifications urged by our anxiety-ridden economy. Are those promises that surge in our midst ones that serious, anxious folk can rest on? Are there impossibilities that well up that will bring relief from the depressing possibilities of the rat race that we can never win? The current nonnegotiable measure is not circumcision as it was for Paul, but it is money and control and power and admission to the right school and the right house and the right entertainment center and the right leisure occupation. Abraham stands alongside Sarah, and they were invited to defy the definitions of reality all around them that seemed obvious and beyond question. They are justified, valorized, reckoned as graced by allowing the promise to extract them from the tired categories of the predictable. Thus, at the beginning in Romans 4:1–7 and at the end in Romans 4:19–24, Abraham and Sarah trust in the promise of God: "He grew strong in faith as he gave glory to God, being fully convinced that God was able to do what he has promised" (vv. 20–21). It is a miracle!

In between verses 1–7 and verses 19–24 Paul writes, in quite convoluted grammatical construction, concerning Abraham and those who share the faith of Abraham, "(for he is the father of us all, as it is written, 'I have made you the father of many nations')—in the presence of the God in whom he believed, who gives life to the dead" (vv. 16–17). The God who justifies by grace is the God who gives life to the dead! This is the Lord of the resurrection. We might have expected Paul here to allude to the new Easter life of Jesus and consequently to that of the church. But he does not. We might have expected him to do a riff on the obvious "resurrection texts" in Isaiah and Daniel. But he does not do that either. Because his subject continues to be Father Abraham, and him as good as dead, death here means without hope for the future, without any prospect in the normal scheme of things.

But then there is Isaac. Thus, the possibility of new life is offered to a withered man and a closed-off woman, a new gift that opens all the future. We can see from this way of reasoning that Paul is not fixed on a single remarkable moment in the life of Jesus, though he clearly knows that from the attestation of the church (see 1 Cor. 15:3–6). Rather, he focuses on God's characteristic action in the world of overpowering death and summoning life, of joining issue with the power of the Nihil and generating new possibility where none was on tap. I suspect that it is the Abraham-Isaac connection that is the ground of the lyric in Romans 8 that we recite at every funeral: "Neither life nor death nor anything else can separate us from the love of God." This is an active, resolved, defiant love that refuses the categories of the world. Abraham is a fearful man. He has risked trading Sarah to Pharaoh for food (Gen. 12:1–20). He risked bringing another woman into the family in order to get an heir (Gen. 16:1–3). But he knows, after these pitiful human efforts at self-securing, that new life comes only from outside of us.

The third theme in verse 17, after the affirmation of God's saving grace and God's power for resurrection, is an even more remarkable affirmation: Abraham believed in the God who "calls into existence the things that do not exist." With this wondrous phrasing one might expect that Paul would talk about creation *ex nihilo,* even though the Old Testament texts do not claim that. The theme might lead to the issues of creation, evolution, and creationism. But of course it does not. It does not because Paul keeps his eye on aged Abraham—him as good as dead—and little Isaac, the lean thread to the future given by promise. What God creates that does not exist is this baby Isaac. What God creates that does not exist is an alternative narrative of promise and covenant and Torah obedience. What God creates that does not exist is a people, and then a book, and then two more peoples of faith that are called and summoned to exist. Or as my own United Church of Christ lyrically affirms, "God calls the worlds into being. . . . God calls us into the church to accept the cost and joy of discipleship." And then come a stream of descendants and witnesses and practitioners and members of the praise choir for the newness—altos and basses and sopranos and tenors and monotones, all called beyond themselves in wonder and awe.

Now we have before us these three great evangelical themes from Paul:

Reckoned to him as righteous

Gives life to the dead

Calls into existence things that do not exist

It turns out that the same God is the subject of all three verbs—*reckons, gives, calls*—perhaps God's three great enactments toward us.

More than that, I have learned from Hans Heinrich Schmid, a noted Swiss interpreter, that these three phrases are precise synonyms.[10] All three phrases testify to the power and willingness of God to impose a transformative purpose and reality upon a huge dysfunction:

The law that never justifies

The dead who never stir or generate newness

Chaos that never grants life

Consider—*law, death, chaos*—and then Abraham and Sarah! In their frail, aging bodies they were beyond productive obedience, were as good as dead, and had in purview no viable future. And then little Isaac arrived—little Isaac as an embodied promise given to them, little Isaac as new life to the dead parents, little Isaac as a sign of the future they had not expected. It is no wonder that Paul holds up little Isaac (even if not named in this text) as the primal sign of the generativity of God.

I propose, then, that Romans 4—a text that reaches all the way back to Genesis and forward to the inventory of the faithful in Hebrews 11—gives the preacher the truthful news for a church that resists unity in dialogue and purity in otherness. This lyrical presentation attests that God moves outside all of our boxes of fear and anxiety, all of our boxes of control and certitude, all of our boxes of doctrine and morality and liturgy and piety, all of our boxes of sociopolitical ideology, and makes available a newness. I do not need to tell you, moreover, that other than the God of the gospel, there is no agent who can do this:

- *There is no other* who reckons trust as righteousness, because all the others are moral bean counters fixed on performance.
- *There is no other* who can give life to the dead, because God has reserved for God's self the mystery of life in all its fullness.
- *There is no other* who can call into existence that which does not exist. All the others simply move the pieces of chaos around, hoping that something new will emerge.

This is a good time for preachers to bring home the big majestic truth of God, not to be sidetracked by pet projects or sidelined by ideological issues. The truth of the gospel not only overrides our preoccupations; it blows away the categories in which we frame the discussion.

So consider this: The unity of the church does not arise from the merger of pension plans or the tedious agreement on creedal formulations or compromises on polity, all of which no doubt need to happen. The unity of the congregation does not come by majority vote or by pastoral manipulation. The unity of the church is given by the majestic power of God, who draws all to God's self and away from our guarded efforts at control. Surely Calvin's famous hymn has it right: "Our hope is in no other save in thee alone." Calvin's theme of hope echoes Paul in Romans 4: "Hoping against hope, he believed that he would become 'the father of many nations'" (v. 18).

The unity of the church will not come by agreement on sexuality or by agreement on anything else. It will come by the glad ceding of our partial claims over to God in exuberant praise that holds nothing back of our most treasured truth.

I understand that such talk is unreal when one considers the plodding of the local congregation with the same invitation and the same affirmation in sermon after sermon. I understand that this moment of utterance after Paul is a call beyond ourselves that has no coercive power or anxiety to it, only an invitation to watch for the newness that will be given.

Unity in the church is not realized by barter. It is realized by recognizing that the others in the church belong in the doxology with us, all of us gathered together in praise and adoration of this gospel God who is beyond our categories. We ourselves, in this gathered presence, are pushed to strange depths of our own being in the presence of God. It is wonder, love, and praise; it is shock and awe before the throne that offers transformation in the church. We do not know how bread becomes body. We do not know how wine becomes blood. And we do not know how contrary folk like us are drawn into the one unified body, except that it is promised. And we are not wanting to be deserters. We find, in this matrix of praise, that all the sisters and brothers in the dialogue of evangelical engagement have a word to speak to all of us. It is most often a word of hurt, but sometimes that word of hurt, when heard, is transposed into a word of hope. But it is a word that must be heard, because we never know when the right word will be spoken, nor from what quarter.

The purity of the church will not come about by rules of excommunication and acts of preemption. It is not possible to arrive at purity by way of exclusion, because Jesus has called together a church and not a sect. Thus, purity cannot be an act of subtraction. Paul's notion of purity in the church is that it does not come through regulation or moral or legal consolidation. It comes through trust, through living into the future without excessive preoccupation with what has gone before: "By faith Abraham obeyed when he was called to set out for a place that he was to receive as an inheritance; and he set out, not knowing where he was going" (Heb. 11:8). The text is from Hebrews; the sentiment, however, is Pauline. He went—to a new place. The purity of the church consists in ready obedience for the future that is not defined by where we come from. As one man was drawn into the future by the God who calls, we find others on the same path—others unlike us, others who come from somewhere else but on the path. The call was not an easy one in ancient Israel or in the early church, because there was always, then as now, an attempt to sort out and rank and grade the qualified. What strikes one about the departure to the future is that there is no such qualification. It is only by faith, by faith, by faith, and all sorts of folk can do it:

> All of these died in faith without having received the promises, but from a distance they saw and greeted them. They confessed that they were strangers and foreigners on the earth, for people who speak in this way make it clear that they are seeking a homeland. If they had been thinking of the land that they had left behind, they would have had opportunity to return. But as it is, they desire a better country, that is, a heavenly one. Therefore God is not ashamed to be called their God; indeed, he has prepared a city for them. (Heb. 11:13–16)

The thinking and living of the church, with its dialogical engagement with all the others, is in the future, not in our several pasts.

But surely the twinned notions of the unity and purity of the church constitute a penultimate agenda. The real issue is what does the church—and the preacher—have to say to the world in its bewilderment? I propose that we reflect on the truth that the God of the gospel is the last resource left that can offer a way to the future of the world. Given its own resources, one could conclude that our Western world (and our own U.S. imperial way in the world) is in shut-down. No one can figure out how to jump-start it. Well, the God of *justification, resurrection,* and *new creation* is the jump-starter who, by the inexplicable gift of Isaac, lets us hope for our world and its future.

It occurs to me that Paul's three great phrases in Romans 4 provide an anti-dote exactly to the pathologies of our society. First, Paul testifies to trust reck-oned as righteousness. It may be too much to call the world "guilty," but try "alienated." The world is indeed alienated in every way imaginable—rich and poor, north and south, east and west, haves and have-nots. The issues are global and acutely local, as local as the killing of a postmaster or a pastor, or the aban-donment of a child, or the exclusion of a lesbian, or the execution of a mentally handicapped person. All acts of violence derive from and feed more fear, anger, and anxiety, and every turn to violence begets more violence and leads to fresh waves of alienation.

And in that ocean of alienation, the gospel invites us to the truth that gifts are yet to be given:

> By faith Abraham obeyed when he was called to set out.
>
> By faith he stayed for a time, living in tents.
>
> By faith he looked forward.
>
> By faith he received power of procreation. (Heb. 11:8–11)

Trust in God beyond our fear and our control unlooses the juices of possibility. The world wonders what to do in its alienation. Here is the preacher's word: alienation can only be countered by risky trust; the future always wells up among the trusters and nowhere else.

In Paul's second great phrase, he testifies to "the God who gives life to the dead." We need not say that the world is "dead." But we could say it is disem-powered, unable to be generative. The world has a way, moreover, of disempow-ering people. And indeed, the church, in its imitation of the world, has a way of hurting people until they are left with no energy. Our great institutions of health and education are now mostly failed institutions, without the impetus to do their work well. It is no wonder, if we pay attention, that we sink into despair that we are mostly unwilling and unable to utter.

Into this world, attests the preacher, comes Easter power. Easter summons a little Isaac to be the foretaste of a new, alternative history in the world. Easter comes, note well pastors, by an uttered word of life that is at the same time summons and assurance. It is assurance: "Yes we can!" It is summons: "You go!" The God of life comes to work newness among the mass of resigned people; here and there comes a stirring to newness that is God-given.

In Paul's third great phrase, he speaks of the God "who calls into existence things that do not exist." We would not say that the world does not exist. But surely it exists only, characteristically, in diminished fashion. The chaos is everywhere, because the power of the Nihil is enormously attractive and determined. That power comes in violence; it comes in devouring selfishness. It comes in greed and a thousand violations of human dignity.

And the Creator "calls," says the preacher—calls to order, calls to fruitfulness, calls to life and joy and well-being. In the long tradition of faith, some fully answer that call in glad obedience. Thus, I propose that while the preacher has work to do on the themes of unity and purity in the church, the preacher may speak over the shoulder of the church to the world:

- The preacher speaks to an alienated world about *trust.*
- The preacher speaks to a disempowered world about *Easter possibility.*
- The preacher speaks to a diminished world about *abundant fruitfulness.*

Preachers have always trusted the news and have refused to give in to the data before them. When we give in to the data, we end in cynicism or despair or moralism or absolutism. But this baby, this Isaac, refuses cynicism or despair or absolutism or moralism. The baby brings a vitality to the old parents and continues even now, even among us, to evidence a new future that is a miracle:

- Vitality issues in trust to ready obedience.
- Vitality issues in an Easter laugh against all the disabilities.
- Vitality issues in new creation where the angels and the morning stars dance before the Creator.

It is no wonder that as the father looked at his beloved son in that acute crisis on the mountain, he told the inquisitive son with confidence, "The Lord will provide" (Gen. 22:8).[11] He knew because the son is a sign that the Lord does provide. And the father, with his withered wife, need only receive.

IV.

David Howell gave me advice on how to speak at the Festival of Homiletics: "Pastors like discussions of upcoming lectionary texts." For the four Sundays in June, consider the psalms assigned in the lectionary that revolve around this collage of miracles.

June 7, Trinity Sunday: *Psalm 29* is an exhibit of the great storm God who twists oak trees and shatters the cedars of Lebanon. The exhibit of divine power by the Creator evidences the power of heaven; all respond by saying, "Glory." All say, "Wow," to divine power. The psalm ends by transposing awesome divine power into a will for *shalom*. The newly crowned divine king sits atop the flood-waters, enthroned above chaos; the king declares that the people will be blessed with *shalom*. This is a dramatic liturgical enactment with loud clashing cymbals. The creator God invites the audience to notice a cosmic will for shalom:

> May the LORD give strength to his people!
> May the LORD bless his people with *peace*!
> Ps. 29:11 (au. emph.)

Then it follows that the preacher says, "The Lord bless you and keep you, the Lord cause his face to shine upon you, and give you *peace*." It is the word of the preacher designed to contradict the chaos by uttering an act of shalom, calling into existence that which does not exist until uttered. It is an awesome echo of the exhibit of the Creator!

June 14, Second Sunday after Pentecost: *Psalm 92:1–4, 12–15*. As you might expect, the reading skips over verses 5–11 because they speak of the dullard and the stupid and the wicked and enemies and evildoers and assailants, and we would not want anything negative to creep into our awareness. Verses 1–4 are a summons to praise:

> To declare your steadfast love in the morning,
> and your faithfulness by night.
> Ps. 92:2

Day and night we are encompassed, so says our doxology, by the utter reliability of God. Verse 4 ends with a grand doxology:

> For you, O LORD, have made me glad by your work;
> at the works of our hands I sing for joy.

Your work in creation and in Easter—at the bottom of our wearisome world is the faithful work of God. And we have been stupid dullards in our self-preoccupation not to notice.

The psalm concludes with an ode to the righteous:

> The righteous flourish like the palm tree,
> and grow like a cedar in Lebanon.
> They are planted in the house of the LORD;
> they flourish in the courts of our God.
> In old age they still produce fruit;
> they are always green and *full of sap*,
> showing that the LORD is upright;
> he is my rock, and there is no unrighteousness in him.
> 92:12–15 (au. emph.)

The righteous are the Torah keepers, the ones who have not had their eyes or their lives distracted from the neighborly ethic ordained into creation. They are the ones who honor God's good order, who trust themselves to God's good future.

And get this: They are full of sap! They are full of energy and generative juices, not withered in despair or cynicism or any of the gifts of self-preoccupation. This is the true story of the righteous. The others are exhausted, anxious, and weary. But these shall mount up with wings like eagles, soar and run and walk—and not be weary (Isa. 40:31). The doxology is a decision to see if you would like to be full of sap, even in your old age. If you are not full of God's sap, you will be played by the world for a sap. Count on it!

June 21, Third Sunday after Trinity: *Psalm 9:9–20.* The verses move through all the notes of prayer.

> Doxology in verses 8–12:

> > And those who know your name put their trust in you,
> > for you, O LORD, have not forsaken those who seek you.
> >
> > v. 10

> Petition in verses 13–14:

> > Be gracious to me, O LORD,
> > See what I suffer from those who hate me;
> > you are the one who lifts me up from the gates of death.
> >
> > v. 13

> Complaint in verses 15–17:

> > The nations have sunk in the pit that they have made;
> > in the net that they hid has their own foot been caught.
> >
> > v. 15

> Hopeful imperative in verses 18–20:

> > Rise up, O LORD! Do not let mortals prevail;
> > let the nations be judged before you.
> >
> > v. 19

Rise up! Do Easter! Show power! Be the equalizer between the innocent and the wicked, between the poor and the aggressive. Imagine summoning God back into Easter. From time to time the poor, who are the only ones who pray for Easter, attest that there is an Easter laugh evoked by the power of new life. It is no wonder that Mother Sarah, the one with the closed womb, laughed!

June 28, Fourth Sunday after Pentecost: *Psalm 130.* This psalm is a prayer out of the depths. It is used often in Lutheran fashion to ponder the depth of human inadequacy. But in fact the psalm says otherwise. It says that the depths are the place from which to pray and from which to expect to be heard and taken seriously. Thus, a prayer from the depths, but a prayer prayed in confidence!

There is forgiveness. YHWH is there and attentive!

I wait for the LORD, my soul waits,
    and in his word I hope;
my soul waits for the Lord,
    more than those who watch for the morning.
                                        Ps. 130:5–6

There is waiting:

- Waiting for the promises to be kept
- Waiting for a long time for the gifts of newness
- Waiting through the night for the dawn
- Waiting, not doubting, even in the depths, trusting!

And then in the concluding verses, there is hope:

O Israel, hope in the LORD!
    For with the LORD there is steadfast love,
    and with him is great power to redeem.
                                        130:7

These psalms will give us weighty grist for a while amid our excessive posture of deference. This voice refuses to give in. So imagine that the piety of
the church, grounded in miracle, is an act of defiance. It refuses the seduction
of being ground down to insignificance. It refuses the arrogance of piety that
excommunicates. It knows that gifts of newness are indeed gifts but also that
they are practices of discipline that require patient intentional waiting, because
we do not in fact live in a world of immediate indulgence. We live in a world
where the gifts of God are adequate, but not in our possession.

What strikes me most about these themes of Romans 4 is that they are lyrical.
I suspect that the gospel is most often defeated when it is prosaic and explanatory. Let me offer one more lyric from Paul about the unity and the purity of the
church. It sounds like an ode about Jesus:

. . . who, though he was in the form of God,
    did not regard equality with God
    as something to be exploited,
but emptied himself,
    taking the form of slave,
    being born in human likeness.
And being found in human form,
    he humbled himself
    and became obedient to the point of death—
    even death on a cross.
Therefore God also highly exalted him
    and gave him the name
    that is above every name,
so that at the name of Jesus
    every knee should bend,

in heaven and on earth and under the earth,
and every tongue should confess
   that Jesus Christ is Lord,
   to the glory of God the Father.

                      Phil. 2:6–11

But this poem is in fact not an ode to Jesus. It is about the church:

Let the same mind be in you that was in Christ Jesus. (2:5)

And the way to do that is given in verse 4:

Let each of you look not to your own interests, but to the interests of others.

The unity and the purity of the church will come not by muscle and power grabs and control; it will come as the mind of the self-emptying Christ is among us.

And the final lyric I cite from Paul is again about Jesus as the model for proper church behavior, in this case stewardship: "For you know the generous act of our Lord Jesus Christ, that though he was rich, yet for our sakes he became poor, so that by his poverty you might become rich" (2 Cor. 8:9). There is no supply-side ideology in the church. Supply-side economics or supply-side doctrine or supply-side morality will never yield unity and will never give purity.

So, dear preachers, the ones with the hardest, most urgent job in the world: Keep your eye on the baby. Faith has been keeping its eye on the baby of the promise all the way from Isaac to the one who is "away in a manger." It is all by faith that defies the world, faith that receives all kinds of impossibilities from the God who justifies, who raises from the dead, and who creates that which does not exist. The great roll call of the saints ends this way: "Yet all these, though they were commended for their faith, did not receive what was promised, since God had provided something better so that they would not, apart from us, be made perfect" (Heb. 11:39–40).

Their faith is made perfect in us! Now the miracle is entrusted to us!

Chapter 9

Prayer as Neighbor Love

In chapters 9 and 10 I will consider the twin themes of prayer and justice. I take these twinned themes to be decisive marks of the church in its contemporary call from God; at the same time, of course, these two evangelical disciplines are too often disputatiously presented as an either/or: either to leave things in the hands of the God whom we trust or to accept singular responsibility for the well-being of the world. In what follows, I will consider the ways in which these two evangelical disciplines are intimately and intrinsically bound together so that they need not be, in any of our heated ideological passions, rent asunder.

The twinning of these themes pertains to varied and immense questions for the church:

- It raises the question of the presence of the church in the public square, since some want to retreat from that public engagement and others want to impose theocratic claims on a pluralistic society.
- It raises the questions of piety and politics, since in modern times the church has mostly practiced a private piety with a silent conformity to dominant culture, wherein a more assertive piety is something of a scandal to the faithful—witness the aggressive condemnation by con-

servative Christians of other conservative Christians who recently have
acknowledged global warming.

- It raises the issue of the relationship between the internal life of the
  church vis-à-vis its external mission, the capacity to practice enough
  internal life to sustain the external mission.
- It raises to visibility the interface of conservatives and liberals, conservatives now who do not want to conserve but to impose and liberals who
  now do not want to practice liberality but only a shrill insistence. The
  interface invites to an alternative posture that is not driven by such blatant ideological absolutisms.
- It raises the issue of whether we shall divide the church in the United
  States between "red" and "blue," or whether *communion with God* and
  societal compassion for the neighbor might pervade the entire life of the
  church.

Thus, I consider that my reflection here may make a modest contribution to
the larger conflicted reality of the church as we think and pray and act together
in the church, somewhere between the urgency of *unity* and a passion for *purity*.

I.

The two themes of prayer and justice correlate, I suggest, with the two great
commandments. Jesus is asked, in rabbinic playfulness, "Which commandment
is the first of all?" (Mark 12:28). It may be a trick question; if it is, Jesus does
not fall for it. More likely it is a conventional exercise in weighing priorities
and passions. Jesus answers that you cannot have one great commandment; you
always get two.

Jesus answers readily out of the tradition, quoting from the familiar and
much used Shema: "You shall love the LORD your God with all your heart, and
with all your soul, and with all your might" (Deut. 6:5). He understands that
the covenantal tradition of Deuteronomy is utterly preoccupied with singular
loyalty to God, a singular loyalty voiced in the First Commandment.[1] It is clear,
moreover, that we *love God* by engaging in *communion in prayer*. Prayer is indeed
an act of loving God.

But alongside the quote from Deuteronomy, Jesus promptly adds a verse
from Leviticus 19, a chapter ironically enough placed between the now famous
sexual prohibitions of Leviticus 18 and Leviticus 20: "You shall not take vengeance or bear a grudge against any of your people, but you shall love your
neighbor as yourself: I am the LORD" (Lev. 19:18).[2]

We love our neighbor when we seek justice for our neighbor as we seek justice
for ourselves. At the end of chapter 19 concerning love of neighbor, moreover,
the text adds a more stunning exegesis of the same conviction: "The alien who
resides with you shall be to you as the citizen among you; you shall love the alien

as yourself, for you were aliens in the land of Egypt; I am the LORD your God"
(Lev. 19:34). You shall love the alien, the undocumented worker, as you love
yourself.

Thus, my argument in what follows is that prayer and justice correlate with
the two great commandments, *prayer as love of God, justice as love of neighbor.* In
this exercise, however, I will consider what happens if we reverse the correlation.
It occurs to me that we should not too readily slot things "toward heaven" and
"toward earth," precisely because the enfleshed character of our God suggests
that such categories be deconstructed. Thus, I ask that we

- see prayer as a way to love neighbor; and
- see justice as a way to love God.

This reversal is, to be sure, counterintuitive, but it strikes me as a way into the
deeper claims of biblical faith.

II.

The practice of prayer and the practice of justice are, in Israel, in the context of
covenant. As a consequence, we cannot begin with either prayer or justice but
must consider the prior, more elemental affirmation of covenant. The narrative
of the covenant at Sinai begins with the exodus, when the kingship of YHWH
is made effective (Exod. 15:18), when the powers of this age are overthrown
(15:4–10), and when Israel is set on a journey of liberty (15:14–17).[3] Whatever
Israel is able to do or to be in time to come is because of a destiny freely given
by YHWH and freely received by those who departed the empire.[4] Israel prays
and does justice in the context of covenantal freedom that is the gift of YHWH.

The covenant of Sinai brings Israel under new sovereignty. The core tradition
of the exodus-Sinai narrative concerns regime change; in this decisive regime
change wherein the incomparable YHWH is enthroned, everything is changed:

> "Who is like you, O LORD, among the gods?
>   Who is like you, majestic in holiness,
>   awesome in splendor, doing wonders?
> You stretched out your right hand,
>   the earth swallowed them."
>   Exod. 15:11–12

The only thing that matters now is learning to live with YHWH, who has power
to bring low and to exalt:

> The LORD makes poor and makes rich;
>   he brings low, he also exalts.
> He raises up the poor from the dust;
>   he lifts the needy from the ash heap,

to make them sit with princes
  and inherit a seat of honor.
For the pillars of the earth are the LORD's,
  and on them he has set the world.
                                                1 Sam. 2:7–8

The grounds for new life under the new regime are given in the *command-ments of Sinai*, commandments that have displaced and abrogated the commands of Pharaoh that required endless productivity (Exod. 5).[5] The intent of the Torah of Sinai is to bring every dimension of life—public and personal, civic and cultic—under the rule and supervision of the new regime. That is why the command of Deuteronomy 6:5 mentions "heart, soul, and strength." As a result, both prayer and justice are placed in the zone of YHWH's command to which Israel has assented.

The commands of Sinai, however, turn out not to be absolutist, unilateral, and monarchal; rather, they constitute a covenantal, interactive, dialogical enterprise.[6] As modeled by the chutzpah of Moses, Israel is a people not only *commanded* by YHWH but *entitled* by YHWH and, therefore, able to engage in contestation with the God of Sinai. Neither prayer nor justice is to be enacted in one-dimensional servility and conformity, no matter how transcended we imagine YHWH to be.

III.

The great models of prayer in ancient Israel, the ones who exercise courage for engagement with YHWH, are those who are members of the covenant community who act out of entitlement and seize the chance to speak in emancipated, dialogic tones. Thus Abraham, in the exchange with YHWH about Sodom, at least in one textual tradition, has YHWH "stand before him," as though YHWH must give an account of himself to Abraham. And Abraham, in a tone of reprimand, dares to say to YHWH, "Far be it from you to do such a thing, to slay the righteous with the wicked, so that the righteous fare as the wicked! Far be that from you! Shall not the Judge of all the earth do what is just?" (Gen. 18:25). And of course Abraham's question is not really a question, but a summons to the God who must now negotiate with Abraham concerning the future of Sodom.

Jacob, in his desperate claim to meet his brother, Esau, whom he has wronged, can appeal to YHWH with an enormous imperative petition: "Deliver me" (Gen. 32:11). Jacob makes his appeal, moreover, by quoting back to YHWH what YHWH had allegedly promised him, so holding YHWH to YHWH's promissory word: "Yet you have said, 'I will surely do you good, and make your offspring as the sand of the sea, which cannot be counted because of their number'" (Gen. 32:12).

More elaborately, Moses, in his determined resolve to ensure the well-being and safe passage of Israel, can urge YHWH to new action. For example, when

YHWH is ready to strike out against the company of Aaron, Moses intervenes in order to appeal both to YHWH's "image" and to YHWH's sworn oath in the book of Genesis:

> Why should the Egyptians say, "It was with evil intent that he brought them out to kill them in the mountains, and to consume them from the face of the earth?" Turn from your fierce wrath; change your mind and do not bring disaster on your people. Remember Abraham, Isaac, and Israel, your servants, how you swore to them by your own self, saying to them, "I will multiply your descendants like the stars of heaven, and all this land that I have promised I will give to your descendants, and they shall inherit it forever." (Exod. 32:12–13)

Likewise, in Numbers 11, when Israel is restless and without food, Moses remonstrates with YHWH and reminds YHWH of YHWH's obligation:

> So Moses said to the LORD, "Why have you treated your servant so badly? Why have I not found favor in your sight, that you lay the burden of all this people on me? Did I conceive all this people? Did I give birth to them, that you should say to me, 'Carry them in your bosom, as a nurse carries a sucking child,' to the land that you promised on oath to their ancestors? . . . If this is the way you are going to treat me, put me to death at once—if I have found favor in your sight—and do not let me see my misery." (Num. 11:11–12, 15)

Moses daringly plays brinkmanship with YHWH and calls the bluff of the unresponsive, delivering God.

In Numbers 14, Moses again reminds YHWH of YHWH's reputation and, like Jacob, quotes YHWH back to YHWH as a motivation for YHWH's alternative act of graciousness:

> And now, therefore, let the power of the LORD be great in the way that you promised when you spoke, saying,
>   "The LORD is slow to anger,
>   and abounding in steadfast love,
>   forgiving iniquity and transgression,
>   but by no means clearing the guilty,
>   visiting the iniquity of the parents
>   upon the children
>   to the third and the fourth generation."
>   Num. 14:17–18

The quote is from YHWH on the mountain in Exodus 34:6–7, and now YHWH is called to account.

Later on, King Hezekiah petitions YHWH to intervene for the sake of Jerusalem when the city is under Assyrian threat. The prayer is a complaint about the Assyrian threat that moves to petition, assuming that YHWH is ready and able to intervene effectively. But the ground of Hezekiah's petition is not about the suffering of or danger to Jerusalem. It is, rather, about YHWH's insecure pride and vanity. Thus, the key charge against the Assyrians is that they have "mocked" YHWH, thus humiliating YHWH before the nations and before the other gods.[7] The key petition in 2 Kings 19:19 is "So now, LORD our God, save us." Most interesting, however, is the motivation attached to the petition in verse 19: "so that all the kingdoms of the earth may know that you, O LORD, are God alone" (2 Kgs. 19:19). Like Moses before him, Hezekiah attends to YHWH's needs as an available patron and plays upon that need. The rescue of Jerusalem is a by-product of the rescue of YHWH's reputation as "God alone." YHWH must outmuscle the Assyrian gods, or at least so the prayer of the king assumes.

In his "lamentations," Jeremiah gets down and dirty with YHWH. It is clear in his final complaint (Jer. 20:7–13) that Jeremiah can be direct and assaulting against YHWH.[8] Before the prayer turns to trustful petition (vv. 11–12) and a doxology (v. 13), Jeremiah can tell the truth about YHWH's betraying fickleness toward him:

> O LORD, you have enticed me,
>   and I was enticed;
> you have overpowered me,
>   and you have prevailed.
> I have become a laughingstock all day long;
>   everyone mocks me.
>   Jer. 20:7

The utterance of the prophet is a vigorous contestation that, at the outset, YHWH is granted no exemption from challenge.

All of these prayers—and eventually the corpus of the lament and complaint psalms—draw YHWH into crises to show that something is at stake for YHWH in the needfulness of Israel that is voiced. In every case, there is an appeal to YHWH's self-regard and YHWH's need to live up to reputation and to previous commitment. These great agents of prayer are not intimidated in their exchange with YHWH. They approach YHWH with powerful expectation and with powerful insistence. When appropriate, they are properly deferential. But they judge that such deference is very often not appropriate, and so they run the risk of speaking otherwise.

IV.

I propose that in the Old Testament, prayer is *entitled dialogue* that is undertaken at some risk. In this regard, then, prayer is sharply distinguished from praise. Praise is an act where all attention is focused on YHWH and YHWH's splendor. Praise is designed to enhance YHWH's reputation and character, and consequently, such utterance is deflected from the needs of the one who offers praise. In prayer, by contrast, for all the "schmeicheling" of YHWH, attention in the big, demanding imperatives is focused on the need of the petitioner and is not primarily focused on YHWH. In prayer the need of the petitioner receives cosmic attention. Indeed, in prayer YHWH is asked to "step aside" and let identified, voiced need occupy center stage. There is a cosmic shift in the center of gravity in prayer; for an instant the petitioner may enjoy being the center of all holy attention.

Karl Barth has made two decisive points that help to assert the contrast of prayer and praise:

1. Prayer is "simply asking." Barth's rendition is clearly that asking is the most genuine act of praise and thanksgiving.[9]
2. "God does not act in the same way whether we pray or not. . . . Prayer exerts an influence upon God's actions, even upon his existence."[10]

This second point, of course, is a most astonishing statement for this theologian who so insisted upon God's "otherness." Barth increasingly came to see that God's otherness is in the service of others. Whatever we may say theologically, it is true that in times of acute need, even the most urbane among us finally appeals to a God who may hear and answer.

In his essay "Prayer," Barth comments on the final question of the Heidelberg Catechism.[11] Question 129 reads, "What is the meaning of the little word 'Amen'"? The answer: "Amen means: this shall truly and certainly be. For my prayer is much more certainly heard by God than I am persuaded in my heart that I desire such things from him."[12] The catechism then offers as supportive texts two citations:

> For in him every one of God's promises is a "Yes." For this reason it is through him that we say the "Amen," to the glory of God. (2 Cor. 1:20)

> Before they call I will answer,
>   while they are yet speaking I will hear.
>   Isa. 65:24; see 2 Tim. 2:13

Of this answer Barth comments, "God is not deaf, but listens; more than that, he acts. God does not act in the same way whether we pray or not. Prayer exerts an influence upon God's action, even upon his existence."[13]

Notice on all counts how different such prayer is from the voice of praise:[14]

* In praise, there is no asking, only wonder.
* In praise, God is not asked to change or to act or to move. Indeed, the great doxologies of Israel celebrate God's constancy; by contrast, Israel's petitions ask YHWH to commit a new act of faithfulness.
* In praise, there is no future act of YHWH asked or expected; all is already in hand.

There is no doubt that praise is an easier task in a modern secular environment. For taken by itself, praise moves in the direction of undifferentiated timelessness. No doubt that is part of the reason that the church is drawn to praise. It is also the case that the most conformist parts of the church are drawn to what are called "praise hymns," because they expect, await, and insist upon nothing.[15] They are contented with what already is.

Prayer, unlike praise, is the work of evoking new futures that have not yet been given by mobilizing YHWH's good power that can alone effect newness. Prayer knows and insists that without newness from God we are caught in a hopeless, closed system of death.[16] There are ideological reasons why the prayer of the church has become conformist and anemic. That is how the church prays when it succumbs to the despair of the world. In its faithful prayer, Israel refuses such despair and insists on the future to which YHWH is deeply pledged.

V.

In my pondering of prayer, I have been led to two texts that will relate prayer to the neighbor, whom we are commanded to love. The first is Luke 18:1–8, in which Jesus tells a parable about the need of the disciples to pray in order that they do not lose heart. In the parable there is a *widow* who seeks *justice*. She petitions the judge, who will not listen. But she keeps bothering him; she nags him to wear him out, and finally the "unjust judge" grants her petition in order that she should go away. It may interest us that in Jesus' instruction on prayer, the model is a *widow*, the exemplar in Israel of a vulnerable member of society who is without leverage or resource, and what she seeks in this narrative about prayer is *justice*. The story lacks specificity, but the main issues are clear. John Donahue comments, "The shock of the parable comes here, not in the exploitation of widows, which was common, but in her public and persistent cry for justice."[17]

In his interpretive comment on the parable, Jesus then continues to say that God will "grant justice" to his chosen ones who cry to him day and night (Luke 18:6–8). This prayer, as it is characterized in this instruction, is a vigorous assertion of covenant entitlement in the interest of securing justice in an unjust context from a God who is able to do justice.

It is remarkable that the introduction to the parable is about praying and not losing heart. Prayer is an antidote to losing heart, to despairing and losing hope, to settling for an unjust circumstance that must be endured because it cannot be changed. The quintessential prayer is on the lips of the widow who refuses despair but who has no recourse except to address God with a vigorous demand rooted in a sense of entitlement.[18]

This text in Luke pushes me back to an Elisha narrative in 2 Kings 8:1–6.[19] In this narrative a woman has lost her house and her field due to a famine-caused absence. She lost her property while absent. The NRSV says that she made "an appeal" to the king. The Hebrew is *sa'aq*, to "cry out." She issued a vigorous, urgent petition stating both her loss and her deep entitlement. The king, apparently because he was in the environment of Elisha the prophet, restores her property plus her lost revenue from the property.

The plots of the parable and of the royal narrative are strikingly parallel. In both cases the key player is a bereft widow; in both cases there is an injustice; in both cases there is an appeal to an authority who responds positively to the appeal; in both cases the voice of the petition is the voice of bereft entitlement that is respected and taken seriously. Donahue comments on the parable, but he might have had both texts in purview: "In the cultural context a woman would rarely, if at all, claim her rights by appearing constantly, and presumably alone, in public, raising a public outcry. . . . The situation of the woman could be one of life and death; she is faced with poverty and starvation if her rights are not respected."[20]

I have taken the plot of these two texts to be the quintessence of prayer:

- the voice of the socially disqualified;
- the assumption of entitlement that is vigorous even when "disqualified"; and
- a relentless and insistence public act of out-loud petition for redress.

And Jesus says, "Pray like that!"

VI.

Those two texts suggest to me, not surprisingly, that vigorous, insistent psalms of lament are the best representatives of prayer, for which I take Psalms 9–10 as a model.[21] The two psalms are, for good critical reason, frequently taken as a single articulation of faith.

Psalm 9:1–12 is a doxology of praise and thanksgiving to the God who sits enthroned in order to enact judgment (v. 7). Judicial imagery permeates the psalm. YHWH will adjudicate with righteousness and equity:

> The LORD is a stronghold for the oppressed,
>   a stronghold in times of trouble.
> . . . .
> For he who avenges blood is mindful of them;
>   he does not forget the cry of the afflicted.
>   Ps. 9:9, 12

It is the cry of the afflicted to which the judge attends, the same cry as that of the woman in 2 Kings 8 and the widow in Luke 18.

The petitioner states a need that reflects a conflicted society and speaks from a posture of vulnerability:

> Be gracious to me, O LORD.
>> See what I suffer from those who hate me;
>> you are the one who lifts me up from the gates of death.
>>> 9:13

The psalm continues to celebrate YHWH's act for the sake of justice:

> The LORD has made himself known, he has executed judgment;
>> the wicked are snared in the work of their own hands.
>>> 9:16

It is as though the verdict has been rendered that redresses affliction and oppression. But then in verse 19 it is as though the justice given in verse 16 is an old case; there is always a new case of injustice, always a new appeal that seeks redress:

> Rise up, O LORD! Do not let mortals prevail;
>> let the nations be judged before you.
>>> 9:19[22]

This petition to "rise up" suggests that this divine judge has been passive, dormant, or indifferent. It is the purpose of the petition to move the judge back into attentiveness about injustice.

Indeed, the summons to God continues in Psalm 10 with a suggestion that God has been remote:

> Why, O LORD, do you stand far off?
>> Why do you hide yourself in times of trouble?
>>> 10:1

And when the judge is indifferent and remote, injustice and economic exploitation readily prevail:

> In arrogance the wicked persecute the poor—
>> let them be caught in the schemes they have devised.
>>> 10:2

In the next verse, the lines of social analysis begin to converge:

> For the wicked boast of the desires of their heart,
>> those greedy for gain curse and renounce the LORD.
>>> 10:3

The "wicked" who face judgment are the "greedy" who are cynical about any theological-ethical restraint on their actions. Thus, the term "wicked" is not to be understood in our usual moralistic way. The indictment pertains to socioeconomic greediness that is socially legitimate but that does damage to the neighbor. Such damage can be enacted with impunity, moreover,

because the God of all justice is, for all practical purposes, denied. And here
that unbridled freedom permits the devouring of the neighbor in ways that
dominant culture approves and that economic practice would regard as legitimate. In the world of greed where there is no God, the poor are endlessly the
defenseless victim:

> Their mouths are filled with cursing and deceit and oppression;
>> under their tongues are mischief and iniquity.
> They sit in ambush in the villages;
>> in hiding places they murder the innocent.
> Their eyes stealthily watch for the helpless;
>> they lurk in secret like a lion in its covert;
> they lurk that they may seize the poor;
>> they seize the poor and drag them off in their net.
>>>> 10:7–9

It is no wonder that by verse 12 the psalmist echoes the summons to "rise up,"
already uttered in 9:19:

> Rise up, O LORD; O God, lift up your hand;
>> do not forget the oppressed.
>>> 10:12

That urgent imperative addressed to YHWH bespeaks an awareness that
YHWH has not yet appeared on the scene in effective ways. Such an imperative
likely could be issued only by the oppressed, who are resourceless in the face of
the ruthless God-deniers. Those less oppressed might care but would not feel the
raw, bodily urgency of life without a protective God. The imperative of verse 12
is followed by the demanding petition in verse 15. The conclusion of the psalm
may be read as an assurance that YHWH will redress the situation of danger or
as yet another petition. Either way, YHWH is now fully summoned to the task
of restorative justice:

> O LORD, you will hear the desire of the meek;
>> you will strengthen their heart, you will incline your ear
> to do justice for the orphan and the oppressed,
>> so that those from earth may strike terror no more.
>>>> 10:17–18

This psalm is a characteristic triangle to which the resourceless faithful cling
tenaciously:

- *The wicked* do not acknowledge God and so are free to exploit and
  oppress.
- *The poor and oppressed* are vulnerable and without resources.
- *YHWH* the God, when summoned, is capable of justice.

The entire transaction is a resolved effort to reshape the social transaction from a two-party to a three-party reality. Prayer is an attempt to alter the map of social power by appealing in *vulnerability* out of *entitlement* to the one who has a capacity to modify social reality. Such prayer is, of course, absurd to those in power—who deny God and are free to exploit—who imagine that social reality is a two-party affair.[23] To those without hope in the two-party affair, however, prayer is the court of last resort and final appeal. Those who speak such prayer do not mind committing an act that is judged absurd by dominant reason. It is this practice of prayer that dominates the life of Israel and the book of Psalms. Psalms 9–10 offers an acute but not atypical representation of this practice among the faithful.

VII.

Prayer characteristically is utterance in *need* out of *entitlement*. It is the voice of the needy poor who no doubt constituted a certain community of piety in ancient Israel. The needy petitioner is no doubt acutely concerned with his or her own trouble; the petitioners pray for themselves, daring to speak their need while in a society that refuses to notice need. These are the needy, vulnerable entitled who risk their voice and their precarious social position for the possibility of an altered future (risk of organizing a union, risk of undocumented workers in the streets). They address the one who has a capacity to alter the world in the way that social power was dramatically altered in the exodus narrative at the behest of the groans of oppressed Israel (Exod. 2:23–25).

The needy pray first of all for themselves. But they pray not only for themselves. In fact, such urgent prayer is a "class action suit." They pray for all needy, powerless poor. They go to court and bring their friends with them, making petition on behalf of all who suffer the same grievance in the same uncaring social system. It is not difficult to locate such "class action" utterances in the Psalter:

1. In Psalm 12:5, after a petition for YHWH's help, YHWH answers the prayer for the sake of all the poor:

> "Because the poor are despoiled, because the needy groan,
>   I will now rise up," says the LORD;
> "I will place them in the safety for which they long."

The response of YHWH concerns not only the petitioner but all who are represented in the petition.

2. In Psalm 35:10, the speaker speaks for himself and "all my bones":

> All my bones shall say,
>   "O LORD, who is like you?"

But then the same utterance moves beyond self to all the others in like circumstance:

> "You deliver the weak
>> from those too strong for them,
>> the weak and needy from those who despoil them."

3. In Psalm 82, the high God of the divine court addresses the lesser gods with a mandate that is the defining mark of Godness:

> Give justice to the weak and the orphan;
>> maintain the right of the lowly and the destitute.
> Rescue the weak and the needy;
>> deliver them from the hand of the wicked.
>> Ps. 82:3–4

The rhetoric concerns no particular individual; God here has in purview all of the denied class who are cut out of social power and social access: the weak, the orphan, the lowly, the destitute, the needy—all those preyed upon by "the wicked" who preside over a rapacious political economy.

4. Psalm 109 is the most aggressive assault on such exploiters. In verse 22 the psalmist identifies himself sociologically, perhaps with a tinge of self-pity:

> For I am poor and needy,
>> and my heart is pierced within me.
> I am gone like a shadow at evening;
>> I am shaken off like a locust.
> My knees are weak through fasting;
>> my body has become gaunt.
> I am an object of scorn to my accusers;
>> when they see me, they shake their heads.
>> Ps. 109:22–25

No doubt the venom of the psalm reflects an intimate experience of raw abuse. The psalmist does not stay within the limits of self, but extends the urgency to others like himself:

> For he did not remember to show kindness,
>> but pursued the poor and needy
>> and the brokenhearted to their death.
>> 109:16

The accused did not show kindness "to me." But in fact the accused did not show kindness to any of "us," any of us poor and needy. Thus, in the prayer the self stands in solidarity with many others for whom the petition to YHWH is addressed. It is a petition for *self*, while at the same time inescapably intercession at the court for *others*.

Such prayer is quite personal and is rooted in particular social pain. But such prayer is knowingly communal. The poor person who prays in this way knows that there is no "private prayer," because the social reality to be addressed concerns many needy persons who stand together in the solidarity of abuse—widows, orphans, immigrants—all of whom are in the same dilemma. A prayer of one is perforce the prayer of the social class, for all are vulnerable, all are without resources, all are entitled—even if all do not find voice. Such prayer, characteristically, is against the "enemy," who is situated at the center of a legitimate social system of uncaring. On occasion, such prayer also spills over against YHWH, when YHWH is carelessly allied with established power and so does not hear and will not act. It is the wager of such prayer that YHWH can be summoned away from such an alliance into solidarity with the petitioners who intercede. That bet, of course, is the whole point of going to court.

VIII.

By following the text, I have myself been surprised to reach the conclusion that prayer is the voice of the *needy* that are *entitled* and able to *cry out* in negating circumstance. Thus, I entertain the notion, given some interpretive leeway, that all prayer must be understood in terms of social need, and that it requires social analysis and social criticism in order to understand theologically what we are doing in prayer. This way of thinking about prayer, I believe, coheres with the prayers of Abraham, Jacob, Moses, Hezekiah, and Jeremiah that I have cited. It coheres, moreover, with Karl Barth's cryptic "Just ask." No prayer is in a social vacuum; for that reason no prayer is innocent or disinterested.[24] Such a judgment about prayer leads me inescapably to this question: What of the prayers of the well-off, if such prayers are, according to political economy, screened off from the poor and the needy?[25]

My thesis is that the well-off, led by way of the Psalter, are summoned by the tradition to move past themselves in order to join the prayer of the needy, to go with those urgent petitioners to court as a friend of the court in order to intercede with the judge. Thus I imagine, in the narrative of Elisha, readers are invited to stand alongside the bereft woman who seeks recovery of her house and her field (2 Kgs. 8:1–6). And in the parable of Jesus, the listening disciples are invited to stand alongside the importunate widow before the judge as she seeks justice (Luke 18:1–8).

I state the matter in this way because, faithful to the Psalter, it is clear that the risk of prayer is cast, characteristically, in judicial language—just what one would expect if the subject matter is justice; it is the court of YHWH that can enact justice for its petitioners (see Ps. 82). When the well-off have no urgent claim to file for themselves, they are asked to join the claims that have urgency to them and that must be filed. They are asked to use privileged friendship with the court in order to gain a hearing for those who lack such easy access in court.

Thus, the social map of prayer includes the vulnerable entitled petitioner, the friend of the court who joins in intercession before the judge, and the real judge who is capable of ruling effectively. The assumption of the transaction is that social power is indeed supple and malleable; things need not remain as they are. Such a possibility, however, requires vigorous petition and authoritative intercession.

There are, of course, seductions in the prayers of the well-off, powerfully suggested in the parable of Luke 18:9–14 that follows immediately after the parable of the importunate widow that I have cited. In the second parable, the Pharisee prays a prayer of self-congratulation, a celebration of social status that is marked by class distinction. I could think of three such seductions amid the prayers of the well-off. First, the well-off are seduced away from a cry for justice by excessive *praise*, which may be sung without the cry. Such prayer amounts to an affirmation of the status quo. It is likely that the "surplus" of praise in the Psalter derives from the Jerusalem temple liturgy, the worship of the urban elites. In such context, the cries of the poor are not likely to be voiced loudly.[26] Second, the well-off are seduced away from the cry for justice by excessive preoccupation with *guilt*, a sense of failure in covenant, a sense that protects against noting the failure of God or the failure of the system over which God presides. Third, the well-off are seduced away from the cry for justice in *trivializing petition* for a life already gifted and well ordered, so that prayer at most expects God to "tweak" an already good arrangement.

In the Psalter, against such temptations to excessive *praise*, excessive *guilt*, or *trivialization*, the well-off, like the needy, are called to love the neighbor. We may do so by intercession, a forceful cry for justice on behalf of the entitled needy. Such a practice of prayer, of course, would make even the worship of the well-off a place of uneasy contestation, a contestation that is undertaken everywhere in the prayers of Israel.

IX.

The flow of my argument is to insist that prayer—the voice of the needy who are entitled but vulnerable, along with their friends—concerns "the weightier matters of the Torah: justice and mercy and faith" (Matt. 23:23). Unless prayer is understood as love of neighbor, love of neighbor in need to whom mercy is to be shown (Luke 10:37), it is likely to fall into "nice prayer" that is bewitched by "the therapeutic" and that issues in rhetorical splendor without the confrontive dimension of contestation and disjunction. There is no doubt that the common tradition of church prayer fails not only in large life-or-death imperatives, but that it fails in the abrasion of rhetoric of contestation. Such failures likely reflect the domestication of the church and its loss of nerve when it subscribes to dominant cultural reason. By contrast, the laments of Israel as primal and characteristic acts of prayer offer a rhetoric of *contestation and expectation* that moves in a juridical direction. Such voiced contestation is not one-dimensional;

it is offered in compelling artistry that is rich in imaginative phrase and image. That artistry is designed to communicate to all those engaged in prayer—God, neighbor, self—that the world is in dispute, that the vulnerable entitled cannot afford rhetoric that is polite and therapeutic, that the world is indeed available for contestation. Change is needed and is expected, even required.

It is plausible to suggest that the introduction to the exodus narrative, an introduction surely patterned after the Psalms, may be a defining notice to us about prayer. In that narrative, after a long historical account in which God is not a player, the text reports that "the Israelites groaned under slavery, and cried out" (Exod. 2:23). The cry is not addressed to anyone in particular; it is just raw human pain that cannot be kept silent. That cry, we are told, "rose up to God." Indeed it would, for the God of Israel is the magnet that draws to itself all voiced pain.[27] That voiced pain—for self and for neighbor—is an act of covenantal brinkmanship. It summons God to see, to hear, to notice, to act. It is a bid that YHWH should be YHWH's true self, so unlike the other gods who are immune to the cry, indifferent to pain, and deaf to need. There is, inescapably, a threat to YHWH in such prayer, a threat grounded in covenant and risked in entitlement. To be sure, the slaves that cry out in Exodus 2 have not yet been to Sinai to make a covenant. But they have been in such a relationship long before in the book of Genesis and in the ancestral narratives, where YHWH has promised attentive presence.[28] Behind that, moreover, all of those slaves and the many other vulnerable persons were present the day after the flood when the covenant of rainbow was enacted (Gen. 9:8–17).[29] Since that moment, all such creatures have been entitled by their very existence to a life better than oppression. For that reason, the cry is deep. The God who hears and answers is the God of Abraham, Isaac, and Jacob. But that God who hears is the creator God, attentive to the creatures, all of those who cry when pain impinges.[30] The human vocation is to cry, matched, so the story goes, by the listening God of all pain.

X.

Prayer as a cry for justice is real prayer, a spiritual act addressed to a real God who hears. While it is real speech by real people in real hurt addressed to God, it is a public act. For that reason, the transaction spills over into the public realm, whereby the *rhetoric of prayer* inescapably becomes *political talk*. The test of the linkage of pain and political talk is the fact that every such vigorous, concrete prayer is sure to evoke political feedback of a hostile kind from those committed to the status quo. Such prayer—in addition to not being "nice" and therefore socially unacceptable—is immediately recognized as subversive of present power arrangements. I cite three elements of prayer that functions as spilled-over public talk.

First, Gerald Sheppard has proposed that in such vocal triangulation prayers, including the prayers of the ones I have cited, are designed to be overheard by "the wicked enemy" in a way that gives the petitioner leverage and legitimacy and that might lead to the cessation of such harmful wrongdoing.[31]

Second, a model for such cries of justice addressed to God performed as political talk are the prayers conducted by Martin Luther King Jr. and other civil rights leaders. Characteristically before a march of protest or demonstration began, the participants knelt in prayer, which they offered before hostile police officers and resentful sheriffs. There is no doubt that such prayers were serious prayers, for the moment was deeply rooted in the faith claims and practices of the church. But there is also no doubt that at the same time such prayers were transformative theater.[32] They were addressed to God; they were also addressed to the media in order to gain public support; and they were no doubt addressed as well to hostile police forces and witnessing crowds in order to evoke shame for such resistance to justice. Such prayers are not an either/or but always a both/and, always genuine prayer and political stratagem. The same was surely true in the ancient world of the Psalter. The prayers are not "mere prayers," but public statements of alternative social possibility. In such utterance of prayer following the Psalter, the church might be aware of such "surplus" in its prayer that is indeed an act of neighbor love.

Third, James Boyd White has published a compelling book on public speech. As a constitutional scholar, he is interested in the First Amendment guarantee of free speech. But his argument is that "free speech" that only practices "the marketplace of ideas" is likely to be speech that is pandering and designed to offer gratification, as does the market, to a variety of desires. Beyond "free speech," White studies and celebrates the importance of "living speech," by which he means public talk that is substantive, seriously located in concrete community, and engaged with foundational ideas of social justice and well-being. His book explores a variety of examples of living speech that run from Dante and Shakespeare to Supreme Court opinions. His most interesting examples, in my view, are higher court opinions that support speech that lower courts have ruled illicit. Thus, White considers as living speech the court ruling on Paul Cohen, who used an obscenity in public to protest the draft for the Vietnam War (*Cohen v. California*), and its ruling on a labor organizer who undertook union organizing that a state court ruled as illegal (*Thomas v. Collins*).[33] In both cases, White shows how the court protected public speech that subverted dominant control but that was in the interest of human justice.

My purpose in citing White is to observe that in the end White concludes that it is a cry for justice received by the court that constitutes the most elemental dimension of living speech:

> The lawyer's belief is not in law as a mechanical system but in what can be done with it, sometimes at least, by an engaged and open mind, alone and with others. The lawyer knows that the language of the law will not work automatically in the world to realize the will or intention of the legislature or any other legal authority. Every case is new, and presents an opportunity to imagine it in new ways; to this end one calls upon other ways of talking,

other languages, new perceptions and understandings, and one's own experience of life. Every case presents an opportunity for the judge or lawyer to call his reader into a fuller life of thought and imagination and feeling, all with the object of achieving justice—not for all time, but for this time, in the knowledge that in the next case it will have to be done again. The lawyer and judge live out of the belief that they can, that we can, create the world anew when we speak, making real for the moment the possibilities of love and justice. . . . This is a vision of the world, and of the law, not as a mechanistic system that can be reproduced in language, reshaped, manipulated, and so forth, all to achieve something called the goals of the system, but as itself a source of life, infinitely renewable. In the end, the belief of the lawyer and judge in the possibility of justice, and love, is a belief in the possibility that they themselves can be called into life by the world—by another person, by a problem—and that they in turn can call others into life.

To resist the empire of force one needs to believe in the possibility of both love and justice, and believe it not merely as a general matter but in one's own writing. One needs to believe, that is, that one's own formulations can actually offer an experience of justice and love, in the way they define and talk about other people; and that they can also, correspondingly, commit what deserves to be called injustice, expressing not love for another person, or for what is most deeply characteristic of the human being, but the opposite—a kind of hatred, or erasure, or denial.[34]

Such a judgment on White's part indicates how much a discernment of engaged judicial rhetoric is closely paralleled to prayer in the Old Testament. In both cases it is a cry for justice. We may marvel about such a parallel between contemporary judicial attentiveness and ancient cries of justice. We may also marvel, with less elation, that the church has largely forgotten the "living speech" that has been entrusted to it.

XI.

I finish with three conclusions. First, good prayer is genuinely interactive, a covenantal transaction between lively engaged partners. Sometimes the prayer is only a raw cry; more often the prayer seeks to show that something is at stake for YHWH as well as for the petitioner. This is especially evident in our much-used cliché, "for thy name's sake . . . for Jesus' sake." These habitual formulas attest that what is asked by the needy entitled, when granted, will enhance YHWH's reputation. This is the ground of Moses' petition in Numbers 14:13–19. The same point is vividly made in two other passages:

- In Isaiah 48:9–11, YHWH speaks in the first person, acknowledging that restorative action for Israel is for YHWH's sake (au. emph.):

  For my name's sake I defer my anger,
      for the sake of my praise I restrain it for you,

> so that I may not cut you off.
> See, I have refined you, but not like silver;
>   I have tested you in the furnace of adversity.
> *For my own sake, for my own sake*, I do it,
>   for why should my name be profaned?
> *My glory* I will not give to another.

- In Ezekiel 36:22, 32, YHWH explicitly denies concern for Israel as a motivation for generous restoration:

> Therefore say to the house of Israel, Thus says the Lord GOD: It is not for your sake, O house of Israel, that I am about to act, but for the sake of my holy name, which you have profaned among the nations to which you came. . . . It is not for your sake that I will act, says the Lord GOD; let that be known to you. Be ashamed and dismayed for your ways, O house of Israel.

These texts show how answered petition benefits the court that makes the ruling for justice. The court is enhanced by such a compassionate, attentive ruling!

My second conclusion is that Job may be taken as a model petitioner. Claus Westermann has shown how Job's "speeches" are in fact laments.[35] These protests stand in the tradition of the Psalms, but here the rhetoric is pushed to extremity. In the end, Job is celebrated by YHWH as one who has spoken "what is right" (Job 42:7–8). What is "right" apparently is the *truth of need* on the *lips of the entitled* in the face of injustice, which in the book of Job is given cosmic scale.

Finally, James Kugel has summarized the biblical argument about the *cry to God* and the *readiness of God* to hear and answer: (1) God is obligated to hear the cry: "It says that hearing the victim's cry is a god's duty and God's duty. It says that if that job is not properly performed, the very foundations of the earth will shake."[36] (2) The cry is taken seriously as a valued constitutive element in the practice of daily life:

> After all, the world is what it is. Why should biblical texts keep saying that it is so different from what it appears to be—that, in the case at hand, God hears the cry of the victim, when so often He apparently does not? Certainly it would have been possible, within the framework of ancient Israelite religion, to maintain the opposite and say that this all-powerful God is quite inscrutable. Sometimes He listens, sometimes He doesn't. There would scarcely be any less reason to worship Him and seek His favor—and of course, such a view of God would seem to better fit everyday reality. Or if that path was, for some unknown reason, unacceptable, then why not simply pass over the issue of innocent suffering in silence—why keep coming back to the cry of the victim when it was only a potential source of embarrassment? The answer, it seems to me, must be that it was not a source of embarrassment. Somehow, the everyday world did not flash "Disconnect" when the subject of the victim's cry came up. Exactly why or how is far from clear, but certainly the fact itself is worthy of consideration.[37]

(3) God's character is constituted by attentiveness to such cries:

> Now, what God actually says to Moses about His being merciful is really
> not news—as we saw in Psalm 82, it was simply any god's job to be com-
> passionate and merciful, and this truth was so universally assumed in the
> Bible that, as we have seen, it underlies the dozens of passages that speak
> of the victim's cry. Yet here, in Exodus, this cliché is presented as a revela-
> tion. God's ultimate self-revelation to Moses: I am by nature [gracious and
> compassionate] (despite all evidence to the contrary). I hear the cry of the
> victim: I can't help it.[38]

Given that defining character of God, how can we do less than stand in
solidarity with neighbors, issuing on their behalf an *entitled petition*? From this
primal act in court, there are, of course, many derivative ways to love the neighbor, incidental acts, sustained strategies, and policy formation. All derive, for the
faithful, from prayer as the quintessential act of neighbor love.

Chapter 10

Justice as Love of God

In chapter 9 I proposed that prayer is the quintessential act of neighbor love. It is an act of standing in solidarity before the court of truth and summoning God to stand in solidarity with you for the sake of the neighbor. As the importunate widow nagged the judge to give justice, so we are to be importunate widows on behalf of that widow and all her ilk (Luke 18:1–8).

That leaves for consideration the second half of our theme: *justice* as *love of God*. That formulation, of course, is as counterintuitive as my first argument, because on the face of it justice might be readily taken as love of neighbor. I would not resist such a judgment but would suggest that the counterintuitive reversal of corollaries lets us see more in the biblical tradition.

In what follows, I shall argue that love of God is not primarily a "religious act," as it might be in some other interpretive traditions. In the tradition of Deuteronomy from whence comes the great commandment to love that Jesus quotes as the first great commandment (Deut. 6:5; Mark 12:30), love of God is faithful, responsible participation in the political economy where God has shown God's self to be present (as in the exodus event) and where God is clearly preoccupied in the corpus of commandments in Deuteronomy.[1] This divine engagement in the political economy is not an add-on to covenantal faith; it is, rather, the real substance of faith that has eventuated in the great interpretive tradition of the credo.[2]

In that great founding tradition of Israel's faith, YHWH is linked to the political economy. Those who would love God must engage themselves in the political economy:

- The *exodus narrative* is the revolutionary overthrow and termination of a political regime that was organized against the neighborhood in rapacious modes.
- The *covenant at Sinai* is nothing less than regime change wherein the will of YHWH is embraced as alternative to the will of Pharaoh: "For they are my servants, whom I brought out of the land of Egypt; they shall not be sold as slaves are sold" (Lev. 25:42).
- The *commandments of Deuteronomy* characteristically—not exclusively but characteristically—concern a neighborly polity. For good reason, Jeffries Hamilton and Moshe Weinfeld regard the provision for the "year of release" as the epitome of Deuteronomic command (Deut. 15:1–18).[3]
- *Prophetic oracles*, both the speeches of judgment and oracles against the nations, concern exactly the will of YHWH in contestation with every other will that is propelled by self-aggrandizement under a variety of ideological pretensions.

In all these traditions, *love of God* is being responsibly engaged in the *body politic*. It is for compelling reason that Karl Barth conducted a sustained polemic against "religion"; what he meant by "religion" is characteristically an escape from the more demanding engagement in the arena of public power, where neighbor may be diminished or enhanced, brought low or lifted up.

I.

Thus, we have for our second theme an odd triad: (1) *love*, an affective desire;[4] (2) *God*, guarantor of cosmic order; and (3) *justice*, guaranteeing and meting out what is deserved for every creature. When these elements are brought into juxtaposition with each other, the several items are transposed to become what they were not:

- Love as affective desire becomes covenantal solidarity as a pattern of mutual obligation and commitment.[5]
- God as guarantor of cosmic order becomes one who presides over the political economy of the earth.
- Justice as meting out what is deserved becomes rehabilitating distributive practice of shared resources.

What had been a conventional arrangement now becomes "thick" with relational engagement due to the peculiar passion of this God who is to be loved by Israel. Love of God is now fidelity to and participation with the Lord of covenant solidarity; such a God, such a people, and such a practice constitute a remarkable alternative to the acquisitiveness of Pharaoh.

II.

YHWH, the God of covenantal solidarity, is a lover of justice. Who could doubt that defining propensity of the God of Sinai and the God of Zion?

- It is this God who intervened against Pharaoh's injustice precisely because YHWH willed a better future for "my first-born son" (Exod. 4:22).
- It is this God who provides Torah guidance and guarantees pertaining to the "quadrilateral of vulnerability"—widows, orphans, immigrants, the poor.
- It is this God who dispatches the prophets with sustained strictures against exploitation, who issues demanding summons to reengage the justice questions, and who, through visionary poetry, imagines an alternative social reality of well-being.
- It is this God, so the wisdom traditions attest, who creates the world according to *Gerichtigkeit*, to an ordered wholeness that gives life for all:

> Yahweh and the world order are related to one another in their initial distinctiveness. In this relationship, the world order does not appear as good, wise, glorious, and righteous by virtue of its own potential. But it has the qualities and the efficaciousness of the goodness, wisdom, glory, and righteousness of Yahweh, who is present in it as its creator. Because of Yahweh's presence, the world order was considered to be intact; and in this intactness, Yahweh was experienced as cosmically present in everyday reality. The intactness of the world order is not a matter of abstract cosmological theory. It is a fact of experience in exactly those realms of cosmic, natural, and cyclic stability to which all creatures owe their sustained existence. It was intensely perceived, understood, and celebrated. It was the reason for much of Israel's hymnic praise of Yahweh. Inasmuch as the world order revealed goodness, wisdom, glory, and righteousness, it also revealed Yahweh's presence in the world in an ultimate way, and did so more directly than human history ever could.[6]

YHWH's primal commitment to justice is tersely affirmed in Israel's poetry:

> Mighty King, lover of justice,
>   you have established equity;
> you have executed justice
>   and righteousness in Jacob.
>   Ps. 99:4

The verb indicates that *mišpaṭ* is YHWH's core commitment and primary devotion. In a poem that envisions Israel's restoration and well-being, the verb "love" is offered in a participle:

> For I the LORD love justice,
>> I hate robbery and wrongdoing,
> I will faithfully give them their recompense,
>> and I will make an everlasting covenant with them.
>>   Isa. 61:8

This portrayal asserts that YHWH loves justice all the time, a most characteristic and recurring practice.[7] It is not immediately clear what the antecedent is of the "them" to whom YHWH makes promises. In the end it is commitment to Israel, who is taken here to be a doer of the very justice to which YHWH is pledged. The Israelites are the ones who are invited into "everlasting covenant."

In Isaiah 59:8–11, the poetry of indictment and hope utilizes the term "justice" three times (au. emph.):

> The way of peace they do not know,
>> and there is no *justice* in their paths.
> Their roads they have made crooked;
>> no one who walks in them knows peace.
> Therefore *justice* is far from us,
>> and righteousness does not reach us;
> we wait for light, and lo! there is darkness;
>> and for brightness, but we walk in gloom.
> We grope like the blind along a wall,
>> groping like those who have no eyes;
> we stumble at noon as in the twilight,
>> among the vigorous as though we were dead.
> We all growl like bears;
>> like doves we moan mournfully.
> We wait for *justice*, but there is none;
>> for salvation, but it is far from us.[8]

In verse 8, "justice" is parallel to "shalom." In verse 9, the same term is parallel to "righteousness," and in verse 11 it is parallel to "save." Thus, "justice" becomes, in this poetry, the term around which cluster all of the other great terms of this defining relationship that pertains both to YHWH's transformative passion and to Israel's responsive obligation.

These verses in Isaiah 59 are a prayer on the lips of Israel, who waits for justice knowing that justice is YHWH's primal agenda in the world, an agenda that intends justice for Israel. Verses 14–15, moreover, recognize that where justice is not practiced, everything unravels as well (au. emph.):

> *Justice* is turned back,
>> and righteousness stands at a distance;
> for truth stumbles in the public square,
>> and uprightness cannot enter.

> Truth is lacking,
>   and whoever turns from evil is despoiled.
>
> The LORD saw it, and it displeased him,
>   that there was *no justice.*

Specifically, absence of justice is twice mentioned and is connected to the absence of truth, whether taken as truth-telling or as reliable relationship. Either way, injustice leads to the unraveling of the social fabric. The lament and petition of Israel confidently affirm that YHWH is passionately committed to a viable infrastructure of a political economy that binds together weak and strong, poor and rich, needy and self-sufficient. It is YHWH's ultimate desire that the world should be a healing neighborhood. In Isaiah 59, Israel speaks as a community of returning exiles. In its bid for such a neighborhood, it acknowledges that there now is no such neighborhood; it sets about the construction of such a neighborhood, which is the primal agenda of newly formed Judaism.

III.

It is not surprising that Moses' core mandate to Israel in Deuteronomy, which is taken to be the core obligation of Judaism, is expressed as love of YHWH and love for the things of YHWH: "Hear, O Israel: The LORD is our God, the LORD alone. You shall love the LORD your God with all your heart, and with all your soul, and with all your might" (Deut. 6:4–5).[9]

Observe four obvious but important dimensions of this text. First, it is a command to love YHWH in every dimension of life. The word "love" surely has *affective* dimensions, but it also moves to covenantal agreements and mandates that are *legal* and *elemental*. It is, of course, that way in any abiding relationship of love. Along with affective devotion, there must very soon be commitment and performance of the important matters that concern the beloved. Without the performative obedience to match affect, the relationship turns to a simple infatuation or sours away.

Second, the opening imperative is "to hear"—to listen, to pay attention, to heed, to do "what I say." It is a term used by impatient and exhausted parents: "I don't know why you don't listen!" As Jews have understood so much better than Christians, the imperative of YHWH is not to a feeling, but it is to act, to do. Indeed in Exodus 24:7, as the rabbis have long noted, the covenant oath of Israel at Sinai in response to the Decalogue is "All that the LORD has spoken we will do and hear." It is taken by the rabbis as crucial that *do* precedes *hear*. We listen and hear through concrete acts of obedience. Following the rabbis, moreover, John Calvin declared, "All right knowledge of God is born of obedience."[10] Everything depends upon active, performative listening.

Third, the opener is to *hear* and to *love*, to love by hearing, but the specificity concerns "these words which I am commanding you"—that is, the Torah. The way to love YHWH (whom we have not seen) is to obey Torah. In the context of Deuteronomy 6:5, moreover, the way to love YHWH is by keeping the Torah requirements of Deuteronomy, which feature first the Decalogue of 5:6–21 but then the long interpretive commentary on the Decalogue in chapters 12–25. Unlike the commands that are given in a priestly manual in Leviticus, the Torah commands of Deuteronomy are addressed to the whole community and concern the infrastructure of the political economy, that is, the neighborhood.[11] Israel is to love God by loving the neighborhood and the neighbor. Israel is to love God whom it has not seen by loving the neighbor whom it has seen and the neighborhood in which it lives (1 John 4:20–21).

Fourth, Deuteronomy 6 continues to accent YHWH's peculiar passion for the political economy among the young. That is, the educational task for loving God and obeying the first great commandment is urgent:

> Keep these words that I am commanding you today in your heart. Recite them to your children and talk about them when you are at home and when you are away, when you lie down and when you rise. Bind them as a sign on your hand, fix them as an emblem on your forehead, and write them on the doorposts of your house and on your gates. (Deut. 6:6–9)

Recite and interpret the commands everywhere, all the time, in order that the young shall be inculcated into the continuing communal act of loving YHWH by way of the neighborhood. I have termed this "saturation education" so that the young should be in no doubt about the primal commandments of the parental generation.[12]

That educational process is reiterated in Deuteronomy 13:4, a characteristic Deuteronomic sequence of verbs in which obedience to YHWH and to YHWH's Torah is urgent and defining for Israel. The verbs have to do with reliability, loyalty, and performative obedience: "The LORD your God you shall follow, him alone you shall fear, his commandments you shall keep, his voice you shall obey, him you shall serve, and to him you shall hold fast."[13] The sequence of verbs—follow, fear, keep, obey, serve, hold fast—binds Israel to YHWH's central passion, the one who does justice. The inverted word order keeps YHWH visible and up front in the requirement.

It is neither possible nor necessary to exegete in a full way that mandate as it is played out in the tradition of Deuteronomy. It is useful nonetheless to supplement the simple mandate by enough data to show that *performance in the neighborhood* is the central concern of this set of commandments.

The "year of release" is commonly taken as *a* if not *the* core command of Deuteronomy (15:1–18). This provision requires Israel to cancel debt on poor people after six years in order that there should be no permanent underclass. I note five elements of this command that indicate that love of God is no easy or convenient matter.

1. The command includes five "absolute infinitives," the odd grammatical usage in Hebrew wherein the verb is reiterated in order to communicate intensity: diligently observe (v. 5), willingly lend (v. 8), open (v. 8), give liberally (v. 10), provide liberally (v. 14). This cluster of verbs in the "absolute infinitive,"

more I think than anywhere else in Scripture, indicates the urgency and centrality of this command.

2. Israel is enjoined to keep practicing this year of release, because there are
always poor people who need relief:

> Since there will never cease to be some in need on the earth, I therefore
> command you, "Open your hand to the poor and needy neighbor in
> your land." If a member of your community, whether a Hebrew man or a
> Hebrew woman, is sold to you and works for you six years, in the seventh
> year you shall set that person free. (Deut. 15:11–12)

3. Israel is assured that if the commandment is practiced, the devastating reality of a permanent underclass can be prevented:

> There will, however, be no one in need among you, because the LORD is
> sure to bless you in the land that the LORD your God is giving you as a pos-
> session to occupy, if only you will obey the LORD your God by diligently
> observing this entire commandment that I command you today. (15:4–5)

4. Israel found the commandment grossly inconvenient and did not
want to obey, did not want to forego economic advantage for the sake of the
neighborhood:

> Be careful that you do not entertain a mean thought, thinking, "The sev-
> enth year, the year of remission, is near," and therefore view your needy
> neighbor with hostility and give nothing; your neighbor might cry to the
> LORD against you, and you would incur guilt. (15:9)

5. The motivation for this commandment, in the face of such predictable
resistance, is exactly the naming of the exodus, indicating that the indebted poor
are, in the economy of the land, yet again subjected to something like pharaonic
enslavement (15:15). Indeed, the indebted poor are always like the Egyptian
slaves, and among them YHWH is always as YHWH was in Egypt, prepared
with an imperative directive, "Let my people go," let them go of indebtedness
back to a viable economic life by the generous management of death.[14]

The "quadrilateral of vulnerability" is front and center to the commands of
YHWH in the tradition of Deuteronomy; the welfare of these vulnerable people
must be a concern and obligation of wealthy Israel. Thus, Moses issues a series
of "welfare reforms" that Frank Crüsemann terms the first social safety net in
history, a social provision for those without resources, a social provision made
possible in concrete ways by the modest curbing of acquisitive economics:[15]

> When you reap your harvest in your field and forget a sheaf in the field, you
> shall not go back to get it; it shall be left for the alien, the orphan, and the
> widow, so that the LORD your God may bless you in all your undertakings.
> When you beat your olive trees, do not strip what is left; it shall be for the
> alien, the orphan, and the widow.

> When you gather the grapes of your vineyard, do not glean what is left;
> it shall be for the alien, the orphan, and the widow. Remember that you
> were a slave in the land of Egypt; therefore I am commanding you to do
> this. (24:19–22)

Of course, the provision about grain, olives, and grapes is not particular to those crops, but it intends to establish a principal that the productivity of creation is abundant enough for *us* and *others*, for the owner-producer class and for those who do not own and who perhaps do not produce.

This provision has an important history in economics. It was the "law of enclosure" in a German state that provoked Karl Marx's first publication when he protested over the decision to keep the poor from foraging in the manor estates.[16] Michael Polanyi, moreover, has traced the great transformation in modern economics to the passing of laws of enclosure in Britain in the eighteenth century that made the operation of the economy the great enemy of the neighborhood.[17] It is not a difficult claim to assert that YHWH loves the neighborhood and intends that the economy be organized for the sake of the neighborhood.

Beyond the two great commandments on *release* and *surplus* in Deuteronomy, I also mention that there is a series of terse commands in Deuteronomy 24 that speak of justice for the poor as YHWH's passion in quite concrete ways:

- concerning no interest on loans (23:19);
- concerning property taken as collateral from the poor (24:10–13); and
- paying day laborers promptly (24:14–15).

It is not easy for us to see how such requirements pertain to a postindustrial economy. But then it was not easy in ancient times to see how the commands pertained to that of an agricultural community. The problem, as we interpret these commandments, is not the lack of pertinence of these commandments. Rather, the problem is a failure of political will, because it requires political will to love YHWH more than we love mammon, an old matter of divided loyalty among us.

IV.

The covenant agenda of the book of Deuteronomy lines out for us *YHWH's core love for justice* and renders *Israel's core work of neighborhood constitution and maintenance* as performance of what the beloved cherishes most. From that covenant agenda of Deuteronomy, we are able to understand more fully the prophetic summons in Israel to the "weightier matters of the Torah . . . justice, mercy, and faith" (Matt. 23:23, au. trans.). There are, to be sure, acute critical problems about relating the prophetic materials to the traditions of Deuteronomy, for it may be that Deuteronomy is later and is dependent upon and derivative of prophetic traditions. There can be no doubt, nonetheless, that in canonical rendition it is Deuteronomy that provides the linkage between *the commands of Sinai* and *the prophetic materials*, a linkage that is accomplished with great imagination through a complex traditioning process. After mentioning a pivotal text in Deuteronomy, I cite three prophetic texts.

1. Deuteronomy 10:17–20, a text in the mouth of Moses, adumbrates all that is to come in the prophetic corpus. The text begins with a doxological characterization of YHWH, perhaps a formulation that belongs to the high liturgies of the Jerusalem temple:

> For the LORD your God is God of gods and Lord of lords, the great God, mighty and awesome, who is not partial and takes no bribe, who executes justice for the orphan and the widow, and who loves the strangers, providing them food and clothing. (Deut. 10:17–18)

The doxology, as the premise for what follows, begins with YHWH's awesome transcendence and asserts YHWH's primacy in the world of the gods, presiding with awesome authority over the council of all the gods and all the lords. The doxology then moves abruptly to social engagement, a move that is characteristic of the biblical God, one celebrated in Christian tradition through the descent of God into human form.

The remarkable claim made for YHWH is not YHWH's sovereign splendor, but the assertion that YHWH acts unlike the alternative capricious gods. It is this God alone who will not be partial and who will not take bribes from those most capable of offering bribes. It is this God who stands in solidarity with orphans, widows, and strangers, those who are not capable of offering bribes (10:17–18). YHWH does not *receive* from these vulnerable members of the community, but *gives* to them. The concreteness of YHWH's gift to the powerless is astonishing—food and clothing! Indeed, "Your heavenly father knows that you need all these things" (Matt. 6:32)!

In verse 19, the text shifts from affirmation of God to mandate for Israel: "You shall also love the stranger, for you were strangers in the land of Egypt" (Deut. 10:19). The mandate picks up the word "stranger" from verse 18. YHWH attends to the *stranger*, you attend to the *stranger*, you were *strangers* in Egypt.[18] The motivation for the mandate, as so often in Deuteronomy, is the exodus. What is remembered as a great, miraculous deliverance in Egypt is now the model that is to be replicated in the daily economic life of Israel. As YHWH reached out beyond the familiar to the slaves in Egypt, so now Israel is to reach out beyond the familiar to those "unlike us."

The text culminates with a bid for exclusionary passion. Israel is to rely *only* on YHWH: "You shall fear the LORD your God; him alone you shall worship; to him you shall hold fast, and by his name you shall swear" (10:20). But the "onlyness" of YHWH is for Israel a direct object of loyalty. YHWH is an object of loyalty mediated through the presence of the needy. Care for the needy is the way in which Israel fears, worships, holds fast, swears. This mode of reasoning, deep in the old covenant traditions, is of course echoed in the later, more familiar texts:

> Then the righteous will answer him, "Lord, when was it that we saw you hungry and gave you food, or thirsty and gave you something to drink? And when was it that we saw you a stranger and welcomed you, or naked and gave you clothing? And when was it that we saw you sick or in prison and visited you?" (Matt. 25:37–39)

The divine answer to the question makes the connection that does not change:

> And the king will answer them, "Truly I tell you, just as you did it to one of the least of these who are members of my family, you did it to me." (25:40)

The answer persists, moreover, to those "at his left hand":

> Then he will answer them, "Truly I tell you, just as you did not do it to one of the least of these, you did not do it to me." And these will go away into eternal punishment, but the righteous into eternal life. (25:45–46)

This connection is at the root of the covenant tradition. There is indeed no other way to love God except to perform YHWH's central passion, the way in which one performs all of our central loves, by doing the things cherished by the beloved. In the case of YHWH, what is cherished, simply and demandingly, is passion for the needy, powerless stranger who images the strangeness of YHWH, always a contemporary mandate for the stranger among us.

2. In Amos 5:4–15, a more familiar passage, the prophet issues a sustained summons to Israel to change its way before it is too late. It is not likely that the primary tradition of Amos is informed by Deuteronomy, but the assumptions are surely covenantal. The theme that it is "very late" for the self-indulgent, consumer-driven Israel pervades the textual tradition of Amos:

> Alas for those who lie on beds of ivory,
>   and lounge on their couches,
> and eat lambs from the flock,
>   and calves from the stall;
> who sing idle songs to the sound of the harp,
>   and like David improvise on instruments of music;
> who drink wine from bowls,
>   and anoint themselves with the finest oils,
> but are not grieved over the ruin of Joseph!
>   Amos 6:4–6

That indictment that evokes the smell of death ends with a "therefore" of awesome danger to that society:

> Therefore they shall now be the first to go into exile,
>   and the revelry of the loungers shall pass away.
>   6:7

The poetry is an indictment for self-indulgence before which justice issues have characteristically evaporated. What interests us here is the summons to do justice, suggesting that a reversal of policy and conduct could avert disaster. In the long poem of Amos 5:4–15, the poet issues five imperative summonses that build to a remarkable climax. At the beginning of the poem are two summonses that sound like a call to worship:

> Seek me and live.
> . . . .
> Seek the LORD and live.
> . . . .
> Ah, you that turn justice to wormwood
>   and bring righteousness to the ground!
>   5:4, 6

Then there are intervening verses that indict—you trample the poor, you take bribes, you push aside the needy (vv. 11–12)—and then more imperatives: seek good and not evil, hate evil and love good, establish justice in the gate.

The sequence of imperatives is remarkable because it moves from "seek me" in verse 4 to "establish justice" in verse 15. These two imperatives form an inclusio around the other three imperatives. The intervening material consists in a doxology asserting YHWH's awesome power (vv. 8–9) and an indictment against injustice (vv. 10–12). The inclusio would suggest that YHWH and justice are intimately related or, as we may dare imagine, they are equated in the poetry so that establishing justice is the visible, concrete, required form of seeking YHWH. This inclusio in Amos is an early and characteristic judgment that is recently and belatedly made by Jacques Derrida that deconstruction is justice:

> 1. The deconstructibility of law (*droit*), of legality, legitimacy or legitimation (for example) makes deconstruction possible. 2. The undeconstructibility of justice also makes deconstruction possible, indeed is inseparable from it. 3. The result: deconstruction takes place in the interval that separates the undeconstructibility of justice from the deconstructibility of *droit* (authority, legitimacy, and so on).[19]

Justice is the truth against every false claim that must be exposed, just as YHWH, the God of Sinai, is the truth that exposes all idols. In the context of Amos or Derrida, we may use a hyphen to say that "YHWH-justice" is the bottom line beyond which one cannot go. YHWH is known in and in answer to neighborly *praxis*. It is for that reason that Amos mocks conventional worship in Israel by a phony call to worship at the two great shrines:

> Come to Bethel—and transgress;
>   to Gilgal—and multiply transgression;
> bring your sacrifices every morning,
>   your tithes every three days;
> bring a thank offering of leavened bread,

and proclaim freewill offerings, publish them;
for so you love to do, O people of Israel!
says the Lord GOD.

4:4–5

And then come verses that refuse these centers of phony religion:

. . . but do not seek Bethel,
and do not enter into Gilgal
    or cross over to Beersheba;
for Gilgal shall surely go into exile,
    and Bethel shall come to nothing.

5:5

Love of YHWH is the performance of justice.

3. Just after Amos comes Micah. I refer to his best-known text:

He has told you, O mortal, what is good;
    and what does the LORD require of you
but to do justice, and to love kindness,
    and to walk humbly with your God?

Mic. 6:8

This famous triad concerns justice, steadfast love, and a humble walk with God—however that last phrase is to be translated. The triad concerns both *love of YHWH* and *love of neighbor* and therefore is rightly taken as a powerful summary of prophetic faith. For our purposes, it is important to notice that the triad of faithful disciplines is set in contrast to a series of valued and seductive commodities:

"With what shall I come before the LORD,
    and bow myself before God on high?
Shall I come before him with burnt offerings,
    with calves a year old?
Will the LORD be pleased with thousands of rams,
    with ten thousands of rivers of oil?
Shall I give my firstborn for my transgression,
    the fruit of my body for the sin of my soul?"

6:6–7

In this list, even one's firstborn son is a valuable commodity available for an economic transaction. The poet offers a transposition of categories, away from *commodities* to *relationships* that are demanding, obligatory, and community sustaining.

The contrast that focuses upon right relationships with YHWH and with neighbor (justice and steadfast love) calls to mind the rebuke of Psalm 50, wherein YHWH refuses commodity transactions but instead calls for actions of gratitude and dependence:

If I were hungry, I would not tell you,
    for the world and all that is in it is mine.
Do I eat the flesh of bulls,
    or drink the blood of goats?
Offer to God a sacrifice of thanksgiving,
    and pay your vows to the Most High.
Call on me in the day of trouble;
    I will deliver you, and you shall glorify me.
                        Ps. 50:12–15

4. A century after Amos and Micah, Jeremiah 22:13–19 moves in the same direction. The poetry castigates Jehoiachim and the royal enterprise in Jerusalem (vv. 13–15) and imagines the death of the king who, in his failure, will not be grieved (vv. 18–19). Between the castigation and the dismissal of Jehoiachim as a king who betrayed his tradition and his office, verses 16–17 contrast Jehoiachim with his father, Josiah, who is reckoned in Deuteronomic circles to be "the good king":

Did not your father eat and drink
    and do justice and righteousness?
Then it was well with him.
                    Jer. 22:15b

Josiah is celebrated and affirmed as a Torah keeper. As Torah keeper, he did justice and righteousness (the same word pair used in Amos 5:7 to indict), and therefore he prospered. Josiah is an exemplar of the Deuteronomic requirement of performance of Torah and blessing, a connection made in places such as Psalm 1. But then verse 16 becomes more specific about justice and righteousness:

He judged the cause of the poor and needy;
    then it was well.
Is not this to know me?
    says the LORD.
                    22:16

The most remarkable claim is the rhetorical question "Is not this to know me?" Knowledge of God, that is, covenantal solidarity, is exactly justice for the poor and the needy. The poetry does not say that performance of justice will result in knowledge of God; the poetry does not say that knowledge of God will result in justice. Rather, it equates the two so that YHWH here, as in Amos 5, is given in neighborly praxis. Love of YHWH is doing justice; this is how we know, this is how we commune.[20]

The sum of these texts makes clear that the prophetic tradition unpacks the Mosaic mandate of love of God toward communitarian justice.

V.

Now I want to change direction and push behind these core claims of covenant in order to suggest a quite particular linkage to our time and place, a time and place overflowing with anxiety because the world as we have known it is falling apart. We may ask about YHWH whom we are to love: Who is this YHWH who loves justice and who brings the world—and the political economy—to well-being?

The answer surely is this: *YHWH is the unanxious Creator* who faces into the recalcitrant reality of chaos and the recurring threat of injustice and who presides over the coming order of justice and *shalom*. The connection between mandates for justice and celebration of the Creator is an important connection in our time when we are so preoccupied with order—and disorder—that we mute the justice question. The accent for what follows is on *unanxious*, and to that end I cite six texts.

1. In Psalm 2:2–4, we have a second introduction to the Psalter after the Torah accent of Psalm 1. The psalm lines out the rebellious state of the world, wherein the kings of the earth resist the rule of YHWH. In this psalm, YHWH is reported not as angry at such resistance, but only amused:

> The kings of the earth set themselves,
>   and the rulers take counsel together,
>   against the LORD and his anointed, saying,
> "Let us burst their bonds asunder,
>   and cast their cords from us."
>
> He who sits in the heavens laughs;
> the LORD has them in derision.
> Then he will speak to them in his wrath,
>   and terrify them in his fury, saying,
> "I have set my king on Zion, my holy hill."
>
> Ps. 2:2–4

YHWH is not threatened by the surging disorder of the nations. The psalm has been mostly noted among us for its unmistakable "messianic" note in verse 7. My point, however, is that the Creator is not threatened by nations at war. God will rule, and the world is safe.

2. Psalm 46 is widely known, perhaps most especially among Lutherans for the derivative "Ein Feste Burg." It was the psalm that we used in our seminary over and over after 9/11, an assurance that the world will hold because it is held by the creator God who is undisturbed by threat:

> Therefore we will not fear, though the earth should change,
>   though the mountains shake in the heart of the sea;
> though its waters roar and foam,
>   though the mountains tremble with its tumult.
>
> There is a river whose streams make glad the city of God,
>   the holy habitation of the Most High.
> God is in the midst of the city; it shall not be moved;
>   God will help it when the morning dawns.
>
> Ps. 46:2–6

The threats are real, but the threats do not happen outside the purview of YHWH's governance. YHWH's commanding voice matters decisively, and the world is safe. It may be that this psalm is simply ideology for urban elites in ancient Jerusalem, but after them the faithful have found the poem a credible assurance in a world under assault.

3. In the great creation psalm, 104, eventually the doxology must come to terms with the primordial threat of Leviathan, the seething power of nothingness. In its confident doxology, Israel can dare to say,

> Yonder is the sea, great and wide,
> creeping things innumerable are there,
> living things both small and great.
> There go the ships,
> and Leviathan that you formed to sport in it.
> Ps. 104:25–26

The evil sea monster, like the nations in Psalm 2, is a source of amusement for the Creator, who is unanxious about the apparent threat.

4. From that taming of Leviathan, I mention the ode to Leviathan in Job 41:1–11. In the midst of YHWH's admiration for this most extreme creature—just a creature and not a threat—God asks rhetorically:

> Who can confront it and be safe?
> —under the whole heaven, who?
> Job 41:11

Who indeed? No one! No human creature! No human creature in aggressive hubris. Carol Newsom observes the congruence between Leviathan and YHWH, a congruence that may lead to the awareness that no human partner can challenge YHWH, the creator God, even as Leviathan is not to be challenged.[21] The effect is to assert that surging chaos (Leviathan) is in fact a witness to the ultimacy of YHWH before whom human strength, human pride, human aggression, or human anxiety constitutes a fraudulent irrelevance. The world, as Leviathan knows and trusts, will be had on YHWH's terms.

5. We may ask—given the seething of disorder that produces anxiety, a seething heretofore embodied by Leviathan who has now become YHWH's creaturely ally—what does the Creator do amid a creation that is as yet not fully tamed? And the answer is, God rests. God rests serenely without anxiety, knowing that the world that YHWH has blessed will hold, will be fruitful, will give and sustain life:

> And on the seventh day God finished the work that he had done, and he rested on the seventh day from all the work that he had done. So God blessed the seventh day and hallowed it, because on it God rested from all the work that he had done in creation. (Gen. 2:2–3)

The creation liturgy that began in Genesis 1:2 with "formless void" now is at peace. The Creator is indeed unanxious about the future of the world.

6. The Creator is not anxious, but in at least one text the Creator is *weary*:

> Therefore the Israelites shall keep the sabbath, observing the sabbath throughout their generations, as a perpetual covenant. It is a sign forever between me and the people of Israel that in six days the LORD made heaven and earth, and on the seventh day he rested, and was refreshed. (Exod. 31:16–17)

"Was refreshed" is a translation of the *hiph'il* of *nephesh*. YHWH was "re-nepheshed," as the work of creation had exhausted YHWH's *nephesh*.[22] For that reason, Sabbath is the quintessential mark of creation. Creation is an antidote to endless, anxious restlessness.

VI.

I offer six texts:

- Psalm 2:2–4, in which the Creator is amused by rebellion;
- Psalm 46:2–6, in which the Creator is unmoved by the roaring and foaming of chaos;
- Psalm 104:26, in which the Creator is at play with Leviathan;
- Job 41:1–11, in which the Creator, like Leviathan, is beyond challenge;
- Genesis 2:2–3, in which the Creator, alongside creation, is at rest; and
- Exodus 31:17, in which the Creator is refreshed.

These texts taken together testify to an unanxious Creator. My purpose in this riff on the Creator is to suggest that Israel knows about the unanxious Creator and is invited at Sinai to imitate the Creator, to keep Sabbath, to pause to acknowledge, in a bodily unanxious way, that the world will hold without our feverish efforts at control.

My thesis is this: Anxiety about self-securing the world is the root cause of aggressive injustice against which prophetic faith testifies. This anxiety is a feverish attempt at more production, more consumption, and more accumulation at the expense of the neighbor, all the way from personal eagerness to the global chase for more oil. The outcome is that the entire globe is kept in turmoil.

Being *unanxious* is the taproot of *justice*, for being unanxious is to break the grip of production and consumption. Sabbath is a sign of being unanxiously in the world, unworried about the world and our place in it. This imitation of God's Sabbath, I propose, is the precondition of justice in the world. For that reason, the Sabbath stands at the center of the Decalogue at Sinai as an invitation to unanxiousness that turns out to be, perforce, an invitation to justice:

> Remember the sabbath day, and keep it holy. Six days you shall labor and do all your work. But the seventh day is a sabbath to the LORD your God;

> you shall not do any work—you, your son or your daughter, your male or
> female slave, your livestock, or the alien resident in your towns. For in six
> days the LORD made heaven and earth, the sea, and all that is in them, but
> rested the seventh day; therefore the LORD blessed the sabbath day and
> consecrated it. (Exod. 20:8–11)

The whole creation and all creatures are to be at rest. Israel is to be at rest like the
Creator. The world, from Sabbath on out, is ordered by God—and by Israel—to
oppose frantic, neighbor-using practices that produce injustice. It is clear in the
commandment that even in a focus on creation, Moses cannot forego the neighbors, slaves, and strangers.

That neighborly accent is even more directly underscored in the second version of the Decalogue. In Deuteronomy 5, here the neighbor has come front
and center:

> But the seventh day is a sabbath to the LORD your God; you shall not do
> any work—you, or your son or your daughter, or your male or female slave,
> or your ox or your donkey, or any of your livestock, or the resident alien
> in your towns, so that your male and female slave may rest as well as you.
> (Deut. 5:14)

Of the phrase "as well as you," Hans Walter Wolff comments, "*Kamoka*—'just
like you'! Thus the commandment about the day of rest inaugurates a position of
equality for all men before God. On this day at least parents should stop giving
orders to their sons and daughters, let alone their subordinates."[23]

Sabbath is the day of social equity, the curbing or cessation of exploitation
of the laboring class by the monied class.[24] On Sabbath, the anxious race to
get ahead is curbed by the disciplines of rest. In that rest, we may fall back into
the reliability of the Creator and the abundance of creation. The command in
Deuteronomy 5:12–15 concludes, "Remember that you were a slave in Egypt."
The dominant memory of Egypt in Israel is the memory of Pharaoh, the ultimate producer and the ultimate consumer, the one who had everything, but
along with everything had nightmares of famine and scarcity (Gen 41:1–7).
Pharaoh could never have enough! And now Sabbath—counter to pharaonic
anxiety—is reengagement with the exodus, one more dramatic departure from
the relentlessly aggressive political economy. Sabbath is a walkout from anxiety
that includes all the neighbors, even the ones unproductive, incompetent, and
therefore undeserving. All are released and relieved in the day of God's serene
freedom that is replicated in the Sabbath practice of God's people.

VII.

Unanxious people, in response to the Lord of the exodus who is also the creator
of abundance, act differently and make justice possible.

Deuteronomy 15:1–18 is concerned with the year of release—seven days and seven days and seven days, and then seven years, a time to cancel debts on poor people because the neighborhood cannot be sustained by exploitative financial leverage: "Remember that you were a slave in the land of Egypt, and the LORD our God redeemed you; for this reason I lay this command upon you today" (Deut. 15:15).

Leviticus 25:1–15. After seven days and seven years and seven years and seven years come forty-nine years and the jubilee of fifty: "The land shall not be sold in perpetuity, for the land is mine; with me you are but aliens and tenants" (Lev. 25:23). The land will rest in Sabbath, and the poor will rest in Sabbath:

> If any who are dependent on you become so impoverished that they sell themselves to you, you shall not make them serve as slaves. They shall remain with you as hired or bound laborers. They shall serve with you until the year of the jubilee. Then they and their children with them shall be free from your authority; they shall go back to their own family and return to their ancestral property. For they are my servants, whom I brought out of the land of Egypt; they shall not be sold as slaves are sold. (Lev. 25:39–42)

It is always about the exodus and the overthrow of the kingdom of aggressive anxiety.

Amos 8:4–6. But the unanxious quality of the Sabbath is not easy to maintain or even easy to bear. When we are totally inured in the narrative of production and consumption, we can hardly bear to be at ease without an effort at controlling productivity. This is not a new issue, for Amos already saw it happening. People could not wait for the sun to go down on Sabbath in order to rejoin the exploitative rat race:

> Hear this, you that trample on the needy,
>   and bring to ruin the poor of the land,
> saying, "When will the new moon be over
>   so that we may sell grain;
> and the sabbath,
>   so that we may offer wheat for sale?
> We will make the ephah small and the shekel great,
>   and practice deceit with false balances,
> buying the poor for silver
>   and the needy for a pair of sandals,
>   and selling the sweepings of the wheat."
>   Amos 8:4–6

The craving is that the Sabbath be suspended or ended early. When enthralled to the market, we would rather cease to imitate the God of rest and be free to assault the neighbor, the poor neighbor, for a pair of shoes.

Isaiah 56:3–6. When the community of Israel was reorganized after the exile there was, predictably enough, dispute over membership—who was in, who is qualified, who was to be excluded. In these verses from Isaiah there is an urging that genuine outsiders—foreigners and eunuchs—should be admitted to the community. For that admission, the only specific stipulation is Sabbath keeping. The test of admission is readiness to engage in a life that is unanxious, that is not propelled by pharaonic modes of social relationships of injustice. It is a small leap, moreover, from Isaiah 56 on Sabbath to Isaiah 58 on the "fast" that is to "loose the bonds of injustice" (Isa. 58:6). From its new beginning, Judaism hopes to be a community of rest-filled justice that is an alternative to the seething disordered society all around.

VIII.

I finish with three texts about loving God.

1. In Psalm 73, the psalmist ponders the seductive world of the cynical pursuit of commodity (vv. 2–14). But then, in a visit "to the sanctuary" (v. 17), the psalmist comes to his senses and realizes that his true love, his single desire, is communion with the God of covenant:

> Whom have I in heaven but you?
> And there is nothing on earth that I desire other than you.
> Ps. 73:25

The psalmist is like the prodigal son; he comes to himself. And when he comes to himself, he comes to YHWH. He departs the cynical pursuit of commodity and rests his life in devotion to God, who is his refuge.

2. In Psalm 27, the psalmist acknowledges his fear and anxiety but stays focused on the utterly reliable YHWH:

> The LORD is my light and my salvation;
>   whom shall I fear?
> The LORD is the stronghold of my life;
>   of whom shall I be afraid?
> Ps. 27:1

The psalm ends in waiting:

> Wait for the LORD;
>   be strong, and let your heart take courage;
>   wait for the LORD!
> 27:14

Waiting is not a common practice among the anxious. It is a habit among those who know that the world as God's creation is a safe place for genuine life. Our society, in its fearfulness, pursues the fever of injustice, believing that if we can trump the neighbor economically we shall be safe. But the people of God—the ones who practice a trusting creatureliness—know better. We know better because we have entered into God's Sabbath rest and refuse the fever of anti-neighborliness. And when we so refuse, the unanxious God of restful justice is pleased, and the angels rejoice.

3. Jesus invited his disciples to follow him out of Egyptian anxiety. He said to them, "Do not be anxious"—do not participate in the anxiety of a craven world about food, clothing, life (Matt. 6:25). He contrasted that kind of Sabbath serenity with Solomon (v. 29), who is the quintessential practitioner of anxious, aggressive injustice in the Old Testament. Then Jesus aligns his disciples with the quintessential Torah act of Sabbath: It is Gentiles—those outside the sphere of Torah serenity—who strive for all this stuff in unanxious, unjust ways.

To be a "Gentile" is to fall outside the restfulness that comes with loving God. To be in faith is to act in the way of the "sevens"—seven days, seven years, seven times seven years—in order to transform the neighborhood, to subordinate the political economy to a fabric of neighborliness. It is the summons of the Shema in Deuteronomy 6:4–5 that obedience to Torah situates the unanxious on the seventh day, a competent serenity that prevails for the next six days in the practice of the economy. Such love of God makes a new world possible, a new world glimpsed in everyday realities of restful neighborliness.

Chapter 11

Prayer and Justice as Disciplines of Identity Maintenance

We are considering the ways in which *prayer* and *justice* are intimately connected in the practice of biblical faith. In chapters 9 and 10, I proposed a correlation with the two great commandments of Mark 12:28–34:

- *Prayer as neighbor love* through vigorous acts of solidarity before the court of mercy
- *Justice as love of God* by performing in the world that which God loves most

I.

In Mark 12:28–31, the conversation partners of Jesus—the scribes, the ones most learned in the Torah—asked him what must have been a favorite question: "Which commandment is first of all?" One can see, in the current ideological wars in the church, why the question is an important one. How we answer that question tends to give shape to all the interpretation that follows. Thus, the answer that Jesus will give is an important one.

He answered readily by reference to Deuteronomy 6:5: "Love the LORD your God with all your heart, and with all your soul, and with all your mind, and with all your strength." But then immediately, without pausing or taking a breath, he continued by reference to Leviticus 19:14: "You shall love your neighbor as yourself." They had asked him for the single most important commandment, the one that would control all subsequent interpretation. But by his answer, he changed their question. He refused to give one commandment and therefore to establish absolute interpretive clarity. You cannot, he said, have "one great commandment." You get two; they come together and are inseparable. You cannot choose between God and neighbor, for the two loves are a single love. You cannot choose *prayer without justice* as a conservative temptation; nor can you choose *justice without prayer*, a liberal seduction. Justice and prayer belong together. Conservatives might be tempted to pray and to leave it all to God. Liberals might imagine that God has no hands but ours. Prayer and justice go together; conservatives and liberals need each other. We need each other in the great ecumenical conversation because the two commandments cannot be separated; neither can be taken without the other.

It occurs to me that Jesus' answer—"two for one"—introduces a playful interpretive responsibility. Were there only one great commandment, one could arrive at an authorized, or even authoritarian, interpretation. There are two that belong together, but they belong together in less than clear ways. That fact introduces a dimension of the indeterminate in our interpretation. We can never arrive at "the right way" of relating the two commandments to each other; we are left with an open-ended, unresolvable interpretive task.[1] This is perhaps the great vexation of the church, but it is also the impetus for further work. In the mainline Protestant ecumenical movement, for example, the interface of the two commandments has been generative for the structural interrelatedness of "Faith and Order" and "Life and Work,"[2] an interrelatedness that is undoubtedly indispensable even though it has become formulaic in the movement.

II.

These two defining acts of obedience have been decisive for shaping canonical reflection on covenantal responsibility. First, the command to *love God* alone has eventuated in the summons to *holiness*: "Speak to all the congregation of the people of Israel and say to them: You shall be holy, for I the LORD your God am holy" (Lev. 19:2). That mandate, moreover, has given impetus for the holiness traditions of Leviticus that are committed to the maintenance of purity as a necessary prerequisite for God's presence amid the community. Second, the command to *love neighbor* has eventuated (in the covenantal traditions of Deuteronomy) in radical requirements for the shaping of the political economy. These two defining disciplines of faithfulness are profoundly countercultural and must be enacted with great critical intentionality.

Clearly, dominant culture is not into prayer that bespeaks dependence, that openly petitions in need, and that eventuates in gratitude. In our dominant culture, popular prayer has become a vehicle for an ideology of self-congratulation that is rarely an act of glad, yielding submissiveness to a will other than our own. Clearly, dominant culture is not open to the practice of neighborly justice, especially if it is inconvenient or if it is costly to one's personal acquisitiveness. Indeed, in our society the primary enactment of justice is of a "law and order" variety that functions to keep "have-nots" in their disadvantaged place and to keep immigrants out of "our place."

Popular embrace of either commandment in dominant culture may keep the letter of the command. But the generous and God-centered intention of the command most often is seriously violated in order to sustain dominant values that are notably anticovenantal, antineighborly, and "without God in the world." For that reason, the commands are a summons to an alternative obedience, just as ancient Israel at Sinai was marked as a priestly kingdom and a holy nation, and just as the early disciples were called to an alternative obedience that is the way of the cross.

Both Israel and the church are called to a *distinct identity*, an identity made evident in both *the talk* of narrative specificity and *the walk* of concrete praxis. Thus, prayer as a way of loving neighbor and justice as a way of loving God are not simply specific acts of faith and obedience, but together they constitute an identity that persists over time. That peculiar identity stands distinct in the world, free from the deathly identities of a society that embraces neither prayer as neighbor love nor justice as love of God.

III.

That distinct identity both evokes and arises from the formation of a counter-community whose life exists to bear witness to life outside the dominant culture. This is an enormous challenge in much of the established church that has been allied with dominant culture and that has accepted its role in the maintenance and legitimization of that dominant culture.[3] The interface of the disciplines of prayer and justice raises profound ecclesial issues.

First, in these twinned acts of prayer and justice, the church engages in activity that is inherently subversive. The church is informed, authorized by, and operates from a *sub-version* of reality that intends to *subvert* dominant culture by its very existence. While such a formulation may strike us as rather grandiose, it is clear that even the local congregation—in its practices of generosity, compassion, forgiveness, and solidarity with "the least"—is definitionally and intrinsically subversive. Much of the time the church has been unable or unwilling to perceive itself in this way, even though the cadences of baptism make the point unmistakably clear each time we sprinkle or immerse and recite the promises.

Second, in these twinned acts of subversion, the church is summoned to impact the public sphere by its insistence that the Holy God to which it testifies is Lord not only of the religious community, but the larger civic community. The church knows the riddle of "rendering to Caesar" and also knows that in the end nothing is to be rendered to Caesar (Mark 12:13–17). In a less intense and direct way, the public community is called to the reality of Divine Providence that persists. Thus, the claim of faith is that in the public realm, the purposes of God are relentlessly, even if covertly, at work, and cannot finally be outflanked. Of course, every civic society imagines, even as the urban elites in ancient Jerusalem imagined, that such hidden workings of Divine Providence can be overcome:

> At that time I will search Jerusalem with lamps,
>   and I will punish the people
> who rest complacently on their dregs,
>   those who say in their hearts,
> "The LORD will not do good,
>   nor will he do harm."
>
> Zeph. 1:12

But such complacency, in the horizon of prophetic poetry, characteristically leads to the enactment of divine reality, albeit through passive verbs:

> Their wealth shall be plundered,
>   and their houses laid waste.
> Though they build houses,
>   they shall not inhabit them;
> though they plant vineyards,
>   they shall not drink wine from them.
>
> 1:13

Third, the twinned disciplines of prayer and justice are modes of gospel proclamation that announce regime change in the world, regime change that in prophetic imagination is taken to be certain, even if not visible. I cite three gospel assertions of regime change, capped by the ringing anticipation of the apocalypse.[4]

In *Isaiah 40:9–11*, the good news to exiles is "Here is your God"—here even though the Babylonians had driven YHWH from the scene, and even though the exiles had, for the most part, accepted Babylonian versions of reality (au. emph.):

> Get you up to a high mountain,
>   O Zion, *herald of good tidings*;
> lift up your voice with strength,
>   O Jerusalem, *herald of good tidings*,
>   lift it up, do not fear;
> say to the cities of Judah,
>   "Here is your God!"
>
> 40:9

In *Isaiah 52:7*, the same gospel to the same exiles in the midst of the same empire asserts the news that YHWH is newly enthroned and lord and sovereign (au. emph.):

> How beautiful upon the mountains
>   are the feet of the messenger who announces peace,
> who brings *good news*,
>   who announces salvation,
>   who says to Zion, "Your God reigns."

The formula "Your God reigns" can, following Sigmund Mowinckel, also be taken as "Your God has just become king," just in this hidden moment of over-riding the force of the empire.[5]

The initial declaration of Jesus in *Mark 1:14–15* is surely intended to be an echo of the exile-ending assertion of Isaiah just cited:

> Now after John was arrested, Jesus came to Galilee, proclaiming the good news of God, and saying, "The time is fulfilled, and the kingdom of God has come near; repent, and believe in the good news."

It is clear, as the gospel narrative unfolds, that Jesus is remembered as enacting regime change, one leper and one widow at a time.

That good news, characteristically, is announced to a particular community—of exilic Jews or of disciples. But the news pertains to the larger community, whether Babylon or Rome or any more contemporary empire that, as a socioeconomic system, imagines itself invincible. Regime change happens as alternative agents chip away at legitimacy and eventually deny the self-confidence of the empire. In the end, of course, the anticipation of regime change is frontal and wholesale:

> Then the seventh angel blew his trumpet, and there were loud voices in heaven, saying,
>
> "The kingdom of the world has become the kingdom of our lord and of his Messiah,
> and he will reign forever and ever."
>
> Rev. 11:15

Such a sweeping anticipation, however, is rooted in daily, concrete practices that await the coming of new power for life:

> And he answered them, "Go and tell John what you have seen and heard; the blind receive their sight, the lame walk, the lepers are cleansed, the deaf hear, the dead are raised, the poor have good news brought to them." (Luke 7:22)

The linkage of *the sweep* of Revelation 11:15 and *the concreteness* of Luke 7:22 is precisely the linkage that valorizes daily acts of ministry and mission, daily acts that in sum constitute an alternative way in the world.

IV.

The twinned disciplines of prayer and justice, as acts of glad obedience to an alternative vision, concern the maintenance and celebration of a distinct alternative identity amid imperial definitions of reality. The act of prayer and the act of justice are out-loud gestures that assert an embraced identity and assert a refusal to conform to dominant reality.

It is clear that Jews have always lived amid empire and have had to sustain a distinct identity.[6] Very often the work of distinct identity done by Jews has been in the face of imperial homogeneity that sought to crush such communal distinctiveness as the Jews practiced. Many examples from the long history of Jewishness could be cited. In the Old Testament itself, it is the crisis of Antiochus IV Epiphanes in the second century BCE that dramatically exhibits the risk and daring of Jewish identity. In the narrative of Daniel 1:1, to cite a dramatic case in point, Daniel and his Jewish friends sign on for civil service in the empire of Nebuchadnezzar, the Babylonian king now become a cipher for every brutalizing regime. The narrative in Daniel 1 is no doubt designed both to encourage a peculiar Jewish identity and to instruct on how such an identity may be practiced. Daniel, through an imperial training program, qualifies for imperial service, but he does so on his own Jewish terms:

> Daniel resolved that he would not defile himself with the royal rations of food and wine; so he asked the palace master to allow him not to defile himself. (Dan. 1:8)

In this telling, Daniel's alternative way in the empire is successful on all counts, an invitation to others to practice such alternative:

> And among them all, no one was found to compare with Daniel, Hananiah, Mishael, and Azariah; therefore they were stationed in the king's court. In every matter of wisdom and understanding concerning which the king inquired of them, he found them ten times better than all the magicians and enchanters in his whole kingdom. (1:19–20)

In a remarkable little book, *The Enchantments of Judaism*, Jacob Neusner has reviewed and exposited specific disciplines and practices of contemporary Judaism, including practices of kosher, Sabbath, circumcision, and ritual baths. Neusner concludes that such prescribed acts are acts of imagination whereby Jews can imagine, over and over again, that they are Jews: "All of us are Jews through the power of our imagination."[7] Neusner's accent is on the fact that it is Jewish imagination that has generated much of the artistic legacy of the West. But implicit in his assertion, I believe, is also the recognition that Jewishness depends upon such bold and sustained acts of imagination.

Mutatis mutandis, progressive Christians in the United States now face a fresh challenge. So long as U.S. society was visibly "a Christian society," no special effort was required to maintain Christian identity. All of the institutional supports and practices of society assumed and affirmed Christian claims, surely much more so than their purveyors recognized. Now, however, in a society gone publicly secular, that social identity is no longer "automatic" but now requires determined intentionality to make a case for "evangelical identity" in the midst of an imperial environment that has lost its way in money, power, and violence.[8] It is clear, moreover, that the work of progressive Christianity is made more urgent by the fervor of right-wing Christianity that is a ruthless, well-funded effort to deal with the secular loss of the human, but in ways that are coercive and exploitative, in ways that are not at all healthy or faithful. It is the work of progressive Christianity to offer a societal alternative that is deeply rooted in the miraculous wisdom of the good news. Thus, I propose that obedient prayer and obedient justice are core ways in which the church can sustain a distinct identity and can muster its energy and its courage to resist "the empire of force" that is organized precisely against the will of the Creator, who is the Torah giver of Sinai.[9]

It is clear that in the New Testament, Jesus' work is to form an alternative community, alternative to Rome, by accentuating the subversive elements of Judaism. Such an accent eventually put the Jesus movement in tension with those segments of Judaism that had, in various ways, succumbed to the pressures of the national security state that was Rome.

In both ancient Israel as an alternative community and in the early church as an alternative community, the accent is recurrently upon positive intentionality that requires attentiveness to discipline and the vigilant resistance required for the maintenance of life under the rule of the covenant God. I understand that such a claim for the church is a bit grand, and I understand how remote such a practice is in most congregations that have settled for conventional accommodation to culture. But I also affirm that the means for such identity in *Word and sacrament* are already fully available in the practice of the congregation. What is required is patient, bold interpretation, so that matters in the church are given their proper names and that the congregation can see, perhaps afresh, what it is that has been entrusted to us.

V.

When I consider the formation and maintenance of an alternative community of obedience in the midst of a defining empire, as an Old Testament teacher I am led, willy nilly, to consider the formative movement of Judaism in the fifth century BCE under Ezra and Nehemiah. It is an indication of how comfortably conventional Christianity has been in the United States and how insistently dismissive it has been of Judaism's struggle for distinctive identity that until recently the fifth century and the work of Ezra and Nehemiah were simply skipped over in most Christian work in the Old Testament. Conversely, it is surely a hint of new interpretive awareness that the fifth century, even poorly documented and scarcely available to us, now is a central preoccupation of scholarship.[10] I believe that scholarship follows, albeit at some distance, the felt needs of confessing communities. I believe that the new focus on the fifth century in scholarship is an inchoate response to the felt need of contemporary faith that life in the empire now requires addressing the issue of distinct identity.

It is now clear that the Persian Empire exercised careful and comprehensive oversight of revitalized Jerusalem after the fall of Babylon and the return of the elite Jews from exile. With the founding of the small western colony of Yehud, returning Jews had the tricky task of negotiating distinct Jewish identity while not only surviving Persian imperial oversight but also receiving protection, support, funding, and legitimacy from the Persians for the reconstitution of Jewishness. The leadership had to walk the fine line that avoided, on the one hand, an excessive submissiveness to and dependence upon Persia that would jeopardize their Jewishness and, on the other hand, an excessive assertiveness that would evoke the might and destructive power of Persia. I do not suggest that Ezra and Nehemiah constitute a complete and adequate model for the maintenance of a counteridentity in our contemporary setting. Indeed, it is easy to see how the Ezra movement includes destructive ideological components, as every such movement potentially does. We can nonetheless learn a great deal from that social crisis and the response to it, because the current situation of the U.S. church concerns roughly the same issue of the maintenance of a baptismal identity in an impervious imperial context. I will take up, in turn, the two dimensions of faithful obedience that have been our focus.

VI.

In the textual tradition, both Ezra and Nehemiah are presented as *persons of prayer*.

Ezra 9:5–15. This prayer on the lips of Ezra the scribe is primarily a confession of guilt. It turns out, however, as such confessions in Israel do, to be a petition.[11] I will identify six themes in this prayer.

1. Faithful to the Deuteronomic tradition, the voice of Ezra is committed to the conviction that the catastrophe of exile and the loss of Jerusalem is divine punishment for sin. Thus, the prayer is one of confession of sin:

> From the days of our ancestors to this day we have been deep in guilt, and for our iniquities we, our kings, and our priests have been handed over to the kings of the lands, to the sword, to captivity, to plundering, and to utter shame, as is now the case. (Ezra 9:7)

This theology is the same as the familiar and conventional formulas of the book of Judges. Divine punishment for "great guilt" takes place in the public domain.

2. The conclusion of verse 8 (see also v. 13) again uses the theme of "remnant" that pervades the prayer. Ezra here speaks for the vulnerable remnant, the ones who have survived the disaster and are now pledged to a new obedience:

> But now for a brief moment favor has been shown by the LORD our God, who has left us a remnant, and given us a stake in his holy place, in order that he may brighten our eyes and grant us a little sustenance in our slavery. (9:8)

The remnant is at risk and continues to carry the guilt of Israel. But the remnant also lives in hope that there may be "bright eyes," "a little sustenance," and "new life" (see v. 9). Even in the acknowledgment of guilt, the remnant is dependent upon YHWH and looks to YHWH for sustenance and succor.

3. The true situation of this remnant is that it is under the coercive surveillance of the Persian Empire:

> For we are slaves; yet our God has not forsaken us in our slavery, but has extended to us his steadfast love before the kings of Persia, to give us new life to set up the house of our God, to repair its ruins, and to give us a wall in Judea and Jerusalem. (9:9)

A great deal has been made in recent interpretation of the generosity and beneficence of the Persian Empire toward Jerusalem. Clearly, the case for generosity should not be overstated. An empire is an empire is an empire. The purpose of empire is to establish zones of security to protect the home base, and to tax the colonies for the sake of the home country. There is no doubt that Persian taxation was a big factor in the life of Yehud, an arrangement that denied economic as well as psychological freedom for the Jews. Colonies exist to benefit empire!

4. In the midst of *guilt, vulnerability,* and *enslavement,* Ezra continues to trust in YHWH's steadfast love (v. 9). The tradition is aware that it must, in the end, rely on YHWH's graciousness, because the remnant is "before you in our guilt" (v. 15). The new beginning is in the awareness that the future for Jews is pure gift from God.

5. The remnant community is now pledged to Torah obedience. It is, of course, this Torah obedience about pollution, abomination, uncleanness, and hoped for purity that leads to ideological passion in later chapters (see vv. 11–12). But before we take this resolve as an ideological surplus, we may recognize that it is in fact a resolve to be different and to maintain an alternative identity in the world. It is worth noting that the resolve never to seek the "peace or prosperity" of the host society is an antithesis to the urging of Jeremiah (see Jer. 29:7). Either way, in Jeremiah and in Ezra, there is a passion for obedience.

6. The conclusion of the prayer in verse 15 keeps the focus on YHWH. "YHWH, God of Israel, is just" ("righteousness"). The prayer is a humble presentation of a community in profound need. In its need it turns to its only source of help. While there is in the prayer a strong note of remorse and even something of self-pity, such notes are designed to move God (in a way that is characteristic

of laments). The conclusion is not finally about Yehud but about YHWH: "You are righteous."[12] YHWH is the God who acquits, who makes right. Given the confession of guilt, the prayer is nonetheless a prayer for justice that is grounded not in Israel's merit, but in YHWH's propensity. While the prayer is not a vigorous intercession for the neighbor (as I have discussed above), in fact Ezra's prayer for his community seeks from God an act of "righteousness." Thus, the prayer is an "importunate" bid for justice for those in the empire who cannot fend for themselves. "New life" depends upon YHWH's faithful generosity (v. 9).

Nehemiah 9:6–37. Ezra's long prayer of petition and trust in Ezra 9 is matched by another long prayer of Ezra. This prayer begins in verses 6–31 with two characteristic motifs. The first is YHWH's great goodness and faithfulness through the history of Israel:

> You are the LORD, the God who chose Abram and brought him out of Ur of the Chaldeans and gave him the name Abraham; and you found his heart faithful before you, and made with him a covenant to give to his descendants the land of the Canaanite, the Hittite, the Amorite, the Perizzite, the Jebusite, and the Girgashite; and you have fulfilled your promise, for you are righteous.
>
> And you saw the distress of our ancestors in Egypt and heard their cry at the Red Sea. You performed signs and wonders against Pharaoh and all his servants and all the people of his land, for you knew that they acted insolently against our ancestors. You made a name for yourself, which remains to this day. And you divided the sea before them, so that they passed through the sea on dry land, but you threw their pursuers into the depths, like a stone into mighty waters. Moreover, you led them by day with a pillar of cloud, and by night with a pillar of fire, to give them light on the way in which they should go. You came down also upon Mount Sinai, and spoke with them from heaven, and gave them right ordinances and true laws, good statutes and commandments, and you made known your holy sabbath to them and gave them commandments and statutes and a law through your servant Moses. For their hunger you gave them bread from heaven, and for their thirst you brought water for them out of the rock, and you told them to go in to possess the land that you swore to give them. (Neh. 9:7–15)

It is notable that in verse 8 Ezra again says, as in Ezra 9:15, "You are righteous." It is YHWH's "righteousness" that is the ground of life for Israel.

The second motif is that Israel has been recalcitrant all through its history:

> But they and our ancestors acted presumptuously and stiffened their necks and did not obey your commandments; they refused to obey, and were not mindful of the wonders that you performed among them; but they stiffened their necks and determined to return to their slavery in Egypt. (9:16–17a)

That same pattern is then reiterated: YHWH's goodness is detailed in verses 17b–25 followed by more data on Israel's sinful resistance to YHWH. The long recital is concluded in verse 31 with a ringing affirmation of YHWH's fidelity:

> Nevertheless, in your great mercies you did not make an end of them or
> forsake them, for you are a gracious and merciful God. (9:31)

The rhythm of *generosity and recalcitrance* is a characteristic read of Israel's life
with YHWH, a rhythm voiced as well in Psalm 106.

The prayer reaches its decisive moment in verse 32 as it turns from a *recital of
the past* to a *present petition* introduced by a characteristic "and now" (*wa'attah*).
The petition is brief and to the point, voiced in the midst of a doxology:

> Now therefore, our God—the great and mighty and awesome God, keep-
> ing covenant and steadfast love—do not treat lightly all the hardship that
> has come upon us, upon our kings, our officials, our priests, our prophets,
> our ancestors, and all your people, since the time of the kings of Assyria
> until today. (9:32)

It is affirmed that YHWH is a faithful covenant keeper. On that basis comes the
petition, "do not treat lightly"—that is, take seriously and deal effectively as you
are able. The petition-cum-doxology is followed by yet another assertion: "You are
righteous." And then verses 33–35 again recite YHWH's past faithful actions of
restorative generosity. As in many laments, YHWH is here reminded of past actions
and is petitioned to do the same yet one more time in this present dire circumstance.

If we bracket out the motivational memory of verses 33–35, we move directly
from the petition in verse 32 to the statement of need in verses 36–37:

> Here we are, slaves to this day—slaves in the land that you gave to our
> ancestors to enjoy its fruit and its good gifts. Its rich yield goes to the kings
> whom you have set over us because of our sins; they have power also over
> our bodies and over our livestock at their pleasure, and we are in great
> distress. (9:36–37)

The citizens of the colony of Yehud are "slaves" in the land of promise. The
implication is that Persia has total control and, consequently, the Jews are in
great distress. In both prayers, Ezra 9:8 and Nehemiah 9:36, the key issue is slavery, an acute form of injustice. With reference to that circumstance, the prayer
in Ezra 9:15 and Nehemiah 9:8, 33, twice asserts, "You are righteous." Appeal
to the "righteousness of God" is an alternative to the reality of slavery. Thus, the
prayer plays off the faithful power of YHWH against the rapacious governance
of Persia and stakes everything on the hope—the hope grounded in remembered
miracles—that YHWH has the will and the power to override Persia.

The two prayers traverse the same ground:

- both confess guilt;
- both describe slavery;
- both affirm that YHWH is "righteous;" and
- both seek action by YHWH in the exploitative context of imperial
  injustice.

Nehemiah 1:4–11. I will only mention a third prayer, this one by Nehemiah. In this prayer, Nehemiah acknowledges again the guilt of the community: "I and my family have sinned" (v. 6). The prayer turns in verse 8 from confession to petition that YHWH will remember a promise:

> ". . . but if you return to me and keep my commandments and do them, though your outcasts are under the farthest skies, I will gather them from there and bring them to the place at which I have chosen to establish my name." They are your servants and your people, whom you redeemed by your great power and your strong hand. (Neh. 1:9–10)

The petition is a bid that YHWH will bring Jews back to the good land of well-being. But the accent on injustice is put poignantly in the final petition of verse 11:

> O Lord, let your ear be attentive to the prayer of your servant, and to the prayer of your servants who delight in revering your name. Give success to your servant today, and grant him mercy in the sight of this man!

The prayer is a bid for mercy "in the sight of this man." "The man"—always the man!—is the Persian king, Artaxerxes. In this prayer, Nehemiah does not yet know, as he will, that the long reach of Persia will extend to the land of the promise. Here he assumes that return to the land will be beyond the reach of "the man."

In this circumstance, Jews pray for justice. The act of dreaming and hoping and petitioning beyond imperial enslavement is a Jewish act. Jewish identity is marked by a will to freedom beyond the empire. Others may succumb to empire. But Jews have a distinct identity rooted in a history of fidelity and hope. Such hope for a better world is the essence of prayer.

VII.

Ezra and Nehemiah, however, are not only men of prayer. They are *men of justice*. I will mention three texts, all of which feature Nehemiah at the work of justice that serves a distinct identity. First, Nehemiah 5 features a quintessential act of justice in the Old Testament, a narrative about exploitative profiteering at the expense of the vulnerable righteous. There was a "great outcry" among the economically vulnerable, a cry not unlike that in Egyptian slavery (Neh. 5:1; see Exod. 2:23–24). The cry is out of *pain voiced*, the most elemental act of justice that may begin the overthrow of regimes of injustice. The cry is about excessive taxation that served the Persian Empire but before that served the urban elites among the Jews in Jerusalem. This is Jews taxing Jews, and the verdict is inescapable:[13]

> Now our flesh is the same as that of our kindred; our children are the same
> as their children; and yet we are forcing our sons and daughters to be slaves,
> and some of our daughters have been ravished; we are powerless, and our
> fields and vineyards now belong to others. (Neh. 5:5)

In response to the cry, Nehemiah intervenes in righteous, impatient indignation:

> I was very angry when I heard their outcry and these complaints. After
> thinking it over, I brought charges against the nobles and the officials; I said
> to them, "You are all taking interest from your own people." And I called a
> great assembly to deal with them. (5:6–7)

In a speech not unlike a prophetic speech of judgment, Nehemiah indicts
the powerful in the community and then summons them to act. The indictment appeals to the Torah—"You are selling your own kin" (v. 8)—because the
process of exacting interest from the poor is a direct violation of the Torah commandment of Deuteronomy 23:19, a Torah provision for covenantal justice.
On the basis of that indictment, Nehemiah issues a summons for restoration of
covenantal relationships:

> Moreover I and my brothers and my servants are lending them money and
> grain. Let us stop this taking of interest. Restore to them, this very day,
> their fields, their vineyards, their olive orchards, and their houses, and the
> interest on money, grain, wine, and oil that you have been exacting from
> them. (5:10–11)

The key verb is "restore" (*shûv*). The summons to restoration is not unlike the
provision for the year of release and the year of jubilee that we have already considered. The community has within itself the capacity to reorder the economy
for the sake of neighborliness. The remarkable outcome of Nehemiah's intervention is the willingness of Jews, still grounded in Torah reality, to concede the
point and resolve to do as Nehemiah urges:

> Then they said, "We will restore everything and demand nothing more
> from them. We will do as you say." And I called the priests, and made them
> take an oath to do as they had promised. (5:12)

The entire drama is an insistence that the old Torah requirements still have
compelling authority for all members of the community, for the exploited who
dare to cry out and for the exploiters who accept the discipline of Torah. The act
commanded by Nehemiah and accepted by the elite in the community overrides
economic advantage for the sake of the neighborhood. This dramatic action is
characteristically Jewish and could not have happened except for a shared distinctive identity.

I mention two other texts. In Nehemiah 10 the community, likely at the
behest of Nehemiah, resolves to refuse commerce on the Sabbath:

> ... and if the peoples of the land bring in merchandise or any grain on the sabbath day to sell, we will not buy it from them on the sabbath or on a holy day; and we will forego the crops of the seventh year and the exaction of every debt. (10:31)

In Nehemiah 13:15–22, moreover, the Jews are contrasted with the traders of Tyre who conduct commerce indiscriminately. When Jews do the same, they "profane" the Sabbath, a day set aside for the enactment of a distinct identity. This tradition knows very well that participating in economics in the way of the world will promptly rob the community of its identity and therefore diminish the moral edge of its life in the world. Nehemiah concludes the unit with a prayer for himself:

> And I commanded the Levites that they should purify themselves and come and guard the gates, to keep the sabbath day holy. Remember this also in my favor, O my God, and spare me according to the greatness of your steadfast love. (13:22)

It is clear that the maintenance of Sabbath as a curb on acquisitive economics is a way of loving God; from that act of love of God, Nehemiah bids YHWH's steadfast love toward him. Economic obedience is a mark of Jewish identity.

There is no doubt that the actions of Ezra and Nehemiah are heavy-handed and become coercive; that cannot be denied. Beyond that however, the self-conscious intentionality of acting *peculiarly* in prayer and in justice ensures the shape of this distinctive community and sustains it in demanding circumstance:

- The prayer is a prayer for YHWH's "righteousness" in a world of slavery, a prayer for the neighborhood.
- The justice is an act of Torah obedience, an act of love toward YHWH.

VIII.

I have one other riff to line out on the theme of distinctive communal identity. Three times Nehemiah prays to be remembered by YHWH for what he has done. First, in Nehemiah 5:19, after his daring economic reform, Nehemiah prays to YHWH: "*Remember* for my good, O my God, all that I have done for this people" (au. emph.). Second, in Nehemiah 13:22, after his rigorous insistence upon Sabbath, Nehemiah prays to YHWH:

> And I commanded the Levites that they should purify themselves and come and guard the gates, to keep the sabbath day holy. Remember this also in my favor, O my God, and spare me according to the greatness of your steadfast love.

Third, at the end of the book, having "cleansed them from everything foreign," Nehemiah prays to YHWH, "I provided for the wood offering, at appointed times, and for the first fruits. *Remember* me, O my God, for good" (13:31, au. emph.).

These petitions strike one as filled with pathos. Nehemiah knows the urgency of his accomplishments for the sake of the community; he also knows that he has not fully succeeded and that his work is in jeopardy. Consequently, he asks and seeks from YHWH long-term approbation for what he has done. In all three cases, Nehemiah alludes to what he has accomplished.

Nehemiah 5:19: "All that I have done for this people" (economic reform)

Nehemiah 13:22: "This also is in my favor" (sabbath enforcement)

Nehemiah 13:31: A claim for cleansing, but no direct reference to it is made in the prayer.

The prayers perhaps reflect the fact that Jewish prayers for the neighbor and Jewish acts for justice—prayers that love neighbor and acts that love God—are always precarious and, in the end, depend upon YHWH's fidelity to give them staying power.

Nehemiah's threefold prayer reflects some anxiety about his status before YHWH and perhaps his status in his community. His prayers pose the question "How do faithful agents of prayer and justice stay at it in the face of recalcitrant community and resistant empire when the prospect of durable success is lean indeed?" In order to answer that urgent question—urgent in ancient times and in contemporary settings—I push behind Ezra and Nehemiah to suggest that in the period of Jewish revival and restoration we may see evidence of the formulation and practice of "Torah piety," a trajectory of biblical faith that is to be contrasted with the great temple liturgies. Or alternatively, this trajectory is what Erhard Gerstenberger terms "family theology."[14] This tradition, reflected in the Psalter and evident in the pathos-filled petitions of Nehemiah, concerns the following:

- humility in its approach to YHWH;
- intimacy with YHWH in one-on-one interaction; and
- modesty but not self-denial before YHWH.

This piety trusts YHWH completely and is confident of YHWH but has no larger agenda that anticipates accomplishment. Thus, I propose that what sustains the venturesome enterprise of Ezra and Nehemiah is exactly the Torah piety reflected in the Psalter. They were working "upstream" to recover a distinct identity that had important public ramifications.

I recite the evidence for that piety in order to suggest that the church, in response to empire, may well practice a piety that is *humble*, *intimate*, and *modest*. It may do so in order to sustain its characteristic acts of prayer as neighbor love and justice as love of God, both acts that the empire characteristically resists. I will not here exposit these particular verses but only invite the reader to consider the cumulative effect of such regularly performed words:

> But I trust in you, O LORD;
>> I say, "You are my God."
> My times are in your hand;
>> deliver me from the hand of my enemies and persecutors.
> Let your face shine upon your servant;
>> save me in your steadfast love.
> Do not let me be put to shame, O LORD,
>> for I call on you.
>>>>>>>>>>>>>>> Ps. 31:14–17a

> This poor soul cried, and was heard by the LORD,
>> and was saved from every trouble.
> . . . .
> When the righteous cry for help, the LORD hears,
>> and rescues them from all their troubles.
> The LORD is near to the brokenhearted,
>> and saves the crushed in spirit.

> Many are the afflictions of the righteous,
>> but the LORD rescues them from them all.
> He keeps all their bones;
>> not one of them will be broken.
>>>>>>>>>>>>>>> 34:6, 17–20

> To you I lift up my eyes,
>> O you who are enthroned in the heavens!
> As the eyes of servants
>> look to the hand of their master,
> as the eyes of a maid
>> to the hand of her mistress,
> so our eyes look to the LORD our God,
> until he has mercy upon us.

> Have mercy upon us, O LORD, have mercy upon us,
>> for we have had more than enough of contempt.
> Our soul has had more than its fill
>> of the scorn of those who are at ease,
>> of the contempt of the proud.
>>>>>>>>>>>>>>> 123:1–4

> If it had not been the LORD who was on our side
>> —let Israel now say—
> if it had not been the LORD who was on our side,
>> when our enemies attacked us,
> then they would have swallowed us up alive,
>> when their anger was kindled against us;

then the flood would have swept us away,
   the torrent would have gone over us;
then over us would have gone
   the raging waters.
124:1–5

Unless the LORD builds the house,
   those who build it labor in vain.
Unless the LORD guards the city,
   the guard keeps watch in vain.
It is in vain that you rise up early
   and go late to rest,
eating the bread of anxious toil;
   for he gives sleep to his beloved.
127:1–2

Happy is everyone who fears the LORD,
   who walks in his ways.
You shall eat the fruit of the labor of your hands;
   you shall be happy, and it shall go well with you.
128:1–2

O LORD, my heart is not lifted up,
   my eyes are not raised too high;
I do not occupy myself with things
   too great and too marvelous for me.
But I have calmed and quieted my soul,
   like a weaned child with its mother;
   my soul is like the weaned child that is within me.
131:1–2

These psalms evidence faith that wears well, that has complete confidence in God, that is not mesmerized by success or deterred by difficulty. It is enough to stay at the task.[15]

IX.

Like fifth-century Judaism, the contemporary church faces many temptations. I can readily think of four:

1. *Nostalgia*, the attempt to escape to a remembered world that is less demanding.
2. *Privatism*, the attempt to settle for a small sphere of safe, manageable relations with our own kind.
3. *Triumphalism*, which imagines the absolute truth of our preferences while failing to notice challenges or alternatives that come with our own credible claims.

4. *The lust for "holy seed,"* which imagines that we can somehow maintain a distinctive identity that yields entitlement (see Ezra 9:2; Neh. 9:2; Esth. 6:13). In the end, the identity that comes via love of God and love of neighbor is given us on quite other grounds than any claim we can make for ourselves. Finally, the faithful cede (pun intended) their identity over to the reality of God, who saves and commands and who calls to prayer and justice. It is this God to whom the faithful bear witness as the creator of heaven and earth:

> You are my witnesses, says the LORD,
>   and my servant whom I have chosen,
> so that you may know and believe me
>   and understand that I am he.
> Before me no god was formed,
>   nor shall there be any after me.
> I, I am the LORD,
>   and besides me there is no savior.
> I declared and saved and proclaimed,
>   when there was no strange god among you;
>   and you are my witnesses, says the LORD.
> I am God, and also henceforth I am He;
>   there is no one who can deliver from my hand;
>   I work and who can hinder it?
>   Isa. 43:10–13

I conclude with a final reference to the book of Acts. One can see in Acts the twinned disciplines of the early church that constitute together a subversive identity. *The internal discipline* is that all was shared in common:

> All who believed were together and had all things in common; they would sell their possessions and goods and distribute the proceeds to all, as any had need. Day by day, as they spent much time together in the temple, they broke bread at home and ate their food with glad and generous hearts, praising God and having the goodwill of all the people. And day by day the Lord added to their number those who were being saved. (Acts 2:44–47)

> Now the whole group of those who believed were of one heart and soul, and no one claimed private ownership of any possessions, but everything they owned was held in common. With great power the apostles gave their testimony to the resurrection of the Lord Jesus, and great grace was upon them all. There was not a needy person among them, for as many as owned lands or houses sold them and brought the proceeds of what was sold. They laid it at the apostles' feet, and it was distributed to each as any had need. There was a Levite, a native of Cyprus, Joseph, to whom the apostles gave the name Barnabas (which means "son of encouragement"). He sold a field that belonged to him, then brought the money, and laid it at the apostles' feet. (4:32–37)

The external discipline was to appear with great frequency before the authorities in order to testify to the regime change that had been accomplished in the person of Jesus. That testimony resulted in imprisonment, but even detention at the hands of the authorities did not diminish the apostolic performance of obedience. The testimony before the authorities is abundant:

- Peter is imprisoned by Herod (Acts 12:1–5).
- Paul is arrested by the tribune (21:27–40).
- Paul appears before a Roman tribune (22:26–30).
- Paul appears before Felix (24:1–27).
- Paul appears before Festus (25:1–12).
- Paul appears before Agrippa (25:13–27).

The internal discipline of *intimate sharing* and the external discipline of *testimony before authorities* yielded energy and courage precisely for the truth of the resurrection. The twinned disciplines are exactly the performance of the two great commandments: It is no wonder that the followers of Jesus are said to be turning the world upside down (17:6). It is further no wonder that Luke has Jesus instructing the church in its appearances before the authorities with the subversive truth of Easter:

> But before all this occurs, they will arrest you and persecute you; they will hand you over to synagogues and prisons, and you will be brought before kings and governors because of my name. This will give you an opportunity to testify. So make up your minds not to prepare your defense in advance; for I will give you words and a wisdom that none of your opponents will be able to withstand or contradict. You will be betrayed even by parents and brothers, by relatives and friends; and they will put some of you to death. You will be hated by all because of my name. But not a hair of your head will perish. By your endurance you will gain your souls. (Luke 21:12–19)

We—you and I—have a long history of timidity. For all of that, however, the commandments to love neighbor and to love God have not been revised or edited. They stand since Sinai as summons and mandate. The exchange about the commandments in the Gospel of Mark ends this way:

> Then the scribe said to him, "You are right, Teacher; you have truly said that 'he is one, and besides him there is no other'; and 'to love him with all the heart, and with all the understanding, and with all the strength,' and 'to love one's neighbor as oneself,'—this is much more important than all whole burnt offerings and sacrifices." When Jesus saw that he answered wisely, he said to him, "You are not far from the kingdom of God." After that no one dared to ask him any question. (Mark 12:32–34)

Chapter 12

Truth-Telling as Well-Making

The lament psalms in the book of Psalms voice a clear, thick, deep, shrewd understanding of the processes that are indispensable for the transformation of the "human condition" from death to life, from sorrow to joy, from anger to energy, from despair to hope. (A fresh understanding of these indispensable processes, so utterly Jewish, was reasserted in the modern world by Sigmund Freud). These lament psalms offer rich variation in particulars. But the general flow of rhetoric that performs these indispensable processes is clear enough to trace, as scholarship has done, as a reliable, persistent pattern that amounts to a describable genre. This genre of speech features a human speaker who is filled with sufficient chutzpah to voice truth in honest ways before the Lord of the covenant. That recurring rhetoric is grounded in the conviction that God's covenant partners have entitlement in the covenant to address God. More than that, these entitled speakers seize the initiative in such speech and dare to summon God into their vexation that is the subject of such lament, protest, and complaint. They assume authority to state their case before God with expectation that God is willing, able, and ready to engage with them in the vexation.

I.

This recurring pattern of speech features the covenantal partner drawing God into trouble with an expectation that if God can be mobilized, the trouble can be assuaged! We may readily identify three features in this patterned speech. First, the psalmist regularly *addresses God by name*: "Lord (YHWH)." The utterance of the holy name affirms that the speaker is intimately and confidently connected to the God who is addressed—thus, "My God, my God" (Ps. 22:1); "O Lord" (3:1); "O God of my right" (4:1); "O Lord my God" (7:1). Second, the speaker voices a specific *complaint*, describing for God the particulars of trouble, often an attack by enemies, being shamed and slandered, being abandoned, being sick, being vulnerable, or being weak:

> O Lord, how many are my foes!
>   Many are rising against me.
>   3:1

> I am distraught by the noise of the enemy,
>   because of the clamor of the wicked.
> For they bring trouble upon me,
>   and in anger they cherish enmity against me.
>   55:2–3

> People trample on me;
>   all day long foes oppress me;
> my enemies trample on me all day long,
>   for many fight against me.
>   56:1–2

> I lie down among lions
>   that greedily devour human prey;
> their teeth are spears and arrows,
>   their tongues sharp swords.
>   57:4

The descriptions are vivid and specific; they are, at the same time, open and imaginative enough that in our use of these psalms we may fill them with imagery from our own experience.

The third feature is that when the complaint has been sufficiently detailed to move God, it is accompanied by vigorous *imperatives* that ask God to rectify circumstances that are unmerited and unbearable and before which the speaker is helpless:

> Rise up, O Lord!
>   Deliver me, O my God!
>   3:7

Answer me when I call, O God of my right!
. . . .
Be gracious to me, and hear my prayer.
4:1

Be gracious to me, O LORD, for I am languishing;
O LORD, heal me, for my bones are shaking with terror.
6:2

Rise up, O LORD, in your anger;
lift yourself up against the fury of my enemies;
awake, O my God.
7:6

O God, break the teeth in their mouths;
tear out the fangs of the young lions, O LORD!
58:6

These imperatives are unrestrained in their vigor, in their emotional force, and
even in their violence. These are acts of urgency that, insofar as they are imperatives, issue commands to God expecting that this covenant partner will be attentive and responsive.

These three elements together amount to framing the God relationship
around the needs of the speaker—in contrast to doxologies, in which all the
attention is given over to God. Thus provisionally, in the lament psalms the
speaker assumes the dominant and primary role in the relationship and is able to
take a daring and necessary initiative.

II.

Two recurring elements in this patterned speech constitute difficulty for those
who want pastoral care (and Christian piety in general) to be "nice." First, the
lament Psalms are permeated with *motivations* that give God reason to be attentive and to act. It is as though when God hears the unrestrained imperatives,
God responds, "Now why should I bother to answer your demand?" Such motivations may seem ignoble to us, because they sound like bargaining that ought
not to happen with God. They are, however, efforts to make clear to God that
God has something at stake in the vexation of the speaker and should act for
God's self-interest. Or as we say, "For your name's sake," that is, for the sake of
your reputation. God should act on behalf of the speaker and so be on exhibit as
a trustworthy God. This act will maintain and enhance God's reputation (about
which God is thought to care!) as a faithful covenant partner. Thus, for example,
the speaker may remind God of God's previous fidelity that ought now to be
continued in the present circumstance:

In you our ancestors trusted;
   they trusted, and you delivered them.
To you they cried, and were saved;
   in you they trusted and were not put to shame.
                       22:4–5

Most daringly, the psalmist warns God that if the speaker dies, there will be one less voice to praise God. This is on the assumption that God relishes praise and enjoys it:

What profit is there in my death,
   if I go down to the Pit?
Will the dust praise you?
   Will it tell of your faithfulness?
               30:9

Do shades rise up to praise you?
Is your steadfast love declared in the grave,
   or your faithfulness in Abaddon?
Are your wonders known in the darkness,
   or your saving help in the land of forgetfulness?
                 88:10–12

The hope is that God will act for the speaker in God's own self-interest. In dire straits it is not a surprise that the petitioner will engage in regressive speech!

The other "objectionable" element in the laments is what scholars term *imprecation*, that is, a wish for vengeance on one's enemies. Most notoriously, in Psalm 109 the speaker inveighs against the enemy at length:

May his days be few;
   may another seize his position.
May his children be orphans,
   and his wife a widow.
May his children wander about and beg;
   may they be driven out of the ruins they inhabit.
May the creditor seize all that he has;
   may strangers plunder the fruits of his toil.
May there be no one to do him a kindness,
   nor anyone to pity his orphaned children.
May his posterity be cut off,
   may his name be blotted out in the second generation.
                 109:8–13

Break the arm of the wicked and evildoers;
   seek out their wickedness until you find none.
               10:15

Let them vanish like water that runs away;
   like grass let them be trodden down and wither.

> Let them be like the snail that dissolves into slime;
> like the untimely birth that never sees the sun.
> 58:7-8

Some of the pious will think that the faithful should not talk this way, and certainly not in the presence of the Holy One. Behind that is the notion that the faithful should not think that way or feel that way. But we do! Israel knew from the outset that what is felt and thought must be said; it must be said out loud, and it must be said out loud in the presence of God. This is the God from whom no secret can be hid![1] Truth-telling through such laments is completely without restraint or reservation because it is truth-telling to the very bottom of the life of the speaker. Of course, the speaker does not herself act out these violent wishes for vengeance but only voices them to God, in whom the speaker has complete confidence.

When we consider these five elements together—address to God, complaint, petition, motivation, and imprecation—we are able to see that this is honest speech in the process of truth-telling. It is an act whereby the self, diminished by many "toils and snares," is now reclaimed and restored in the presence of God. The utterance amounts to a moment of "omnipotence" for the speaker in which she dares presume that her cause deserves and will receive the full attention of the Holy God.[2]

This moment of utterance is an instance of *being heard*, that is, being heard back to full personhood. Thus, the opening imperative of such speech is often "Listen to me!":

Answer me (4:1)

Give ear . . . give heed (5:1)

Hear, O Lord (30:10)

Hear my prayer (54:2)

Give ear to my prayer . . . attend to me and answer me (55:1–2)

Self-announcement is the first step in the recovery of a self that has been depleted. But self-announcement counts only if it is addressed to someone in whom there is confidence of being taken with utmost seriousness. Utmost seriousness on the part of God grounds this daring, unrestrained speech of the self who is ready to risk full exposure.

III.

At this point in this patterned speech there is often a turn in rhetoric or at least a pause. One can see this in the abrupt newness of Psalms 13:5–6 and 22:21a, in which there is inexplicable resolution for the speaker. It is as though the speaker has spent his energy and has no more to say. Or perhaps the speaker pauses in the hope of receiving a response from the one addressed. The outcome of such speech is not automatic or guaranteed. It is a leap to the faithfulness of God that God enacts in freedom. It is risky speech, given fidelity-in-freedom on God's side, but these prayers characteristically end in a good resolve of being heard by God:

> The LORD has heard the sound of my weeping.
> The LORD has heard my supplication;
>> the LORD accepts my prayer.
>>>> 6:8–9

> In my distress I called upon the LORD;
>> to my God I called.
> From his temple he heard my voice,
> and my cry to him reached his ears.
>>>> 2 Sam. 22:7

> But you heard my supplications
>> when I cried out to you for help.
>>>> 31:22b

> This poor soul cried, and was heard by the LORD,
>> and was saved from every trouble.
>>>> Ps. 34:6

> I waited patiently for the LORD;
>> he inclined to me and heard my cry.
>>>> 40:1

> I love the LORD, because he has heard
>> my voice and my supplications.
> Because he inclined his ear to me,
>> therefore I will call on him as long as I live.
>>>> 116:1–2

Being heard when engaged in truth-telling is a moment of verification, recognition, valorization, being taken seriously. It is an act of emancipation. This is indeed truth-telling that makes free and that makes well. Such a prayer characteristically ends in joyous thanksgiving, perhaps expressed in a thank offering:

> What shall I return to the LORD
>> for all his bounty to me?
> I will lift up the cup of salvation
>> and call on the name of the LORD.
> I will pay my vows to the LORD
>> in the presence of all his people.
>>>> 116:12–14

Or it may issue in glad testimony to the community:

I have told the glad news of deliverance
   in the great congregation;
see, I have not restrained my lips.

$$40:9$$

Or endless doxology into future generations:

From you comes my praise in the great congregation;
   my vows I will pay before those who fear him.
. . . .
Posterity will serve him;
   future generations will be told about the Lord.

$$22:25, 30$$

In a variety of forms, these laments culminate in gladness, well-being, and readiness for a new life fully in sync with the faithful God who has restored. The truth that makes free and that makes well is a part of the process of *the reconstitution of the self* that has been depleted by a variety of assaults.

Of course, we must reckon with the occurrences of this patterned speech when it does not eventuate in such good resolve. This is evident in the individual laments of Psalms 39 and 88 and in the communal lament of Psalm 44. These psalms serve as reminders that in the free interaction of covenant partners, there are no guarantees. The entire interaction is risky. That same risk, of course, is present in every serious relationship of honest truth-telling.

IV.

How odd it is that these rich resources of the community of faith that occupy so much of the book of Psalms have been almost completely lost in the life of the church, being absent (except for Psalm 22) in the liturgical sequence of the church.[3] Such an absence from the liturgy is in the interest of a polite spirituality that thinks that such abrasive truth-telling has no proper place in the life of the congregation. Such an absence in the practice of the church is an invitation to denial, the bet that such truth-telling is inappropriate before the God of all truth.

The church has devised two strategies for embarrassed silencing of these texts and their best practice. The positive strategy is the development of pastoral care and particularly (at least in the United States) the "pastoral care movement" with its protocols and accrediting apparatus. In a segue from the lament psalms to pastoral care, the church has made two bargains. First, it has moved the indispensable truth-telling processes from the congregation into "private practice" so that the normative form has become one-on-one counseling. There are, to be sure, some remaining practices of group interaction as in recovery groups, but those tend to be at the margins of congregational life. The *privatism* of such pastoral care is most often done in a vacuum, as though the resources of the community did not matter to well-being. Second, we have agreed to a *secular* form of truth-telling with a *human listener*, because the notion of *God as listener* is too embarrassing for us; we imagine that God is too timid or too fragile for such abrasive interaction. (I do not denigrate such a privatized secularized practice, because I have benefited greatly from such interaction.) But we may be aware that entrusted to us (and only to us) is a reliable script for a more public practice of voiced *I*'s who receive fresh valorization from this holy *Thou* who is made available through the practice of the congregation. Recovery of such public practice is, in my judgment, a powerful desideratum.

The other (less noble) strategy for scuttling the lament psalms is that the church has taken the full range of emotional needs and extremities and reduced them all to only one note, namely, guilt. Thus, liturgically the only aspect of the complex human self about which we regularly tell the truth is our guilt in the regularity of confession. Moreover, we tend to do even that in rote innocuous articulation. Such a singular accent reduces to silence all the other undeniable dimensions of the self that concern our life with each other and with God.

The contemporary Swedish interpreter Fredrick Lindstrom has carefully and compellingly shown that in the fifty or so lament psalms, there is not one admission of guilt: "It is highly doubtful if we can speak of a motif of sin in the individual Psalms. . . . The confession of sin is not an element in the classical individual complaint Psalms, and the motif of sin, in the few cases in which it occurs, hardly functions as indication of the reason for the affliction."[4]

In its lament-protest-complaint, Israel is not willing to accept responsibility for what has gone awry in its life. Often the fault is assigned to unnamed adversaries. Sometimes the fault is said to belong to God as the troublemaker through acts of infidelity toward Israel. It would be well, in my judgment, if the church moved beyond such reductionism and created room in the liturgy for the full truth-telling of the diminished self without such reductionism. Among other liabilities in an excessive focus on guilt is that it amounts to collusion with the political-economic oligarchy. That oligarchy of money and power is wont to "blame the victim" for his sorry state of disadvantage and vulnerability, when in fact the oligarchy itself is most often the perpetrator of such vexation for the vulnerable. Israel in its prayer will have none of that!

V.

I suggest that the church would do well to recover the truth-telling processes of the lament psalms, because a greedy culture of despair will never make free and will never make well. The oligarchy, with its passion for control, predictably ends in despair, whereas the laments are acts of hope that God will make all things new.

In the "posthistory" of the laments, we may refer to Luke 18:1–8, in which Jesus instructs his disciples to pray like a nagging widow who insists on justice before a cynical, indifferent judge. Her insistence on justice sounds very much like a lament psalm. When Jesus taught his disciples in this way, he might have said to these early Jewish followers, "Pray like you know to do in the lament psalms." Jesus does not promise that such prayer will be answered. Rather, he promises that with such prayer we will never "lose heart." Tepid practices of prayer, like so much prayer in the life of the church, end in denial about what dare not be uttered and become a sure way to "lose heart." What is required in order not to lose heart is engagement in self-announcement before one who reliably listens in a way that valorizes. The widow insists on being heard and finally is heard by the judge: "I will grant her justice, so that she may not wear me out by continually coming" (v. 5).[5]

When the church loses heart, its witness is tepid, its mission is weak, its courage is limited, and its imagination is domesticated. At the end of the text, Jesus wonders if the coming Son of Man will find faith to pray as truth-tellers. That same question is put to us. How we answer it indicates a great deal about our practice of pastoral care. There is no other resource than the lament psalms that is so rich and inexorable in its prospect for truth-telling that makes for well-being.

Chapter 13

Colonialism and Migration

2 Kings 24–25

The recharacterization of "exile" as "forced migration" is now a centerpiece in recent scholarly work. That recharacterization invites the question "Forced by whom?" The new formulation of the topic invites the question of agency, to which the biblical narrative characteristically responds with "double agency," thus twinning divine agency and human agency. The notion of double agency—divine and human—is integral to a covenantal-Deuteronomic-prophetic articulation of history. It is voiced, perhaps, already in the Song of Deborah, wherein victory is celebrated and credited to both agents:

> To the sound of musicians at the watering places,
>   there they repeat the triumphs of *the* L ORD,
>   the triumphs of *the peasantry* in Israel.
>   Judg. 5:11 (au. emph.)

The same doubleness is likely reflected in the narrative of Gideon, though agency is not made explicit, in the rhetoric of the army: "For the L ORD and for Gideon" (Judg. 7:18). The doubleness is reflected in the divine verbal assurance to Gideon: "But *I* will be with you, and *you* shall strike down the Midianites, every one of them" (6:16, au. emph.). (That assurance, moreover, is reminiscent of the initial divine confrontation with Moses, wherein YHWH makes a series of first-person assurances to Moses about direct engagement but then decisively turns the task to Moses: "So come, *I* will send *you* to Pharaoh to bring my people, the Israelites, out of Egypt" [Exod. 3:10, au. emph.].)

The assurance to Gideon in 6:16 is answered with the narrative report of the way in which divine agency ("spirit of God") empowered human agency: "The spirit of the LORD took possession of Gideon; and he sounded the trumpet, and the Abiezrites were called out to follow him" (6:34).

I cite these cases, likely earlier than our text, to indicate that double agency constitutes no problem in the narrative form of Israel's historiography, even when we recognize that from a critical modernist perspective "forced migration" requires only an explicit human agent. In what follows, I will consider the problematic of double agency, not in order to resolve it but to see how these traditions articulate the theological claims that Klaus Koch identifies as "metahistory."[1] It is clear that without this doubleness (that our rationality might regard as problematic), there could be no articulation of what passes for biblical historiography.

I.

Our text, 2 Kings 24–25, is readily divided into seven distinct rhetorical units, two of which are explicit about divine agency—that is, YHWH is agent of "forced migration":

1. *2 Kings 24:1–7* summarizes the final days of Jehoiakim and concerns his rebellion against Nebuchadnezzar that led to the first Babylonian incursion into Judah in 598 BCE. Verses 2–4, sandwiched by the chronicle of verses 1, 5–7, voice a "metahistory" that is patterned after prophetic speeches of judgment. The indictment is twofold concerning the "sins of Manasseh" and "the innocent blood that he shed." The divine judgment is the command of YHWH to "remove" Judah and not to pardon. The pivotal term is "remove" (*sur*), which is reinforced by a verdict, "Unwilling to pardon" (*slh*). The verb *sur* has already been used twice with reference to the Northern Kingdom: (1) "Therefore the LORD was very angry with Israel and *removed* them out of his sight (17:18); and (2) ". . . until the LORD *removed* Israel out of his sight, as he had foretold through all his servants the prophets" (17:23). In 23:27, moreover, YHWH pledged to remove Judah from the land, a pledge now enacted in our verses: "The LORD said, 'I will *remove* Judah also out of my sight, as I have *removed* Israel; and I will reject this city that I have chosen, Jerusalem, and the house of which I said, "My name shall be there"'" (au. emph.)

In each case, YHWH is unmistakably the agent.[2] The sequence in 24:1–7 is characteristically Deuteronomic: sanction follows conduct; curse follows disobedience. In the curse recital of Deuteronomy 28:64–65, displacement from the land is the ultimate threat for disobedience:

> The LORD will scatter you among all the peoples, from one end of the earth to the other; and there you shall serve other gods, of wood and stone, which neither you nor your ancestors have known. Among those nations you shall find no ease, no resting place for the sole or your foot. There the LORD will give you a trembling heart, failing eyes, and a languishing spirit.

Thus the threat voiced against Jehoiakim fits squarely as an instance of covenantal history. This will all come "at the command of the LORD" (2 Kings 24:3). In verse 1, it is "Nebuchadnezzar . . . came," followed in verse 2 by "the LORD sent." Though the object of YHWH's verb is not explicitly Nebuchadnezzar, the point in any case is clear. Thus "come," "sent," and "commanded" evidence the delicate way in which the two agents are rhetorically intertwined, though there is no ambiguity about ultimate causation.

2. *2 Kings 24:8–12* reports on the forced removal of Jehoiachin in the wake of his father's rebellion. In verse 9, it is noted in a formulaic way that he "did evil in the sight of the LORD," but that is all. The actual removal is by the hand of Nebuchadnezzar, so that YHWH is not explicitly implicated in the forced migration. Divine agency here is minimal but surely implied.

3. *2 Kings 24:13–16* offers a report on the Babylonian plundering of the temple and the population. Strikingly, it is all Nebuchadnezzar. In verses 13–15, the agent is only "he," but the "king of Babylon" is twice named in verses 16–17. There is no explicit theological reference in these verses. The verb *glh* (forced migration) is used three times, so Nebuchadnezzar is clearly the one who forces the migration.

4. *2 Kings 24:17–25:7* reports on the final disposition of Zedekiah as the last king. The rhetoric of these verses suggests an intentional juxtaposition of the two agents. In 25:1–7, with considerable detail, the actor is Nebuchadnezzar, who breaches the city, pursues the fleeing king, and eventually brings him to Riblah for a final abuse. In these verses, YHWH is absent. In 24:18–20, however, it is all YHWH, according to the rubrics of a prophetic speech of judgment:

- In verse 19 there is a generic indictment, echoing verse 9 on Jehoiachin: "He did what was evil in the sight of the LORD."[3]
- In verse 20: "Jerusalem and Judah so angered the LORD that he expelled them from his presence."

It is important in this usage, as with *sur* in verse 4, that it is not exclusion from the land but from "his presence." The judgment of verse 20 is noteworthy: "He expelled them from his presence. . . . Zedekiah rebelled against the king of Babylon." The narrative suggests no particular connection between the two, though the sequence would seem to suggest that rebellion follows expulsion from the presence, an acting out of a divine mandate that had not yet been implemented.

5. *2 Kings 25:8–21* provides a long inventory of the ways in which Nebuzaradan, on behalf of Nebuchadnezzar, plundered the temple and "every great house." In addition, he brought leading Jerusalem officials to Riblah, where the

king put them to death (v. 21). This long note may be of interest for us for two reasons. First, YHWH is nowhere mentioned. This is completely a Babylonian accomplishment. Second, the inventory is bracketed by the term *glh* in verses 11 and 25. Forced migration is a costly business for property and risky business for life.

6. *2 Kings 25:22–26* summarizes the poststate condition of Judah as a Babylonian colony under the governorship of Gedaliah. We need linger over Gedaliah only long enough to remember that he is a scion of the family of Shaphan, a great supporter of Jeremiah and an advocate of ready surrender to Babylon. Thus, the forced migration opened the way for accommodation of local officials to the claims of empire. The paragraph is dominated by Gedaliah's assurance, "Do not fear" (v. 24). This local accommodator promises that cooperation with empire will lead to *shalom*. The rhetoric of Gedaliah closely parallels the divine assurance on the lips of Jeremiah in Jeremiah 42:9–12, suggesting that the formulation is a standard line of the accommodators who pledge that the forcing regime will be benign.

The report on Gedaliah reflects the deep conflict in Judean society between pro-Babylonian and anti-Babylonian factions, the latter led by Ishmael "of the royal family," a conflict that ends with the assassination of the accommodator and the laconic conclusion "They were afraid of the Chaldeans" (v. 26). While the party of Gedaliah had confidence in Babylon (and should have, given its privilege given by the empire), this confidence was not shared by others, notably those identified with the royal family. Given the internecine conflict, the people "high and low" (or "young and old") fled to Egypt in fear of Babylon (v. 26). Here there is no explicit agent of displacement, but the "forcer" is undoubtedly Babylon. While this narrative lacks one of the signature verbs of expulsion, it may nonetheless be slotted along with the usage of "remove," "expel," and "exile" as a way of speaking of forced migration.

7. *2 Kings 25:27–30*, on the survival and continued recognition of Jehoiachin as king in displacement, completes our text. Elsewhere I have suggested that this paragraph, of itself, has been made to carry more interpretive freight than it is able to carry.[4] Against the promissory accent of Gerhard von Rad, I have suggested that the paragraph is deliberately indeterminate; the narrator does not know what comes next. The paragraph is designed to leave everything open, even against our interpretive propensities. In any case, it does not relieve at all the condition of forced relocation.

In sum, *Nebuchadnezzar* is all through this passage as agent:

He is the one who came against Jehoiakim (24:1).

He is the one who laid siege and took Jehoiachin as prisoner (24:10–12).

He is the one who plundered temple and city (24:13–17).

He is the one who pursued Zedekiah and executed him (25:1–7).

He is the one who—through his captain—plundered the great houses and executed the leading citizens of the city (Jer. 52:13–14).

He is the one who appointed Gedaliah as governor (40:5).

It is his successor, Evil-Merodach, who released Jehoiachin from prison (52:31).

The narrative is straightforward and offers an account of a fierce, demanding imperial force vis-à-vis a restless, vulnerable colony.

But of course this narrative is unlike other narratives because it cannot leave matters as clear as that. The narrative relentlessly attests *a second agent, YHWH,* who "removes," "expels," and—if we reason from the explicit assertions of 2 Kings chapter 17—"exiles" or forces the displacement of this people that knew itself to be chosen.

It is clear that the narrative has no trouble at all with double agency and could not, I suppose, construe the history of Jerusalem in any other way. It has no trouble, moreover, in representing this first agent as bent on a relentlessly destructive course of action toward Jerusalem. Given the starchy premises of the tradition of Deuteronomy, it is not a problem to have two agents or a senior agent who could readily mobilize a junior agent against the chosen people, chosen land, chosen city, chosen dynasty, and chosen temple.

II.

The parallel version of "forced migration" in the tradition of Jeremiah is equally committed to double agency. Thus in Jeremiah 25:9 and 27:6, Nebuchadnezzar is well credentialed as "my servant." Nonetheless, it is remarkable that 39:1–10 reports the actual taking of the city and in the narrative account of 52:1–27, which parallels our narrative in 2 Kings, any mention of YHWH is absent. This is public history of an "ordinary" kind. Here there is nothing of divine anger, divine mandate, or divine action. It is now all Nebuchadnezzar, all Babylon, all empire. Only the last sentence, as an editorial conclusion, uses the term *glh*: "So Judah went into exile" (52:27). To be sure, there is a series of forceful verbs necessary to report imperial action: *captured, killed, burned, broke down, carried, broke, carried, took away, took, struck down, put to death.* All of these terms, however, serve nothing more than as description of the aggression of empire.

In Jeremiah 52:28–30, a text without parallel in Kings, Nebuchadnezzar is the agent of the threefold displacement with the threefold use of *glh*. Clearly, the Jeremiah tradition cannot do without double agency, for it has no interest in the actions of Nebuchadnezzar as such. The case for double agency has already been clearly established elsewhere in the Jeremiah tradition. It need not be explicit here in the actual reportage on displacement.

The matter is not fundamentally different in the Chronicler's account of the demise of Jerusalem in 2 Chronicles 36; we may nonetheless note important variations. In verses 1–14, the text disposes tersely of four kings in succession: Jehoahaz (vv. 1–4), Jehoiakim (vv. 5–8), Jehoiachin (vv. 9–10), and Zedekiah (vv. 11–14). In each case, the "empire of force" is effectively at work:[5]

- Necho, king of Egypt, dispatches Jehoahaz.
- Nebuchadnezzar takes Jehoiakim to Babylon in fetters.[6]
- Nebuchadnezzar brought Jehoiachin to Babylon.
- Nebuchadnezzar made Zedekiah "swear by God," an odd variation indeed.

In the first three cases, YHWH's agency is at best formulaic:

- Concerning Jehoahaz, we have only realpolitik; the reference to "evil in the sight of the LORD" from 2 Kings 23:32 has been omitted. This may be no more than a scribal error; in any case, the result is a one-dimensional statement about the agency of the king of Egypt.
- Concerning Jehoiakim, he "did what was evil in the sight of the LORD his God."
- Concerning Jehoiachin, he "did what was evil in the sight of the LORD."

It is the case of Zedekiah wherein theological interests are much more central. We have the same formula, "did what was evil in the sight of the LORD." But then this royal evil is specified:[7]

- He "did not humble himself before the prophet Jeremiah" (2 Chr. 36:12).
- He "stiffened his neck and hardened his heart against turning to the LORD, the God of Israel" (2 Chr. 36:13).
- In addition to Zedekiah, priests and people are indicted for being "exceedingly unfaithful, following all the abominations of the nations; and they polluted the house of the LORD that he had consecrated in Jerusalem" (2 Chr. 36:14).

The final judgment against the city is no longer grounded in "the sins of Manasseh." Now the cause is much more immediate and contemporary (with Zedekiah) and not deferred from Manasseh. The most intense terms of infidelity cluster in this climactic statement. It is of note that in verses 12–13, the royal rebellion against Nebuchadnezzar is sandwiched between (a) not humbling himself before the prophet and (b) stiffening his neck and hardening his heart against YHWH, as though all three elements (including rebellion against Nebuchadnezzar) are taken with equal theological seriousness. It is astonishing, for all of that, that the narrative does not report on the flight, arrest, or execution of Zedekiah that we have in the report in Kings. In all but the first of these royal reports, the double agency is intrinsically linked to the destruction of the city.

In verses 15–16, the text appropriates from 2 Kings 17:13–14 concerning the sustained warnings of the prophets that are consistently disregarded by royal Judah; the tradition simply transfers them to the south. Again the terms cluster: *mock, despise,* and *scoff* occur in a sentence that attests to intense willfulness against YHWH. In verses 10–17, double agency is again explicit: "[The Lord] brought up against them the king of the Chaldeans." The follow-up consists in brutalizing imperial action, culminating in "exile" that lasted "until the establishment of the kingdom of Persia" (v. 20).

It is evident that in the episode with Zedekiah (vv. 11–14) and the prophets (vv. 15–16), the theological dimension of the destruction is acute. The Chronicler has intensified the centrality of divine agency in the retelling of the end.

In the final paragraph of the chapter, the report on Jehoiachin in 2 Kings 25:27–30 and Jeremiah 52:31–34 is displaced by yet a third appeal to Jeremiah, this time apparently with reference to the prophetic oracle of Jeremiah 50:9, with the "stir up" of *yet another human agent,* Cyrus (2 Chr. 36:22–23). This verb, "stir up," is of interest because it is an attempt to articulate the linkage of the two agents beyond the usual "command, send," now a usage that allows for maneuverability in interpretation.

Given these distinct nuances of chapter 36, it is nonetheless the case that this third report, after Kings and Jeremiah, does not vary in its primary claim from the first two reports. The intent in all three reports is to connect divine will and realpolitik—indeed, to subordinate realpolitik to the sovereignty of YHWH, to whom the king in Jerusalem, like all kings, is subject.

III.

Our task here is to consider the "theological problematic" of this text, and I will do so under five topics.

1. At the outset, we must wonder whether "problematic" is the right word, and if so, "problematic" to whom? It is clear that the claim of such double agency is problematic to Enlightenment rationality, even though we have chosen to mumble about that until exposed by the likes of Langdon Gilkey.[8] But long before that modern problematic, it is surely the case that the commitments to the Deuteronomic-prophetic categories expressed in our text were persuasive for only a segment (a small segment) of the Jerusalem population. No doubt much of the population and certainly many of the opinion makers of that population must have found these claims problematic as well, though not likely for reasons of Enlightenment rationality. Rather, the ground for the problematic was more likely the deeply grounded exceptionalism upon which the Jerusalem claims were based. That *exceptionalism* may logically be the very antithesis

of *Enlightenment rationality*, but the two may also go together in resisting this rendering of the displacement and the forced migration. We may continue to ponder what the affront of the text may be for our reading in the end, for the interface of *exceptionalism* and *Enlightenment rationality* continues to hold powerful sway among us.

2. The recurring formulation of double agency is employed in order to enact the covenantal-Deuteronomic assumption of "deed-consequence," of commandment and sanction.[9] With variations, the formula of "the ways of life and death" is ironclad and nonnegotiable (Deut. 30:15–20). And because, in this purview, knowing disobedience was systemic and intense, the whole matter could be readily reduced to a formula. The ironclad formula served to give a reason for the forced migration, served to protect the legitimacy of YHWH, and provided a warrant for the imperial intrusion of Nebuchadnezzar in Judah.

There are, however, signs that this ironclad formulation was recognized as difficult; there are signs of restlessness with the claim. Bernard Levinson has written recently of the ways in which the ongoing interpretive tradition moved against this simplistic formulation of intergenerational punishment; his exposition is important for our theme of forced migration:

- In Lamentations 5:7, the new generation of the deportees complains that it must bear the iniquities of the fathers: "Our ancestors sinned; they are no more, and we bear their iniquities." Levinson comments:

  The injustice of the doctrine raises important practical difficulties as well. It inevitably creates an overwhelming sense of the futility of historical action altogether, inasmuch as the progeny cannot free themselves from the consequences of the past. In the grim circumstance of Israel after the catastrophe of destruction and exile, the future would have seemed radically foreclosed, the direct result not of one's own but of a previous generation's action.[10]

- In his reading of the proverb of Ezekiel 18:1–4, Levinson suggests that by appeal to Deuteronomy 24:16, Ezekiel reduces the claim of the doctrine of intergenerational punishment to a folk saying and thereby subverts it. By that reduction, a case can be made that the claim is "morally repugnant."[11] It should be noted that Levinson shows the way in which Ezekiel anticipates the moral breakthrough of Immanuel Kant concerning "moral freedom as independence from the burden of the past."[12]
- In Deuteronomy 7:9–10, the new generation is exempted from the punishment that is guaranteed by the Decalogue. Thus, the interpretation that claims to exposit in fact subverts the original claim of intergenerational punishment. YHWH does not delay but repays in their own person those who reject him.[13]

To Levinson's inventory, I add two more:

- In Lamentations 3, the appeal to "return" is grounded in a confession of
  sin, exactly according to the formula of punishment:

> Let us test and examine our ways,
>   and return to the LORD.
> Let us lift up our hearts as well as our hands
>   to God in heaven.
> We have transgressed and rebelled,
>   and you have not forgiven.
> Lam. 3:40–42

That much is conventional. But remarkably, only a few verses later, the poet says,

> Those who were my enemies *without cause*
>   have hunted me like a bird;
> they flung me alive into a pit
>   and hurled stones on me;
> water closed over my head;
>   I said, "I am lost."
> 3:52–54 (au. emph.)

The astonishing term is "without cause" *(hinnam)*, suggesting that the punishment and suffering are gratuitous. What follows in verses 56–61 is an assurance
that YHWH has heard and has broken the cycle of punishment.[14]

- In Isaiah 47:6, in what I regard as a full articulation of a prophetic sense
  of historical dynamics, the poet concedes that Nebuchadnezzar had a
  mandate from YHWH but indicts the Babylonian king, who had fero-
  ciously overstepped that divine mandate:

> I was angry with my people,
>   I profaned my heritage;
> I gave them into your hand,
>   you showed them no mercy;
> on the aged you made your yoke
>   exceedingly heavy.

The general indictment of the empire is premised on the claim that Nebuchadnezzar had gone beyond YHWH's intent in forced migration for, in the end,
YHWH intended mercy for Jerusalem. Such a remarkable claim is surely a surprise
to the circles of Deuteronomy, both concerning the symmetrical formulation of
deeds and consequences and the poetry of Jeremiah that celebrated Babylon as one
dispatched by YHWH who was sent to "have no mercy" (Jer. 6:23).

It is clear that the main line of the tradition continues to hold to a symmetrical calculus. It is equally clear that all around the edges, that symmetrical
calculus is resisted and evokes protest. In the end, that tradition refuses a simplistic explanation of its experience of displacement, a refusal that must have been

increasingly important to subsequent generations of the migrants who had been forced away. Given such a refusal, we are left either with a God who cannot be trusted or a human agent acting autonomously and without divine mandate.

3. From outside the Deuteronomic calculus, among other factions in the Jerusalem population, it is clear that this hard-nosed divine resolve amounted to a drastic reneging on Jerusalem promises to king and to temple, that is, to the foundation of exceptionalism. The pathos about this divine reneging is voiced in Psalm 89 where, after elaborate affirmation of David, the psalm arrives at its unanswerable question: "Lord, where is your steadfast love of old, which by your faithfulness you swore to David?" (Ps. 89:49).

In the ongoing tradition beyond Deuteronomic closure, it is equally clear that the divine promises could not be so lightly dismissed. In a conviction perhaps held by Ishmael "of the royal family" (2 Kings 25:25), the royal promises reemerge concerning the migrants, remarkably even in the tradition of Jeremiah that was so deeply against the Jerusalem entitlement:

> Then I myself will gather the remnant of my flock out of all the lands where I have driven them, and I will bring them back to their fold, and they shall be fruitful and multiply. I will raise up shepherds over them who will shepherd them, and they shall not fear any longer, or be dismayed, nor shall any be missing, says the LORD.
>
> The days are surely coming, says the LORD, when I will raise up for David a righteous Branch, and he shall reign as king and deal wisely, and shall execute justice and righteousness in the land. In his days Judah will be saved and Israel will live in safety. And this is the name by which he will be called, "The LORD is our righteousness." (Jer. 23:3-6; see also 33:14–17)

The reassertion of the royal promise indicates that the migrant community, upon further reflection, found Deuteronomic closure if not unacceptable, at least penultimate and not the final word. And of course the Jehoiachin report attests, perhaps, to this wistful conviction as well (2 Kgs. 25:27–30; Jer. 52:31–34).

4. One cannot fail to observe the silence and absence of YHWH in the detailed inventory of the sacking of the temple (2 Kgs. 25:9–17; Jer. 52:17-23). The silence of YHWH in great stretches of the report of the forcing of the migration leaves the field to the empire. There is no doubt that forced migration was imperial policy. But from a theological perspective, one must wonder about the silence of YHWH in the midst of the dismantling. Perhaps the silence is nothing more than an invitation to imperial rapaciousness over which YHWH exercises no oversight. Or perhaps YHWH is fully implicated in the action. If YHWH is implicated in the action, then the migrants might have wondered about this God who cares not at all for God's own majesty, let alone the people to whom promises have been made.

The issue is even more acute because it is the temple of YHWH (about which YHWH has made promises) that is being sacked. Perhaps the migrants could not conceive of YHWH acting against YHWH's own interest in such a blatant way, so that they permitted YHWH to "take a walk" during that dismantling act.[15]

Or perhaps we are to imagine YHWH watching the imperial plunder—noticing and pondering and weeping—and then blaming Nebuchadnezzar, as in Isaiah 47:6. Or perhaps the absence and the silence are in the service of a transcendence that refuses such blasphemy. In any case, in these passages, the narrative falls short of double agency. Perhaps the tradition simply could not implicate YHWH directly in such destruction, which might suggest that there are limits, even for YHWH, in the stringent calculus. Surely they must have wondered, If YHWH will trash YHWH's own house in this way, why not YHWH's own people as well? And they have departed with grief and longing as they refused to forget the city and its temple.[16]

5. The singular appeal to the "sins of Manasseh" in 2 Kings 24:3–4 led to the conclusion that YHWH "was not willing to forgive" *(slh)*. That verdict surely anticipates what follows in these chapters and is echoed in Lamentations 3:42: "We have transgressed and rebelled, and you have not forgiven." The point is paralleled in Deuteronomy 29:19 and leads to a rigorous defense of YHWH's harsh action:[17] "The LORD will be unwilling to pardon them, for the LORD's anger and passion will smoke against them" (Deut. 29:20).

It is clear in the tradition, nonetheless, that unwillingness to forgive, the decisive claim of our chapters, is not the final word. The term *slh* reappears in continued reflection, because it will not do finally, among this people, to attest to such an intransigent and unresponsive God. The migrants who kept at the tradition could not and would not let that be their permanent fate from YHWH. For that reason, we get the term again, first as petition among the migrants (1 Kgs. 8:34, 36) and then as assurance:[18]

> I will forgive their iniquity, and remember their sin no more. (Jer. 31:34)

> I will cleanse them from all the guilt of their sin against me, and I will forgive all the guilt of their sin and rebellion against me. (Jer. 33:8)

> Let them return to the LORD, that he may have mercy on them,
>   and to our God, for he will *abundantly pardon*. (Isa. 55:7, au. emph.)

The developing interpretive conviction among the migrants moved beyond what seemed a settled verdict in the normative calculus.

All of these points, taken together, attest to the restlessness of the tradition and to the inchoate recognition that no explanatory formula, not even from the magisterial voice of Deuteronomy, can adequately corral history.[19] After the tight calculus of sin and punishment, there is more that must be said. Some of it cannot be said yet. Some of it awaits more pondering. Some of it anticipates the daring imagination of the next generation. Some of it perhaps attests to YHWH's own restlessness and YHWH's refusal of any "final solution," even concerning the unbearable recalcitrance of Jerusalem. The outcome is a dynamic interpretive tradition that can be understood as generative literary energy, as historical requirement in new circumstance, but also as theological buoyancy of an agent who refuses closure.[20] I judge that for the ongoing community of the migrants, the verdict rendered in 2 Kings 24–25 is a credible one that asserts moral sensibility as long as it is not taken as final word. The community of migrants, so permeated with song and oracle, had both a historical yearning and a theological conviction that led to a "returning" (1 Kgs. 8; Deut. 30:1–10) but also to an amazing gift received without any returning.[21]

IV.

I draw two conclusions that are reflective of my thesis concerning double agency. First, the text may be taken as an effort at realpolitik in which the defining terms are *empire* and *colony*, or *imperial system* and *vulnerable migrant community*, for I take the colony and the displaced migrants together as a contrast to the imperial system. With the presence of Gedaliah (grandson of Shaphan and the royal folk), it is clear that the accommodators to Babylon and the resisters to Babylon must exist side by side. Indeed, without the accommodators, that is, without Shaphan and Jeremiah and Baruch, Jerusalem would not have been so readily taken. While the memory and action of Ishmael are not seen in a kindly light in the text, he is an agent of resistance to the empire. It would be no easy thing in biblical teaching to make a systemic case for resistance or for accommodation, because resisters and accommodators dwell together in empire; in both cases, they seek to sustain a distinct identity that is partly sociopolitical and partly theological. When seen as realpolitik, the theological dimension of the attestation may be seen as a function of a very real life-or-death dispute about response to empire—a dilemma that recurs endlessly in a world of empires that characteristically transgress moral coherence.

Second, the God of the Deuteronomic calculus is not exactly winsome. YHWH is portrayed variously as patriarchal and violent and not a happy camper in downtown Jerusalem. In much contemporary interpretation, this God is mostly dismissed as an ideological construct as the voice of the "urban elite" who lust for power, even as we who say these slogans to each other are urban elites with tenure. It is not for me to defend the Deuteronomic syllogism in either its cold form or with its more accommodating nuance. We are, however, obligated to ponder what that formulation intended. Surely its intention was to insist that the coming and going of historical vagaries—dynastic, sacerdotal, and imperial—are all penultimate, and that behind them (or in, with, and under them) is a resolved moral intentionality that will not yield. It is convenient among us, in a common interpretive move, to dismiss such hard-nosed conviction as a "paper god" constructed for ideological purposes. Of course! But not more so than other paper gods we may prefer at the moment, for in the end we traffic in paper gods. Thus, one obligation in interpretation is to entertain the claim of this voice, problematic as we may regard it.

Because my comments constitute a theological venture, I dare to move from that ancient world of abrasion to the one that we inhabit when we interpret. Such a move toward contemporeneity is, in my judgment, required in fruitful theological work, even if it is every time risky and inescapably subjective. That is, it is an act of theological imagination that seeks to move from and remain faithful to the act of imagination that constitutes the text itself. In my attempt, I arrive at this first amid the dominant superpower in the world today; we as residents of that superpower may consider the colonial contours of faith. In that contemporary mode, the issue remains as it did in ancient Judah, a mix of accommodation and resistance. These old interpreters understood with great clarity that displaced people must accommodate or perish. They also understood that uncritical accommodation without resistance will inevitably result in the loss of historical identity. It is exactly the work of vigorous interpretation to continue to parse the dilemma of accommodation and resistance.

The Deuteronomic syllogism is, in the end, an effort to articulate an underlying, unaccommodating moral order that pertains amid the rawness of realpolitik. That unaccommodating moral order is not user-friendly. Every concentration of power that imagines autonomy will, in the end, pay dearly. It is a lesson every such power learns, always too late. Before learning, such powers, with theological appeal, can always imagine with Babylon:

> I shall be mistress forever.
> . . . .
>   I am, and there is no one besides me;
> I shall not sit as a widow or know the loss of children.
> . . . .
>   No one sees me. . . .
> I am, and there is no one besides me.
>
> Isa. 47:7, 8, 10

Sometimes the tradition teaches us otherwise; sometimes it is the raw reality of history that is a substitute teacher. Either way, the lesson is very hard and requires, like every hard lesson, repetitive learning.

Notes

Foreword

1. "What Millennials Want When They Visit Church," Barna Group, March 4, 2015, https://www.barna.com/research/what-millennials-want-when-they-visit -church/. See also the recent *New York Times* piece "It's Getting Harder to Talk about God" by Jonathan Merritt, October 13, 2018.
2. This figure is from the United Nations High Commissioner for Refugees.
3. This figure is from "Syrian Refugee Crisis: Facts, FAQs, and How to Help," World Vision, https://www.worldvision.org/refugees-news-stories/syrian-refugee-crisis -facts. According to Susan F. Martin, "The UN High Commission for Refugees (UNHCR) reports that there are more than 60 million refugees and internally displaced persons (IDPs) as of the end of 2014, the largest number since World War II. Syria is only the most visible crisis, affecting some four million refugees and about eight million internally displaced persons."(Susan F. Martin, "The Global Refugee Crisis," *Georgetown Journal of International Affairs* 17, no. 1 (Winter/Spring 2016): 5). Martin observes that the "solidarity expressed in . . . earlier crises appears to be in abeyance today" (7), and she concludes that "political leadership is greatly needed to reverse today's trends and find new approaches" (10).
4. Samantha-Jo Roth, "Donald Trump Can Tell Refugee Children 'You Can't Come Here,'" HuffPost, February 8, 2016, https://www.huffpost.com/entry/donald -trump-syrian-refugee-children_n_56b8e1d4e4b01d80b24743ea.
5. Daniel Burke, "Pope Suggests Trump 'Is Not Christian,'" CNN, updated February 18, 2016, https://www.cnn.com/2016/02/18/politics/pope-francis-trump -christian-wall/index.html.
6. Jerry Fallwell Jr., interview by Jeanine Pirro, "Moderate Republicans Make My Blood Boil," *Justice with Judge Jeanine*, Fox News, April 29, 2017, https://video .foxnews.com/v/5416587832001/?playlist_id=937116552001#sp=show-clips.
7. See the incisive piece by Molly Worthen, "A Match Made in Heaven: Why Conservative Evangelicals Have Lined Up behind Trump," *Atlantic*, April 18, 2017. For a broad critique of violence, see Jacques Ellul, *Violence: Reflections from a Christian Perspective* (New York: Seabury Press, 1969), 27–79, esp. 27–30.

8. This is manifest especially in *winning* the so-called cultural wars, in appointments of conservative judges, and in advocacy in central institutions of power. Interestingly, two years later at a meeting with evangelical leaders, Donald Trump gave a dire prediction of violence against conservative Christians if the GOP would lose the midterm (2018) elections. He noted at the same gathering that the leaders were only "one election away from *losing* [my emphasis] everything" (August 28, 2018). Winning is apparently the current currency exchange.

9. "Reclaiming Jesus," http://www.reclaimingjesus.org.

10. "Reclaiming Jesus."

11. See the penetrating introduction to Richard Kearney, *Anatheism: Returning to God after God* (New York: Columbia University Press, 2011), xi–xix; see also Henri J. M. Nouwen, *Reaching Out: The Three Movements of the Spiritual Life* (New York: Doubleday, 1966).

12. Sean Salai, SJ, "God Chooses the Despised: An Interview with 2015 Templeton Prize Laureate Jean Vanier," *America*, August 5, 2015, https://www.americamagazine.org/content/all-things/god-chooses-despised-interview-2015-templeton-prize-laureate-jean-vanier.

Chapter 1: Holiness as Ground for Knowing Mercy

1. John J. Collins, *The Apocalyptic Vision of the Book of Daniel* (Chico, CA: Scholars Press, 1976), 84–85. I am indebted to Daniel Smith-Christopher for this reference.

2. Daniel L. Smith, *The Religion of the Landless: The Social Context of the Babylonian Exile* (Bloomington, IN: Meyer-Stone, 1989), 164.

3. Smith, *Religion of the Landless*, 8, quoting Nelson H. H. Graburn, ed., *Ethnic and Tourist Arts: Cultural Expression from the Fourth World* (Berkeley and Los Angeles, CA: University of California Press, 1976), 1.

4. Susan Jacoby, *The Age of American Unreason* (New York: Penguin, 2008), chapter 9 and passim, considers the way in which "junk thought" has eroded critical capacity in U.S. culture. Her notion of junk thought, it seems to me, is very like the yeast of the Pharisees and the yeast of Herod about which Jesus warns (Mark 8:15).

5. This statement calls to mind the earlier poetic lines from Isaiah 55:1–2 that offer free food and then ask, in a tone of reprimand, "Why do you labor for that which does not satisfy?" The contrast in those verses between real food and junk food is parallel to being thirsty and never thirsting again.

Chapter 2: Dialogic Thickness in a Monologic Culture

1. Walter Brueggemann, *Theology of the Old Testament: Testimony, Dispute, Advocacy* (Minneapolis: Fortress Press, 1997), 450–91.

2. This essay was originally presented to the National Conference of the Association for Clinical Pastoral Education.

3. The theme of "the many selves of the self" is an ancient one in Christian spirituality. In more recent study, see Roy Schafer, *Retelling a Life: Narrative and Dialogue in Psychoanalysis* (New York: Basic Books, 1992).

4. The most helpful model for such close reading is Phyllis Trible, *Rhetorical Criticism: Context, Method, and the Book of Jonah* (Minneapolis: Fortress Press, 1994).

5. For a helpful introduction to the work of Bakhtin, see Gary Saul Morson and Caryl Emerson, *Mikhail Bakhtin: Creation of a Prosaics* (Stanford, CA: Stanford University Press, 1990).

6. Barbara Green, *How Are the Mighty Fallen? A Dialogical Study of King Saul in 1 Samuel*, JSOT Supp. 365 (Sheffield, UK: Sheffield Academic Press, 2003); Carol A. Newsom, *The Book of Job: A Contest of Moral Imaginations* (Oxford: Oxford University Press, 2003).

7. Emmanuel Levinas, *Totality and Infinity: An Essay on Exteriority* (Pittsburgh: Duquesne University Press, 1969).

8. I am in general familiar with this literature and have found the work of D. W. Winnicott most accessible for an outsider. Special attention may be given to the study of Daniel J. Price, *Karl Barth's Anthropology in Light of Modern Thought* (Grand Rapids, MI: Eerdmans, 2002), in which the interface between Barth's work and that of object relations is explored to great effect.

9. I cite only one title from each of these authors, but their entire writing merits attention in this regard: Jon Levenson, *The Death and Resurrection of the Beloved Son: The Transformation of Child Sacrifice in Judaism and Christianity* (New Haven, CT: Yale University Press, 1993); Michael Fishbane, *Biblical Interpretation in Ancient Israel* (Oxford: Clarendon Press, 1985); James L. Kugel, *The God of Old: Inside the Lost World of the Bible* (New York: Free Press, 2003).

10. See Susan A. Handelman, *The Slayers of Moses: The Emergence of Rabbinic Interpretation in Modern Literary Theory* (Albany, NY: SUNY Press, 1982); and Geoffrey H. Hartman and Sanford Budick, eds., *Midrash and Literature* (New Haven, CT: Yale University Press, 1986).

11. This reiterated formula of assurance is termed by scholars "salvation oracle." See Patrick D. Miller, *They Cried to the Lord: The Form and Theology of Biblical Prayer* (Minneapolis: Fortress Press, 1994), chap. 4.

12. See the powerful articulation of this point in Harold Fisch, *Poetry with a Purpose: Biblical Poetics and Interpretation* (Bloomington: Indiana University Press, 1988), 104–35.

13. Fredrik Lindström, *Suffering and Sin: Interpretations of Illness in the Individual Complaint Psalms*, Coniectanea Biblica Old Testament Series 37 (Stockholm: Almqvist & Wiksell, 1994) has made a compelling case that evil and destructiveness are effective only because YHWH is absent and inactive. The purpose of the prayers then is to activate YHWH, for evil will flee before YHWH.

14. See Erhard Gerstenberger, "Der klagende Mensch: Anmerkungen zu den Klagegattungen in Israel," in *Probleme biblischer Theologie: Gerhard von Rad zum 70. Geburtstag*, ed. Hans Walter Wolff (Munich: Chr. Kaiser Verlag, 1971), 64–72.

15. The connection between the exodus narrative and the psalms of lament has been clearly articulated by James Plastaras, *The God of Exodus* (Milwaukee: Bruce Publishing Co., 1966).

16. On the book of Lamentations, see Kathleen M. O'Connor, *Lamentations and the Tears of the World* (Maryknoll, NY: Orbis Books, 2002).

17. See the comments in Tod Linafelt, *Surviving Lamentations: Catastrophe, Lament, and Protest in the Afterlife of a Biblical Book* (Chicago: University of Chicago Press, 2000), chap. 3, on the relation of Lamentations and Second Isaiah.

18. There is no doubt that the salvation oracle of the Psalms is a divine response. The response is not given until Israel brings its need and pain to speech. This is modeled in the exchange of Exodus 2:23–25; Israel must speak first, and only then does YHWH effectively respond.

19. See Brueggemann, *Theology of the Old Testament*, 139–44.

20. Claus Westermann, *Praise and Lament in the Psalms* (Atlanta: John Knox Press, 1981), 165–213.

21. Hans Walter Wolff, *Das Zitat im Prophetenspruch: Eine Studie zur prophetische Verkuendigungsweise* (Munich: Chr. Kaiser Verlag, 1937), has surveyed the way

in which prophets in Israel can place alleged statements in the mouths of their opponents. The same rhetorical strategy recurs in the Psalter. What the adversary allegedly says is more often enacted rather than spoken.

22. Schafer, *Retelling a Life*, 25–26:

> Here is the puzzle: How many selves and how many types of self are stated or implied in the following account? A male analysand says to his analyst: "I told my friend that whenever I catch myself exaggerating, I bombard myself with reproaches that I never tell the truth about myself, so that I end up feeling rotten inside, and even though I tell myself to cut it out, that there is more to me than that, that it is important for me to be truthful, I keep dumping on myself."
>
> I count eight selves of five types. The first self is the analysand self talking to his analyst, and the second is the social self who had been talking to a friend. These two selves are similar but not identical in that self-organization and self-presentation are known to vary to some extent with the situation a person is in, and in many ways the analytic situation is unlike any other in life. The third self I count is the bombarding self; the fourth, the derogated self that exaggerates; and the fifth, the exaggerated self itself. The sixth is the truthful self the man aspires to be; the seventh, the conciliatory advisor of the bombarding self, the self that advises cutting out the reproaches; and the eighth is the defended self, the one with redeeming features. As to type, there is what is presented as the actual self (whether exaggerated, reproached, or defended), the ideal self (truthful), the self as place (the one with the rotten inside and the one that can be dumped on), the self as agent or subject (the teller, the bombardier, the aspirant, and the advisor), and the self as object (the self observed, evaluated, reproached, and defended).
>
> My answer to the puzzle introduces once again my thesis that there is value in viewing the self in narrative terms.

23. Gerald T. Sheppard, "'Enemies' and the Politics of Prayer in the Book of Psalms," in *The Bible and the Politics of Exegesis: Essays in Honor of Norman K. Gottwald on His Sixty-Fifth Birthday*, ed. David Jobling, Peggy L. Day, and Gerald T. Sheppard (Cleveland: Pilgrim Press, 1991), 72.

24. Sheppard, "'Enemies' and the Politics of Prayer," 73–75.

Chapter 3: On Knowing, Not Knowing, and Being Known

1. This chapter was originally presented at my alma mater, Elmhurst College, in a conference entitled "The Church and Higher Education."

2. For a consideration of the impact of Bacon's categories, see Brian Wren, *What Language Shall I Borrow? God-Talk in Worship: A Male Response to Feminist Theology* (New York: Crossroad, 1989). See further Cameron Wybrow, *The Bible, Baconianism, and Mastery over Nature: The Old Testament and Its Modern Misreading* (New York: Peter Lang, 1991).

3. See Walter Isaacson and Thomas Evan, *The Wise Men: Six Friends and the World They Made* (New York: Simon & Schuster, 1986).

4. On the brothers Bundy, see Kai Bird, *The Color of Truth: McGeorge Bundy and William Bundy: Brothers in Arms* (New York: Simon & Schuster, 1998).

5. See especially Alister E. McGrath, *A Scientific Theology: Nature* 1 (Grand Rapids, MI: Eerdmans, 2001).

6. Roy Shaffer, *Retelling a Life: Narration and Dialogue in Psychoanalysis* (New York: Basic Books, 1992), 94–95.

7. Wiesel has reiterated this rabbinic tale to characterize the remarkable dialogic nature of faith in Judaism.

Chapter 4: Three Waves of Certitude

1. See Walter Brueggemann, *Solomon: Israel's Ironic Icon of Human Achievement* (Columbia, SC: University of South Carolina Press, 2005).
2. Brueggemann, *Solomon*, 87–103.
3. Francis Fukuyama, *The End of History and the Last Man* (New York: Free Press, 1992).
4. From Alfred Lord Tennyson, introduction in "In Memoriam" (1850). It is often used in a church hymn titled "Strong Son of God, Immortal Love."
5. On the proviso, see Brueggemann, *Solomon*, 139–159.
6. On the impact of Deuteronomic theology on the Psalter, see Patrick D. Miller, "Deuteronomy and Psalms: Evoking a Biblical Conversation," *Journal of Biblical Literature* 118 (1999): 2–18.
7. On this usage, see Claus Westermann, *Basic Forms of Prophetic Speech* (Philadelphia: Westminster Press, 1967).
8. See the classic article on "deeds-consequences" by Klaus Koch, "Is There a Doctrine of Retribution in the Old Testament?," in *Theodicy in the Old Testament*, ed. James L. Crenshaw (Philadelphia: Fortress Press, 1983), 57–87.
9. The most important discussion of these issues in the book of Job is by Carol A. Newsom, *The Book of Job: A Contest of Moral Imaginations* (Oxford: Oxford University Press, 2003).
10. Samuel E. Balentine, "'What Are Human Beings, That You Make So Much of Them?' Divine Disclosure from the Whirlwind–'Look at Behemoth,'" in *God in the Fray: A Tribute to Walter Brueggemann*, ed. Tod Linafelt and Timothy K. Beal (Minneapolis: Fortress Press, 1998), 259–78.
11. See Frederick Schleiermacher, *On Religion: Speeches to Its Cultured Despisers*, ed. Richard Crouter, Cambridge Texts in the History of Philosophy (Cambridge, UK: Cambridge University Press, 1996).
12. Newsom, *The Book of Job*, 257.
13. Newsom, *The Book of Job*, 257.
14. Newsom, *The Book of Job*, 258.
15. Newsom, *The Book of Job*, 170.
16. Newsom, *The Book of Job*, 181.

Chapter 5: Crisis as a Mode of Public Faith

1. See Klaus Scholder, *The Birth of Modern Critical Theology: Origins and Problems of Biblical Criticism in the Seventeenth Century* (Philadelphia: Trinity Press International, 1990).
2. On the current crisis of U.S. exceptionalism, see Gary Dorrien, "Consolidating the Empire: Neoconservatism and the Politics of American Dominion," *Political Theology* 6, no. 4 (October 2005): 409–428. More recently, Richard T. Hughes, *Myths America Lives By: White Supremacy and the Stories That Give Us Meaning*, 2nd ed. (Chicago: University of Illinois Press, 2018), has shown how the claim of exceptionalism is in the service of white supremacy.
3. See Walter Brueggemann, "Always in the Shadow of the Empire," in *The Church as Counterculture*, ed. Michael L. Budde and Robert W. Brimlow (Albany, NY: SUNY Press, 2000), 39–58.
4. On the dynamics of this social location, see Daniel L. Smith-Christopher, *A Biblical Theology of Exile*, Overtures to Biblical Theology (Minneapolis: Fortress Press, 2002).
5. On Solomon as the point person for predation in Israel, see Roland Boer, *The Sacred Economy of Ancient Israel* (Louisville, KY: Westminster John Knox Press, 2015), 128–30 and passim.

6. Frank Crüsemann, *The Torah: Theology and Social History of Old Testament Law* (Edinburgh: T. & T. Clark, 1996), 57.
7. On this text and the narrative of the trial of Jesus, see Paul Lehmann, *The Transfiguration of Politics: The Presence and Power of Jesus of Nazareth in and over Human Affairs* (New York: Harper & Row, 1975), 48–70.
8. See Walter Brueggemann, *The Prophetic Imagination* (Minneapolis: Fortress Press, 1978), and William T. Cavanaugh, *Torture and Eucharist: Theology, Politics, and the Body of Christ* (Oxford: Blackwell, 1998).
9. Gerhard von Rad, *Wisdom in Israel* (Nashville: Abingdon Press, 1972), 65.
10. On the theological urgency of dialogue, George Steiner, *Real Presences* (Chicago: University of Chicago Press, 1989), 225, comments, "It is the Hebraic intuition that God is capable of all speech-acts except that of monologue." On current interest in dialogue as it is presented in the literary theories of Mikhail Bakhtin, see Barbara Green, *Mikhail Bakhtin and Biblical Scholarship: An Introduction* (Atlanta: SBL Press, 2000).
11. Thomas S. Kuhn, *The Structure of Scientific Revolutions* (Chicago: University of Chicago Press, 1962).

Chapter 6: "It's the Economy, Beloved"

1. This chapter was originally presented at a Zacchaeus Society conference at Montreat Conference Center, May 31, 2004.
2. See Peter J. Kearney, "The P Redaction of Exodus 25–40," *Zeitschrift für die alttestamentliche Wissenschaft* 89 (1977): 375–87.
3. Marva Dawn, *Keeping the Sabbath Wholly: Ceasing, Resting, Embracing, Feasting* (Grand Rapids, MI: Eerdmans, 1989), 203–204, 210.
4. Nicholas Wolterstorff, *Justice in Love* (Grand Rapids, MI: Eerdmans, 2012).
5. Frank Crüsemann, *The Torah: Theology and Social History of Old Testament Law* (Edinburgh: T. & T. Clark, 1996), 224–34.

Chapter 7: Full of Truth and Hope

1. The consultation was held in Stevens Point, Wisconsin, on September 25, 2007.
2. The German church crisis was the original context for the term "cheap grace." While the phrase has an obvious generic meaning, its particular point in the German church crisis was the sense that no decision needed to be made concerning the contradiction of the gospel and German National Socialism.
3. The programmatic denial of the dominant system in U.S. society recalls for me the ballad of Nat King Cole, "Pretend you're happy when you're blue, it isn't very hard to do."
4. Patrick D. Miller, *The Way of the Lord: Essays in Old Testament Theology* (Grand Rapids, MI: Eerdmans, 2004), 241.
5. William T. Cavanaugh, *Torture and Eucharist: Theology, Politics, and the Body of Christ* (Oxford: Blackwell, 1998).
6. Robert McAfee Brown, ed., *Kairos: Three Prophetic Challenges to the Church* (Grand Rapids, MI: Eerdmans, 1990), 157.
7. Brown, *Kairos*, 50, 58.

Chapter 8: Purity, Unity, Miracle

1. See Bill Bishop, *The Big Sort: Why the Clustering of Like-Minded America Is Tearing Us Apart* (Boston: Houghlin Mifflin, 2008).

2. See Edwin H. Friedman, *A Failure of Nerve: Leadership in the Age of the Quick Fix* (New York: Seabury Books, 2007).
3. See Aarne Siirala, *The Voice of Illness: A Study of Therapy and Prophecy* (New York: Mellen Press, 1964).
4. See D. W. Winnicott, *The Maturational Processes and the Facilitating Environment: Studies in the Theory of Emotional Development* (Madison, CT: International Universities Press, 1965), especially pp. 145–54.
5. See Walter Brueggemann, *Theology of the Old Testament: Testimony, Dispute, Advocacy* (Minneapolis: Fortress Press, 1997), 317–403, where I use "countertestimony" to refer to "voices to the contrary."
6. See Walter Brueggemann, *Finally Comes the Poet: Daring Speech for Proclamation* (Minneapolis: Fortress Press, 1989).
7. Erhard Gerstenberger, *Der bittende Mensch* (Neukirchen-Vluyn, Germany: Neukirchener Verlag, 1980). For a convenient English summary of his argument, see Patrick D. Miller Jr., *Interpreting the Psalms* (Philadelphia: Fortress Press, 1986), 6–7.
8. Kevin J. Madigan and Jon D. Levenson, *Resurrection: The Power of God for Christians and Jews* (New Haven, CT: Yale University Press, 2008), 121–31: "Both the birth of a child to an infertile couple and the resurrection of a dead person testify to the triumph of the wonder-working God (and the validity of his wonder-working prophet, the 'man of God') over the cruel course of nature" (123).
9. For a probe of the thick ways in which Paul makes use of the Genesis traditions, see Richard B. Hays, *Echoes of Scripture in the Letters of Paul* (New Haven, CT: Yale University Press, 1989), 34–83.
10. Hans Heinrich Schmid, "Rechtfertigung als Schöpfungsgeschehen," in *Rechtfertigung: Festschrift für Ernst Kaesemann zum 70. Geburtstag*, ed. Johannes Friedrich, Wolfgang Pöhlmann, and Peter Stuhlmacher (Göttingen, Germany: Vandenhoeck & Ruprecht, 1976), 403.
11. Jon D. Levenson, *The Death and Resurrection of the Beloved Son: The Transformation of Child Sacrifice in Judaism and Christianity* (New Haven, CT: Yale University Press, 1993), has exposited the way in which the Isaac narrative has been understood in Judaism and appropriated in Christian tradition.

Chapter 9: Prayer as Neighbor Love

1. On the First Commandment and its impact on Deuteronomy, see J. G. Janzen, "On the Most Important Word in the Shema," *Vetus Testamentum* 37 (1987): 280–300; and S. Dean McBride, "The Yoke of the Kingdom: An Exposition of Deuteronomy 6:4–5," *Interpretation* 27 (1973): 273–306.
2. On Leviticus 19 in the midst of chapters 18 and 20, see Mary Douglas, "Justice as the Cornerstone: On Interpretation of Leviticus 18–20," *Interpretation* 53 (1999) 341–50.
3. On the kingship of YHWH at Sinai, see Martin Buber, *Kingship of God*, 3rd ed. (London: Humanities Press International, 1990), 121–62. On the scope and pertinence of the exodus tradition, see Georg V. Pixley, *On Exodus: A Liberation Perspective* (Maryknoll, NY: Orbis Books, 1987), and Jon D. Levenson, *The Hebrew Bible, the Old Testament, and Historical Criticism* (Louisville, KY: Westminster John Knox Press, 1993), 127–59, and more broadly, Michael Walzer, *Exodus and Revolution* (New York: Basic Books, 1985).
4. On the symbolic implications of "empire," see James Boyd White, *Living Speech: Resisting the Empire of Force* (Princeton, NJ: Princeton University Press, 2006). His analysis of rhetoric is of enormous importance for my reflections.

5. On the Sinai commandments in relation to the demands of Pharaoh, see Patrick D. Miller, *The Way of the Lord: Essays in Old Testament Theology* (Grand Rapids, MI: Eerdmans, 2004), 68–79.

6. On this quality of the commandments, see Walter Brueggemann, *Interpretation and Obedience: From Faithful Reading to Faithful Living* (Minneapolis: Fortress Press, 1991), 145–58; and Miller, *Way of the Lord*, 17–36.

7. The same motif is expressed in the exodus narrative, wherein the emancipation of Israel is in order that YHWH may "get glory" over Pharaoh (Exod. 14:4, 17).

8. See Kathleen M. O'Connor, *The Confessions of Jeremiah: Their Interpretation and Role in Chapters 1–25*, SBL Dissertation Series 94 (Atlanta: Scholars Press, 1988).

9. Karl Barth, *Church Dogmatics*, III/3, *The Doctrine of Creation* (Edinburgh: T. & T. Clark, 1960), 268.

10. Karl Barth, *Prayer*, 50th anniversary ed. (Louisville, KY: Westminster John Knox Press, 2002), 13.

11. Barth, *Prayer*, 33.

12. *The Heidelberg Catechism*, 400th anniversary ed. (Philadelphia: United Church Press, 1962), 126. This is the final answer of the catechism.

13. Barth, *Prayer*, 13.

14. See Walter Brueggemann, *Israel's Praise: Doxology against Idolatry and Ideology* (Philadelphia: Fortress Press, 1988).

15. "Praise hymns," with their repetitious, unmoving mantras, are the extreme case of status quo singing. Such hymns have no plot or development or characters, and they require nothing by way of commitment. It is no wonder that in the most co-opted churches, this abdicating form of praise is popular and much utilized.

16. It is the thesis of Fredrik Lindström, *Suffering and Sin: Interpretations of Illness in the Individual Complaint Psalms*, Coniectanea Biblica Old Testament Series 37 (Stockholm: Almqvist & Wiksell International, 1994), that in the psalms of complaint YHWH is summoned into presence and action precisely because in the absence and neglect of YHWH, the power of evil and death will hold sway. Conversely, when YHWH is mobilized, the power of evil and death flees and has no power. On such flight before YHWH, see Psalm 114:3–6.

17. John R. Donahue, *The Gospel in Parable: Metaphor, Narrative, and Theology in the Synoptic Gospels* (Philadelphia: Fortress Press, 1988), 182.

18. On the readiness of the God of Israel to hear such urgent cries for help, see James L. Kugel, *The God of Old: Inside the Lost World of the Bible* (New York: Free Press, 2003), 109–136.

19. On this text, see Walter Brueggemann, *Testimony to Otherwise: The Witness of Elijah and Elisha* (St. Louis: Chalice Press, 2001), 89–106.

20. Donahue, *Gospel in Parable*, 182.

21. On this pair of psalms, see Walter Brueggemann, "Psalms 9–10: A Counter to Conventional Social Reality," in *The Bible and the Politics of Exegesis: Essays in Honor of Norman K. Gottwald on His Sixty-Fifth Birthday*, ed. David Jobling, Peggy L. Day, and Gerald T. Sheppard (Cleveland: Pilgrim Press, 1991), 3–15; and Miller, *Way of the Lord*, 67–177.

22. For good reason, Enrique Nardoni, *Rise Up, O Judge: A Study of Justice in the Biblical World* (Peabody, MA: Hendrickson, 2004) has taken this lead phrase of the psalm as the title for his book on justice in the Bible. It is this plea, "Rise up," that voices both the urgent need of Israel at prayer and Israel's confidence in the God to whom it prays.

23. For example, the self-sufficient in Psalm 73:11 have confidence that there is no God who sees and knows what they do. They imagine themselves to be autonomous without fetters or answerability.

24. Lack of innocence is evident in the prayers of ancient Israel if we pay attention to the variety of "motivations" that are offered to YHWH as grounds for divine response to Israel's petition.

25. Concerning prayers of the privileged, see my collection of such prayers, *Prayers for a Privileged People* (Nashville, TN: Abingdon Press, 2008).

26. Miller, *Way of the Lord*, 203–13, makes the case that lament and complaints are not situated in the public worship of ancient Israel but are more intimate and personal. Certainly that is the case in the dramatic example he cites concerning Hannah. I am, however, not convinced that one can generalize in such a way. In any case, whatever may have been ancient practice, I have no doubt that such cries of the poor and needy need to be part of public worship in contemporary practice, because the well-off in worship can practice intercession alongside those in need. Public worship, in our time and place, cannot be immune to such social reality and urgent petitionary practice.

27. Kugel, *God of Old*, 124, nicely summarizes the point in commenting on Psalm 82: "It says that hearing the victim's cry is a god's duty and God's duty."

28. I am here playing upon the canonical connection made by the juxtaposition of the books of Genesis and Exodus. In historical critical terms, there are, of course, immense complex problems in linking these traditions to each other. See R. W. L. Moberly, *The Old Testament of the Old Testament: Patriarchal Narratives and Mosaic Yahwism*, Overtures to Biblical Theology (Minneapolis: Fortress Press, 1992).

29. Again I appeal to canonical order without reference to the complexities of critical analysis. My point is to insist that these slaves, like all creatures, are participants in the postflood covenant of YHWH with creation. The text on the covenant in Genesis 9:8–17 follows verses 1–7, in which human life is guaranteed and protected by the Creator. Certainly these slaves in the Exodus narrative are in purview of that covenant along with all other creatures.

30. In Psalms 145 and 146, two psalms that have all of creation in scope, the creator God is celebrated as the one who attends to the needy and bowed down. The references are inclusive and not limited to Israel; see 145:14–19 and 146:5–9.

31. Gerald T. Sheppard, "'Enemies' and the Politics of Prayer in the Book of Psalms," in Jobling et al., *Bible and the Politics of Exegesis*, 61–82.

32. Amos Wilder, *Theopoetic: Theology and the Religious Imagination* (Philadelphia: Fortress Press, 1976), 28, has shrewdly referred to such texts, like the contestation in Job and in lament psalms, as "guerilla theater."

33. White, *Living Speech*, 86–90, 175–78.

34. White, 218–219.

35. Claus Westermann, *The Structure of the Book of Job: A Form-Critical Analysis* (Philadelphia: Fortress Press, 1981).

36. Kugel, *God of Old*, 124.

37. Kugel, 129.

38. Kugel, 136.

Chapter 10: Justice as Love of God

1. On participation in the political economy, see the suggestion of Norbert Lohfink, "Distribution of the Functions of Power," in *Great Themes from the Old Testament*, ed. Norbert Lohfink (Edinburgh: T. & T. Clark, 1982), 55–75, and S. Dean McBride, "Polity of the Covenant People," *Interpretation* 41 (1987): 229–44, that Deuteronomy represents something like a constitution for ancient Israel.

2. On the political economy in relation to faith, see the careful study of M. Douglas Meeks, *God the Economist: The Doctrine of God and Political Economy* (Minneapolis: Fortress Press, 1989).

3. Jeffries M. Hamilton, *Social Justice and Deuteronomy: The Case of Deuteronomy 15*, SBL Dissertation Series 136 (Atlanta: Scholars Press, 1992); Moshe Weinfeld, *Social Justice in Ancient Israel and in the Ancient Near East* (Minneapolis: Fortress Press, 1995), chap. 8.

4. On the affective dimension of love in Deuteronomy, see Jacqueline E. Lapsley, "Feeling Our Way: Love for God in Deuteronomy," *Catholic Biblical Quarterly* 65 (2003): 350–69.

5. On love as covenantal solidarity in Deuteronomy, see William L. Moran, "The Ancient Near Eastern Background of the Love of God in Deuteronomy," *Catholic Biblical Quarterly* 25 (1963): 77–87.

6. Rolf Knierim, *The Task of Old Testament Theology: Method and Cases* (Grand Rapids, MI: Eerdmans, 1995), 200–201. See also H. H. Schmid, *Gerechtigkeit als Weltordnung* (Tübingen: Mohr, 1968).

7. For a survey of the texts linking YHWH to justice, see Enrique Nardoni, *Rise Up, O Judge: A Study of Justice in the Biblical World* (Peabody, MA: Hendrickson, 2004).

8. On the theme of justice in this text, see Gregory I. Polan, *In the Ways of Justice toward Salvation: A Rhetorical Analysis of Isaiah 56–59* (New York: Peter Lang, 1986).

9. See J. G. Janzen, "On the Most Important Word in the Shema," *Vetus Testamentum* 37 (1987): 280–300, and S. Dean McBride, "The Yoke of the Kingdom: An Exposition of Deuteronomy 6:4–5," *Interpretation* 27 (1973): 273–306.

10. John Calvin, *Institutes of the Christian Religion* 1.6.2, ed. John T. McNeill, Library of Christian Classics (Philadelphia: Westminster Press, 1960), 72.

11. See Gerhard von Rad, *Studies in Deuteronomy*, Studies in Biblical Theology 9 (Chicago: Henry Regnery, 1953).

12. See Walter Brueggemann, *Biblical Perspectives on Evangelism: Living in a Three-Storied Universe* (Nashville: Abingdon Press, 1993), chap. 4.

13. Note should be taken of the inverted word order of these sentences. The accent is on YHWH, even though YHWH is the object of the verbs. The purpose of the rhetoric is to draw the listener toward YHWH in loyalty and obedience.

14. Patrick D. Miller, "Luke 4:16–21," *Interpretation* 29 (1975): 417–421, has made a succinct case that forgiveness in the Bible is rooted in an economic transaction of the forgiveness of debts; more generally, see David Daube, *The Exodus Pattern in the Bible* (London: Faber & Faber, 1963), especially pp. 55–61.

15. Frank Crüsemann, *The Torah: Theology and Social History of Old Testament Law* (Minneapolis: Fortress Press, 1996), 224–34.

16. See David McLellan, *The Thought of Karl Marx: An Introduction* (London: Macmillan, 1971), 11–15.

17. See the study of Michael Polanyi, *The Great Transformation* (New York: Farrar and Rinehart, 1944), wherein he observes that the laws of enclosure in England were decisive in the introduction of new economic assumptions into European thought and practice.

18. On the "stranger" in Old Testament tradition, see Frank A. Spina, *The Faith of the Outsider: Exclusion and Inclusion in the Biblical Story* (Grand Rapids, MI: Eerdmans, 2005).

19. Jacques Derrida, "Force of Law: The 'Mystical Foundation of Authority,'" *Cardozo Law Review* 11 (1989–1990), 945.

20. See Jose Miranda, *Marx and the Bible: A Critique of the Philosophy of Oppression* (Maryknoll, NY: Orbis Books, 1974), 62–64.

21. Carol A. Newsom, *The Book of Job: A Contest of Moral Imaginations* (Oxford: Oxford University Press, 2003), 250–53.

22. See Walter Brueggemann, *Mandate to Difference: An Invitation to the Contemporary Church* (Louisville, KY: Westminster John Knox Press, 2007), 141–58.

23. Hans Walter Wolff, *Anthropology of the Old Testament* (Mifflintown, PA: Sigler Press, 1996), 139–40.

24. See Barbara Ehrenreich, *Nickel and Dimed: On (Not) Getting By in America* (New York: Henry Holt, 2002).

Chapter 11: Prayer and Justice as Disciplines of Identity Maintenance

1. See Patrick D. Miller, *The Way of the Lord: Essays in Old Testament Theology* (Grand Rapids, MI: Eerdmans, 2004), 17–36; Walter Brueggemann, *Interpretation and Obedience: From Faithful Reading to Faithful Living* (Minneapolis: Fortress Press, 1991), 145–58.

2. These are the two branches of the World Council of Churches and of the ecumenical movement more broadly. "Faith and Order" deals with theological questions whereas "Life and Work" deals with ethical social problems. These are together "talking the talk" and "walking the walk."

3. Slavoj Žižek, "Attempts to Escape the Logic of Capitalism," in *The Universal Exception*, ed. Slavoj Žižek (New York: Continuum, 2006), 137–50, has considered the case of the courage of Václav Havel and has concluded that even Havel could not escape the claims of dominant culture. The case indicates what a demanding, if not impossible, vocation it is to live outside that culture.

4. On the use of the term "gospel" in the Isaiah tradition, see Walter Brueggemann, *Biblical Perspectives on Evangelism: Living in a Three-Storied Universe* (Nashville: Abingdon Press, 1993), chap. 1.

5. See the recent positive review of Mowinckel's hypothesis and his translation in J. J. M. Roberts, "Mowinckel's Enthronement Festival: A Review," in *The Book of Psalms: Composition and Reception*, ed. Peter W. Flint and Patrick D. Miller Jr. (Leiden: Brill, 2005), 97–115.

6. See Walter Brueggemann, "Always in the Shadow of the Empire," in *The Church as Counter-culture*, ed. Michael L. Budde and Robert W. Brimlow (Albany, NY: SUNY Press, 2000), 39–58.

7. Jacob Neusner, *The Enchantments of Judaism: Rites of Transformation from Birth through Death* (New York: Basic Books, 1987), 212.

8. The embrace of a faithful evangelical identity needs to be clearly and sharply distinguished from the current anxious wave of right-wing religion in the United States with its nostalgic effort to establish a theocracy amid the republic.

9. I take the phrase "empire of force" from James Boyd White, *Living Speech: Resisting the Empire of Force* (Princeton, NJ: Princeton University Press, 2006), which he has appropriated from the study of *The Iliad* by Simone Weil. The phrase refers to the will and capacity of hegemonic culture to impose its will on society, even if that imposition requires a show and use of force. White's point is that the "force" of such empire is characteristically hidden and subtle, but nonetheless insistent.

10. A reliable guide to recent scholarship is Jon L. Berquist, *Judaism in Persia's Shadow: A Social and Historical Approach* (Minneapolis: Fortress Press, 1995).

11. Even in Israel's best-known confession of sin, Psalm 51, the confession ends in verse 9. The remainder of the psalm is a petition that offers a note of buoyant hope. Even in this psalm, the hope voiced in petition overrides the confession itself. It is only the "tortured conscience" of Western readers that has caused us not to notice this characteristic shift in Israel's prayers.

12. See the helpful discussion of this formula and its wider implications by Sara Japhet, "Theodicy in Ezra-Nehemiah and Chronicles," in *From the Rivers of Babylon to the Highlands of Judah: Collected Studies on the Restoration Period* (Winona Lake, IN: Eisenbrauns, 2006), 367–98.

13. This description of social exploitation sounds like an echo of the taxing arrangements of Pharaoh instituted by Joseph in Genesis 47:13–26.

14. Erhard Gerstenberger, *Theologies in the Old Testament* (Minneapolis: Fortress Press, 2002), 25–110 and passim.

15. A dramatic case of such modest piety is evidenced by Philip Paul Hallie, *Lest Innocent Blood Be Shed: The Story of the Village of Le Chambon and How Goodness Happened There* (New York: HarperPerennial, 1994). In his reviews of the village, Hallie discovered that the courage of church people who hid Jews from the Nazis was not regarded as heroic, but simply as the natural and inescapable outcome of serious faith. The ones who ran the risks regarded what they did as a normal and proper working out of their faith.

Chapter 12: Truth-Telling as Well-Making

1. See Walter Brueggemann, *From Whom No Secrets Are Hid: Introducing the Psalms*, ed. Brent A. Strawn (Louisville, KY: Westminster John Knox Press, 2014).

2. On the cruciality of an experience of omnipotence for personal health, see D. W. Winnicott, *The Maturational Processes and the Facilitating Environment: Studies in the Theory of Emotional Development* (Madison, CT: International Universities Press, 1965), 180 and passim.

3. See Walter Brueggemann, "The Costly Loss of Lament," in *The Psalms and the Life of Faith* (Minneapolis: Fortress Press, 1995), 98–111.

4. Fredrik Lindstrom, *Suffering and Sin: Interpretations of Illness in the Individual Complaint Psalms* (Stockholm: Almqvist & Wiksell, 1994), 350.

5. John R. Donahue, *The Gospel in Parables* (Philadelphia: Fortress Press, 1988), 183, translates the response of the judge this way: "Because this widow is 'working me over' I will recognize her rights, so she doesn't give me a black eye by her unwillingness to give up."

Chapter 13: Colonialism and Migration

1. Klaus Koch, *The Prophets: The Assyrian Period* (Philadelphia: Fortress Press, 1982), 5, 73, 88, 99, 156, and passim.

2. The same term figures twice in pivotal ways in the David narrative. In 2 Samuel 7:15, YHWH will not remove love from David; in 2 Samuel 12:10, the sword will not be removed from David's house. The double usage is perhaps intentional, as the Davidic house lives between divine fidelity and the sword.

3. In 2 Samuel 11:25, 27, the narrative makes a contrast between "evil in your eyes" and "evil in the sight of the Lord" (my trans.). The inability to distinguish between the two, of course, vexes the regime forever.

4. Walter Brueggemann, "Heir and Land: The Royal 'Envelope' of the Books of Kings," in *The Fate of King David: The Past and Present of a Biblical Icon*, ed. Tod Linafelt, Claudia V. Camp, and Timothy Beal, Library of Hebrew Bible/Old Testament 500 (New York: T. & T. Clark, 2010), 85–100.

5. I allude to the remarkable study of James Boyd White, *Living Speech: Resisting the Empire of Force* (Princeton, NJ: Princeton University Press, 2006), in which he ponders the phrase "force of empire" from the study of *The Iliad* by Simone Weil,

who saw that *The Iliad* is all about violence, the kind of violence that Nebuchadnezzar exhibited and that YHWH sanctioned.

6. This narrative account of Jehoiakim departs significantly from that of 2 Kings 24; see Leslie C. Allen, "The First and Second Books of Chronicles," in *The New Interpreter's Bible*, vol. 3 (Nashville: Abingdon Press, 1999), 654–55.

7. The Jeremiah tradition exposits the interaction of Zedekiah and Jeremiah in some detail; Jeremiah 37:2 summarizes the royal resistance to prophetic summons that is crucial for the Chronicler.

8. Langdon Gilkey, "Cosmology, Ontology, and the Travail of Biblical Language," *Journal of Religion* 41 (1961): 194–205.

9. The normative discussion is by Klaus Koch, "Is There a Doctrine of Retribution in the Old Testament?" in *Theodicy in the Old Testament*, ed. James L. Crenshaw (Philadelphia: Fortress Press, 1983), 57–87. I am aware that Koch's argument is primarily concerned with wisdom teaching, but the same points pertain to the structure of the Deuteronomic tradition.

10. Bernard M. Levinson, *Legal Revision and Religious Renewal in Ancient Israel* (Cambridge: Cambridge University Press, 2008), 59.

11. Levinson, *Legal Revision and Religious Renewal*, 63.

12. Levinson, 67.

13. Levinson, 72–84.

14. The same term is used in the same way in the famous query of Job 1:9.

15. It is perhaps not too farfetched to note that Fredrik Lindstrom, *Suffering and Sin: Interpretations of Illness in the Individual Complaint Psalms* (Stockholm: Almqvist & Wiksell, 1994), makes a compelling case that in the Psalms trouble comes because YHWH is absent or indifferent. In a parallel way, it is possible to think that Nebuchadnezzar can do what he does in the Jerusalem temple because YHWH is "on leave" for an instant.

16. Perhaps there is some irony in Psalm 137 that the migrants are more passionate than is YHWH about the city and its temple.

17. I am citing the English versification. See the long diatribe of verses 20–28 that justify YHWH's harsh action. The punishment is based on the verdict: "It is because they abandoned the covenant of the Lord, the God of their ancestors" (v. 25).

18. On the verb, see Walter Brueggemann, "The Travail of Pardon: Reflections on *slh*," in *A God So Near: Essays on Old Testament Theology in Honor of Patrick D. Miller*, ed. Brent A. Strawn and Nancy R. Bowen (Winona Lake, IN: Eisenbrauns, 2003), 283–97.

19. Levinson, *Legal Revision and Religious Renewal*, 63, shrewdly uses the terms "devoice" and "revoice" for the ways in which interpretation plays on and against the older tradition. Even the loud, majestic voice of YHWH cannot finally dominate the lived reality of Israel.

20. Benjamin D. Sommer, "Dialogical Biblical Theology: A Jewish Approach to Reading Scripture Theologically," in *Biblical Theology: Introducing the Conversation*, by Leo G. Perdue, Robert Morgan, and Benjamin D. Sommer (Nashville: Abingdon Press, 2009), 1–53, has richly explored the way of biblical theology and interpretation that refuses closure.

21. Jacqueline E. Lapsley, *Can These Bones Live? The Problem of the Moral Self in the Book of Ezekiel*, Beihefte zur Zeitschrift für die alttestamentliche Wissenschaft 301 (Berlin: Walter de Gruyter, 2000), has shown the way in which the tradition of Ezekiel, for example, must move from summons to return to a gift of new heart and new life. The tradition continues to play between the summons and the gift as circumstance requires and permits.